A Critical Examination
of the Doctrine of Revelation
in Evangelical Theology

A Critical Examination *of the* Doctrine of Revelation *in* Evangelical Theology

Carisa A. Ash

Foreword by Glenn R. Kreider

PICKWICK Publications · Eugene, Oregon

A CRITICAL EXAMINATION OF THE DOCTRINE OF REVELATION IN
EVANGELICAL THEOLOGY

Copyright © 2015 Carisa A. Ash. All rights reserved. Except for brief quotations in critical publications or reviews, no part of this book may be reproduced in any manner without prior written permission from the publisher. Write: Permissions, Wipf and Stock Publishers, 199 W. 8th Ave., Suite 3, Eugene, OR 97401.

Pickwick Publications
An Imprint of Wipf and Stock Publishers
199 W. 8th Ave., Suite 3
Eugene, OR 97401

www.wipfandstock.com

ISBN 13: 978-1-4982-0193-3

Cataloguing-in-Publication Data

Ash, Carisa A.

    A critical examination of the doctrine of revelation in evangelical theology / Carisa A. Ash.

    xii + 190 p. ; 23 cm. —Includes bibliographical references.

    ISBN 13: 978-1-4982-0193-3

    1. Revelation. 2. Evangelicalism. I. Title.

BT127.2 A8 2015

Manufactured in the U.S.A.   07/02/2015

Contents

Foreword by Glenn R. Kreider | vii
Acknowledgments | xi

1 Introduction | 1
2 Review of Systematic Theologies | 25
3 Review of Integration Practices | 59
4 Problems with Current Definitions and Categorizations | 79
5 A Theology of Revelation | 98
6 Conclusion | 155

Bibliography | 161

Foreword

"The earth is filled with your love, LORD;
Teach me your decrees" (Ps. 119:64)[1]

My father is a man of great wisdom. He is a quiet man who has never said much but when he does speak his words are almost always filled with grace and truth. I do not recall ever hearing him say anything negative about anyone, even if they deserved it. Like most men of his generation, he passed down to my two sisters and me many proverbial sayings. One that I recall hearing regularly is, "What you do speaks so loudly I cannot hear anything you are saying."[2] Or, similarly, he would advise us to "practice what you preach."[3] One of my father's goals was to raise his children to live consistently with the faith we professed, to avoid duplicity and hypocrisy, to demonstrate what we believed by what we did. He embodied the admonition often attributed to St Francis, "Preach the Gospel at all times; if necessary, use words."[4] I have tried to emulate his example, to varying levels of success.

---

1. All Scripture quotations in this essay are from *The Holy Bible, New International Version* (Colorado Springs: Biblica, 2011).

2. Once I reached my teenaged years, I realized that my father probably was not the originator of this quote. But in those days, prior to the ubiquity of access to the internet, I never cared to track down the source. I recently, however, did a search and discovered that although the quote is often attributed to Ralph Waldo Emerson, apparently Emerson never actually said it. See Bloch, "What Ralph Waldo Emerson Really Said."

3. This saying seems to have its origin in St. Jerome, "Do not let your deeds belie your words; lest when you speak in church someone may mentally reply 'Why do you not practise what you profess?'" Jerome, "Letter to Nepotian," 93.

4. It seems unlikely that St. Francis ever said these words, but they resonate with me, having grown up in an Anabaptist home and church. Stanton, "Misquoting Francis of Assisi."

Christianity is rooted in the grace of God; every human is guilty of the sin of Adam and can be saved only by the grace of God, through faith in the work of the Lord Jesus Christ. According to the Scriptures, saving faith is never alone. As James puts it, "Faith by itself, if it is not accompanied by action, is dead" (James 2:16) and "faith without deeds is useless" (James 2:20). In short, the faith that saves demonstrates that it is genuine by what it does. Faith practices what it preaches, it speaks in perfect harmony.

As I studied systematic theology in seminary, I came to understand how profoundly my father had influenced me. Inconsistencies in theology bother me and motivate me to pursue resolution of the tension. The goal is not to remove the mystery of the inscrutability of the infinite, but to avoid obvious lack of consistency; in short, to avoid contradictions between theological claims and between what is professed and what is practiced. This is one of the tasks of systematic theology: "The attempt to summarize religious truth or the belief system of a religious group (such as Christianity) through an organized system of thought carried out within a particular cultural and intellectual context. . . . A common systematic order in Christian theology begins with God and God's self-revelation."[5]

Christian theology is a response to divine revelation. God reveals himself in a variety of ways, through a diversity of means. Humans respond to that revelation, in faith seeking understanding. Theologians pursue the comprehension of who God is and how this knowledge impacts the way we should live. Since theology is a task carried out by fallen humans, it is not surprising that it would be finite and incomplete and even that there would be inconsistencies in practice, inconsistencies between what is affirmed and what is practiced. Such inconsistencies are often more easily seen by others than by the practitioners themselves. Thus, theology must be done in community.

Carisa Ash is a systematic theologian. Like me, she is troubled by inconsistencies. As she studied the doctrine of divine revelation, she observed what appeared to be several inconsistencies in evangelical theology. The more she researched, the more she was convinced that she had a topic for her dissertation. She was right.

What Ash observed is that evangelical theologians, almost without exception, affirm that God reveals himself in creation. When evangelicals describe their theological sources and when they discuss divine revelation, a number of biblical texts are cited as support for general revelation, that God has revealed himself in creation and providence. Chief among them are Psalm 19 and Romans 1, but support for general revelation is more extensive than several isolated texts. Yet when these systematic theologians

---

5. Grenz, et al., *Pocket Dictionary*, 111.

actually do theology, when they write systematic theology textbooks, they generally ignore this resource in their theologizing. Instead, these systematicians tend to produce works that are limited to interaction with the biblical texts. In short, they are doing biblical theology, rooting their claims about God and his world in the Scriptures alone.

That these evangelical theologians trust the Scriptures, find them to be a reliable source for knowledge of God, and go to them for truth is not the problem. Ash is not critical of their use of Scripture in theological method. Surely those who believe that the Bible is God's inspired, inerrant, sufficient, and authoritative word should ground their theology in the Scriptures. She argues that the problem is not what is included in evangelical theological method; it is what is excluded. For if the Scriptures teach that God is revealed in the heavens (Ps. 19), in ants and other creatures (Prov. 6:6–8), in flowers and sparrows (Matt. 6:25–34), and in the world that God has made (Rom. 1:18–32), then to exclude such revelation in the construction of theological systems is to be less than obedient to the Scriptures. After all, Proverbs 6:6 ("Go to ant, you sluggard") and Matthew 6:26 ("Look at the birds of the air") are imperatives. Surely these commands should impact the method and the content of evangelical theology.

Ash's study of revelation also led her to investigate the history and helpfulness of the common categorization of revelation as "general" and "special."[6] She argues that these labels are relatively recent and that they might not be the best way to classify revelation. Among other concerns, she shows that it is common for the differences between the two to be emphasized at the expense of the commonalities and for the two to be seen in a hierarchical relationship, at least implicitly. As a result, general revelation is often seen as inferior to special revelation, which perhaps explains its relative unimportance in the work of these evangelical theologians.

Ash's comprehensive survey of evangelical systematic writing is impressive. It would be hard to argue with her documentation of a problem; she provides sufficient evidence of this inconsistency. Her critique of the classification of general and special is helpful and compelling. But her work does not stop with the identification of a problem. She then begins to build a constructive theology of revelation. As an alternative to the traditional categories of general and special revelation, she proposes three categories; Word, World, and the Word who has come into the World. "Word" delineates propositional revelation. In short, God speaks. Sometimes he himself

6. General revelation is "a term used to declare that God reveals something about the divine nature through the created order" and special revelation is "God's self-revelation evidenced specifically in salvation history and culminating in the incarnation as understood through Scripture." Grenz, et al., *Pocket Dictionary*, 55, 109.

speaks and other times he speaks through others, particularly prophets and angels, but one time through a donkey (Num. 22). God's word is preserved for us in the Scriptures. "World" delimits creation. Several texts of Scripture, including Romans 1, affirm that the Creator is revealed in and by what he has made. "The Word who has come into the world" refers to the Incarnate Son of God, the Word made flesh (John 1:1–18). The incarnation of God the Son is the Creator's condescension to enter the world he created, to become a creature, to take on himself the consequences of human rebellion, and to be the redeemer of his creation. The incarnation is eternal; all creation groans as it hopes for the day of liberation, when it will be set free from its bondage to decay and the Creator will make his home on the new earth forever (Rom. 8:18–25; Rev. 21:1–5).

Ash has provided a great service to the discipline of evangelical systematic theology in this work. She has done painstaking research and has produced a helpful classification and critique of evangelical systematic theology texts. She has developed a view of divine revelation that is rooted in the authoritative Word of God and informed by the Christian tradition. And she has charted a course for a generation of evangelical systematicians to follow, one which takes seriously the teaching of Scripture that God is revealed in his world as well as his word and that reads both through the lens of the incarnate Jesus Christ.

It has been a pleasure for this teacher to watch a student grasp the significance of the doctrine of revelation for theological method, to see her develop as a researcher, thinker, and writer, and to produce a work that makes an important contribution to the discipline. It is an honor to commend this work in the hopes that it will help evangelical theologians consider ways to integrate truth about God and his work from what he has revealed in the world he created into their theological systems. Following this course will help all of us to be more consistent in our theological method, to put into practice the implications of what Scripture teaches when it affirms that "what may be known about God is plain to them, because God has made it plain to them. For since the creation of the world God's invisible qualities—his eternal power and divine nature—have been clearly seen, being understood from what has been made" (Rom. 1:19–20). If we believe that God is revealed in what he has made, then our practice of doing theology must include insights from the created order. We must practice what we preach.

Glenn R. Kreider
Professor of Theological Studies
Dallas Theological Seminary
7 November 2014

Acknowledgments

Standing atop the mountain and peering out over the land traversed I am reminded of the debt I owe to others. In many ways, this particular journey began while studying at Spring Arbor College. Conversations with faculty and students set me on a track leading toward this mountain. I am grateful for my education and particularly the faculty who challenged me to ask questions about the relationship between general and special revelation.

The questions that began forming in college were reignited through my Th.M. and Ph.D. training at Dallas Theological Seminary. Numerous conversations with friends helped me clarify central issues and questions. Unfortunately, I cannot mention the names of everyone, but each name runs through my mind as I type these words. Two in particular, Laurie Norris and Garland Dunlap, bear mentioning because of the sheer number of hours spent discussing the importance of such matters. The Norris home also became a vacation retreat where I could both relax and write. Thanks for opening your home.

Many served as encouragers along the journey. The ability to persevere often requires the simple words "keep going" from family, friends, and colleagues. In addition to those are the many others who reminded me that "this topic is needed." They provided a concrete reason for its usefulness and thereby contributed to its completion.

Honestly, this journey would not have happened without the specific contributions of two key people. Friend, colleague, and supervisor, Glenn Kreider helped me become a better theologian by pushing me to think more precisely. Numerous emails and conversations with him enabled me to articulate the issue and address it with more clarity. His excitement for the topic also spurred me on toward completion. I cannot express the magnitude of the role he played. His role in this is a gift from God.

Mentor, friend, colleague, and reader, Mike Lawson has served as a voice of encouragement over a number of years. I cannot imagine this journey without his involvement. A class taught by him in my master's degree refueled my interests in the topic of integration. Numerous casual conversations over flawed outlines contributed to clarifying key issues and solutions.

Finally and most significantly, I am humbled by and grateful for the gift of eternal life made possible by the atoning work of my Savior, Jesus the Christ. I am astounded that he would select a daughter of factory workers to write on the topic of revelation. I ask that he would continue to open my eyes to the truths written on the pages to follow. Ultimately, I hope that this offering brings glory to him and is somehow useful for his church.

> "The earth is filled with your love, LORD;
> Teach me your decrees" (Ps. 119:64)

Carisa Ash

1

Introduction

Introduction

God teaches through his written Word that he reveals himself outside of Scripture. In other words, Scripture instructs that divine revelation precedes the written Word and continues after its canonization (Ps 19 and Rom 1).[1] On the basis of these texts evangelicals bear witness to the reality of "general revelation" or revelation given through the created order.[2] God reveals himself and his ways through that which he created.

Since God alerts the redeemed to the fact that he reveals through the created order, Christians must "develop eyes to see, ears to hear, and senses to experience—all in the light of God's revelation in Scripture—what our Creator and Sustainer is telling us about Himself, His purposes, and His ways through the things He has made."[3] Moore identifies that "we need to

---

1. Simply stated, revelation is divine disclosure. An expanded explanation of "revelation" appears below under "definitions." See also chapter five "A Theology of Revelation."

2. For example, Johnson, "Between Two Wor(l)ds," 75; Ryrie, *Basic Theology*, 31; Erickson, *Christian Theology*, 179–99; and Thorsen, *Christian Theology*, 17–18. See chapter four for an examination of how evangelicals define and categorize revelation. I use "evangelical" in reference to those who emphasize the Bible, activism, the centrality of the cross, and the necessity of a conversion experience. Bebbington, *Evangelicalism*, 2–3.

3. Moore, *Consider the Lilies*, 55. In brief, the term "created order" refers to everything created by God as well as that which those created in his image create. The created order joins Scripture and the Incarnation as a major form of revelation (see "Forms"

be convinced that this is *real* revelation, not just the reporting of perceptions or the recording of highly subjective impressions, and that it can enrich and deepen our experience of the Lord and, presumably, our service to Him in this world."[4] Revelation through the creation is real revelation.[5]

Bonaventure, the thirteenth-century mystic, observes that "all the creatures of the sense world lead the mind of the contemplative and wise man to the eternal God. For these creatures are shadows, echoes and pictures.... They are vestiges, representations, spectacles proposed to us and signs divinely given so that we can see God."[6] Bonaventure expresses two important things: (1) God reveals through creation, and (2) revelation, through the created order, leads the wise to see God.

Like Bonaventure, evangelicals strongly affirm that God reveals through the created order. However, in contrast to Bonaventure, contemporary evangelicals focus on the salvation of humanity when speaking of general revelation.[7] The focus on salvation results in overlooking other effects of revelation.[8] In turn this narrow focus fosters neglect of the created order as a form of revelation.[9] Johnston believes, "Theology's bias toward the

---

below in chapter five).

4. Moore, *Consider the Lilies*, 55.

5. For example, by studying the monarch butterfly one may learn of God and his amazing works. The span of their migration is amazing. That they take the same path each time is astounding. However, the fact that several generations pass between migrations, and still the great-grandchildren take the same migratory path certainly communicates something about God, his relationship to the created order, and the created order itself. Ryden, "Monarch Butterfly."

6. Bonaventure, *Soul's Journey into God*, 75–76.

7. For example, Oden focuses his article regarding general revelation on the issue of salvation. He argues that the early church taught that God reveals through the created order. Classic Christianity "confirms with Paul that all humanity is offered some true, even if limited, knowledge of God by contemplating the majesty and goodness of God in the whole of creation." He concludes, "But the ancient Christian writers did not presume or imagine from this that such knowledge could constitute a *saving knowledge* of God." Oden, "Without Excuse," 68; emphasis added. Due to the popularity of pluralism, among other issues, Demarest saw the need for "a careful reconsideration of the character, scope, and content of general revelation." Demarest, *General Revelation*, 14–15. See "Effects" in chapter five for other examples.

8. A few effects of revelation include worship of God, knowledge of God, and points of contact with unredeemed. See "Effects" in chapter five for other effects of revelation.

9. Evangelicalism's focus on the salvation of people directly relates to this dissertation. Other factors potentially lead to neglect of the created order as revelation; such as a misunderstanding of *sola scriptura*, the impact of common sense realism, and the modernist-fundamentalist debates in early twentieth century America. However, these factors extend beyond the scope of this dissertation. For those interested in other factors that potentially contribute to evangelicals neglecting the created order as divine

redemptive over the creational and towards propositional over the narrative is perhaps one explanation for the relative paucity of theological thinking on general revelation."[10]

Indeed, mention of general revelation leads to the following conclusion, "Natural revelation is God's witness to man through nature . . . But natural revelation has inbuilt limitations. It is fair to say that in general no man can come to a saving knowledge of Jesus Christ through natural revelation alone, as much as it may bear an indirect witness to the existence of God."[11] Evangelicals affirm the reality of revelation through the created order. They mention that such revelation does not provide knowledge leading to salvation. They, then, label revelation given through the creation as limited or insufficient.[12]

The issue of where people find reliable knowledge for salvation is important, but outside the purview of my work. Instead, I return to the insight of Bonaventure. I explore the significance of the created order as a form of revelation. Before plunging into a critical examination of the beliefs and practices of evangelicals and proposing a theology of revelation I must address preliminary issues. These items include: definitions for terms central to the work, need for the study, thesis of the study, and method of the study. We now turn to definitions.

Definitions

Evangelicalism

A simple definition of "evangelical" or "evangelicalism" looks to etymology and states that an evangelical emphasizes the "good news" or the gospel.[13]

---

revelation, please see Hatch and Noll, *Bible in America;* Mathison, *Sola Scriptura;* Beck, "Sola Scriptura," 293–302; Whidden, "Sola Scriptura," 211–26; Allert, "What are We Trying to Conserve?,"327–48; Bray, "Sola Scriptura," 99–104; Thorsen, "Sola Scriptura," 7–27; and Sawyer, *Survivor's Guide to Theology,* 109–10, 116–17.

10. Johnston, "Discerning the Spirit in Culture," 54–55.

11. Lindsell, *Battle for the Bible,* 17.

12. For example, Street, "Biblical Counseling," 217; Shedd, *Dogmatic Theology,* 88; and Phillips and Okholm, *Welcome to the Family,* 43. See "Characteristics" in chapter five for others who label general revelation as insufficient or inadequate because it does not lead to salvation.

13. Such people treat "evangelicalism as synonymous with Protestantism," as Elwell observes. Elwell, "Preface," vii. The term "evangelical" in a very general sense "means being characterized by a concern for the essential core of the Christian message, which proclaims the possibility of salvation through the person and work of Jesus Christ." Grenz et al., *Pocket Dictionary,* 47–48.

Those offering such a definition succeed in accuracy on one point, but fail to shed light on any true distinctiveness of evangelicalism. Boyd and Eddy narrow the concept a little more focusing on evangelical commitment to historic Christian belief. They seek to distinguish evangelicalism from Catholicism and liberalism by explaining that "evangelicals are united in their commitment to the core beliefs of historic, orthodox Christianity as expressed in the ecumenical creeds and to the primacy of Scripture in all matters of faith and practice."[14]

Sawyer identifies American evangelicals with the convictions of fundamentalists of the early twentieth century. He describes an evangelical as a "Protestant who believes in the inspiration and authority of Scripture, the depravity of man, the need for God's gracious gift of salvation through faith in Christ, Jesus' commission to evangelize the lost, and the second coming of Christ."[15] Similarly, Alister McGrath identifies six "controlling convictions."[16] In brief, these convictions are the "supreme authority of Scripture," "the majesty of Jesus Christ," Spirit's lordship, personal conversion, "the priority of evangelism" and "the importance of the Christian community."[17]

The Evangelical Theological Society defines "evangelical" by two key doctrinal beliefs. The society requires adherence to: (1) "The Bible alone, and the Bible in its entirety, is the Word of God written and is therefore inerrant in the autographs;" and (2) "God is a Trinity, Father, Son, and Holy Spirit, each uncreated person, one in essence, equal in power and glory."[18] All Christians affirm (2), so while this last proposal narrows the definition it still fails to differentiate evangelicals from other Christians. Furthermore, all evangelicals defend the authority and infallibility of Scripture, but not all agree on the doctrine of inerrancy.[19]

No simple or "universally accepted" definition of "evangelicalism" satisfies the unity and diversity within the camp while also separating

---

14. Boyd and Eddy, *Across the Spectrum*, 7.

15. Sawyer, *Survivor's Guide to Theology*, 556. Pierard offers a similar description of evangelism. Pierard, "Evangelicalism," 379–80.

16. McGrath, *Evangelicalism*, 53–87. McDermott follows McGrath as he describes evangelicals. McDermott, *World Religions*, 28–34.

17. McGrath, *Evangelicalism*, 55–56.

18. Evangelical Theological Society, "ETS Constitution, Article III," lines 7–8.

19. Both Lindsell and Erickson explain various positions of this doctrine. Lindsell, *Battle for the Bible*; and Erickson, *Christian Theology*, 246–65. See Marsden for a discussion of neo-evangelicals and the doctrine of inerrancy. Marsden observes, "Progressives thought inerrancy too narrow a way to define biblical authority; more fundamentalistic neo-evangelicals insisted on inerrancy as a test of faith." Marsden, "Fundamentalism and American Evangelicalism, 30.

it from other forms of Christianity.[20] Stackhouse observes, "It is an irony that in a tradition that prizes plain, clear speech, the very word *evangelical* is patient of at least half a dozen definitions, and some of those are hotly contested by interested parties within and without any particular form of evangelicalism."[21] Resultantly, some call for a "moratorium on the use of the term" due to its lack of helpfulness.[22] Hart suggests that "Evangelicalism . . . does not exist" and therefore "born-again Protestants would be better off if they abandoned the category altogether."[23] Those who claim the term vary greatly and often fail to share the same core definition.

Although defining "evangelicalism" proves difficult, value for the term exists for those who call themselves "evangelical." Mouw encourages his reader to think of the term as a "theological modifier rather than a noun."[24] The central ideologies of evangelicalism "are best seen as theological *emphases* that have come to have importance in the context of certain kinds of theological struggles."[25] The brief historical survey that follows sheds light on the key foci that unite evangelicals despite their differences and set evangelicals apart from other Christians.

Evangelicalism expresses a specific form of Protestantism. The movement originated "in the later European Renaissance, especially in France, Germany and Italy," but it "appears to have consolidated itself in England and North America."[26] Evangelicalism took shape in mid-eighteenth century Britain and America as a particular manifestation of the Protestant Reformation marked by revivals in Britain and America.[27] The concern among evangelicals for spreading the gospel stems from this heritage. The importance of conversion and evangelism led to the great missionary movement of the nineteenth century, which in turn spread evangelicalism around

---

20. Boyd and Eddy, *Across the Spectrum*, 7. See also Collins, *Evangelical Moment*, 20; and Dayton and Johnston, *American Evangelicalism*.

21. Stackhouse, "Evangelical Theology," 40–41. Collins explains that Reformed and Wesleyan [for example] evangelicals at times even vie with one another for a definition of American evangelicalism that best suits their own interests and agendas." Collins, *Evangelical Moment*, 20. He points out that many evangelical stories exist which "employ different people, places, and events." Ibid., 21.

22. Dayton, "Evangelical," 251. See also Hart, *Deconstructing Evangelicalism* 187–8.

23. Hart, *Deconstructing Evangelicalism*, 16.

24. Mouw, *Smell of Sawdust*, 72.

25. Ibid.

26. McGrath, *Evangelicalism*, 26.

27. Noll, *Rise of Evangelicalism*, 18. As McGrath points out, "evangelicalism emerged and developed primarily within an English-speaking context." McGrath, *Evangelicalism*, 26. The theologies examined here reflect this context.

the world. Both Puritanism and Pietism mark the evangelical movement.[28] An emphasis on a personal conversion experience evidenced by changed life comes from the Puritan and Pietistic lineages of evangelicalism. The awakenings and in particular Jonathan Edwards likely cemented the stress on conversion in American evangelicalism.[29]

Fundamentalism (1920s–1960s) denotes a specific representation of evangelicalism in America. The decline of cultural prominence coupled with the rise of modernism led to a focus on the fundamentals of the faith.[30] The Bible's authority took the foreground in debates against modernism (or twentieth century liberalism). Key doctrinal issues include defending the unique authority of the Bible, the reality of the Incarnation, the physical second coming of Christ, and a defense of miracles. A greater concern for the souls of people and less involvement in social action also marked the fundamentalist period. Marsden summarizes the place of fundamentalists within evangelicalism:

> [A]lmost all nineteenth-century American Protestants had been evangelical, that is, part of a coalition reflecting a merger of pietist and Reformed heritages and growing out of the eighteenth- and nineteenth-century awakenings in America. . . . All fundamentalists wanted to preserve this nineteenth-century heritage, and so all fundamentalists were evangelicals. But in the early twentieth century, by no means all evangelicals were fundamentalists. . . . [M]any who still called themselves evangelicals were liberals or modernists who had abandoned most of the distinctive emphases of the awakenings; so the term *evangelical* had lost its usefulness. Fundamentalists nonetheless thought of themselves simply as preserving the evangelical heritage.[31]

Rifts between evangelicals began during the early twentieth century and continue today. Bebbington states that the "unity of Evangelicalism broke during the 1920s. The movement had always been marked by variety in doctrine, attitude and social composition, but in the years after the First World War it became so sharply divided that some members of one party did not recognize the other as Evangelical—or even, as Christian."[32] Though

---

28. Bingham, *Pocket History*, 161.
29. Ohlmann, "Baptists and Evangelicals," 157.
30. Hatch, *Democratizing of American Christianity*, 214–5.
31. Marsden, "Fundamentalism and American Evangelicalism," 23–24.
32. Bebbington, *Evangelicalism*, 181.

here Bebbington speaks of British evangelicalism, he remarks, "at the same period there was a comparable division" in the United States.[33]

As fundamentalists seek to preserve the evangelical heritage in response to liberalism, so neo-evangelicals desire to retain the evangelical heritage while maintaining contact with the world around them. Ockenga and Henry represent evangelicals that "would combine the best of both [liberalism and fundamentalism], the social involvement and activism of the former with the theology and evangelistic zeal of the latter."[34] Henry attempted to return evangelicals to the right use of reason through his rationalistic defense of written divine revelation in his series *God, Revelation and Authority*.[35]

A new group of evangelicals arose to face old concerns in a new culture at the end of the twentieth and the beginning of the twenty-first century. These new, younger, or post-evangelicals once again seek to correct their tradition in light of contemporary culture. Tomlinson offers a description of post-evangelicism: "[T]o be post-evangelical is to take as given many of the assumptions of evangelical faith, while at the same time moving beyond its perceived limitations."[36]

In summary, four key issues mark evangelicalism from its earliest days to post-evangelicalism. Bebbington states,

> There are four qualities that have been the special marks of Evangelical religion: *conversionism*, the belief that lives need to be changed; *activism*, the expression of the gospel in effort; *biblicism*, a particular regard for the Bible; and what may be called *crucicentrism*, a stress on the sacrifice of Christ on the cross. Together they form a quadrilateral of priorities that is the basis of Evangelicalism.[37]

This description takes into consideration the great diversity among evangelicals (Wesleyan, Charismatic, Reformed, for example), even in the finer details of key doctrines (the timing and nature of the millennium, for example). Bebbington also notes that particular emphases largely set evangelicalism apart from other Christians. For these reasons, I use Bebbington's description of evangelicalism in this work.[38]

33. Ibid.
34. Hart, *Deconstructing Evangelicalism*, 25.
35. Henry, *God, Revelation and Authority*.
36. Tomlinson, *Post-Evangelicals*, 28.
37. Bebbington, *Evangelicalism*, 2–3.
38. Others making use of his definition include Noll, *Rise of Evangelicalism*, 19; Stackhouse, "Evangelical Theology," 41–55; Bingham, *Pocket History*, 162; Collins,

Revelation

In chapter five of this work I propose a theology of revelation. The brief definition provided here helps orient the reader to my use of the word. Most simply, revelation is divine disclosure. Revelation refers to both process and product.[39] God reveals whenever he discloses himself and truths regarding himself, creation, and the relationship between the two. The term "revelation" also applies to the product of this activity. Although, "revelation" applies to both the divine activity and the product the current work focuses on the product. God reveals using numerous forms. The chief forms include created order (world), Scripture (written Word), and the Incarnation (Word who came into the world created through him).

Systematic Theology

Evangelical definitions of systematic theology tend to fit one of three categories: (1) systematizing biblical texts, (2) systematizing doctrines, or (3) systematizing all truth. Though all truly evangelical systematic theologies use the Bible as the authority (or norm) for theology, the description of what one systematizes differs. The first group systematizes verses from the entire Bible on an issue. The second group systematizes doctrines built from the Bible. The third group synthesizes biblical and extra-biblical truth concerning an issue. Below I provide examples from each category.[40]

Systematizing Biblical Texts

Some evangelicals explain the task of systematic theology as collecting and ordering passages of Scripture. Pieper states that "Christian doctrine is *not produced by the theologian;*" instead the theologian "compiles the doctrinal statements contained in Scripture (in the text and context), groups them under their proper heads, and arranges these doctrines in the order of their relationship."[41] Likewise, Charles Ryrie explains that systematic theology "correlates the data of biblical revelation as a whole in order to exhibit

---

Evangelical Moment, 21; and McGrath, *Christian Theology*, 121.

39. I am indebted to Glenn Kreider for mentioning this distinction in a conversation.

40. See chapter two for an examination of evangelical systematic theologies categorized by each author's stated methodology.

41. Pieper, *Dogmatics*, 1:52; emphasis added. See also Mueller, *Christian Dogmatics*.

systematically the total picture of God's self-revelation."[42] In sum, systematic theology reflects the teaching of the entire Bible on an issue.

Wayne Grudem describes systematic theology as systematizing biblical texts: "Systematic theology is any study that answers the question, 'What does the whole Bible teach us today?' about any given topic."[43] He continues, "This definition indicates that systematic theology involves collecting and understanding all the relevant passages in the Bible on various topics and then summarizing their teachings clearly so that we know what to believe about each topic."[44] Grudem admits the possibility of calling the process "biblical theology." However, in an effort to avoid confusion with common usage of the term "biblical theology" he prefers "systematic theology."[45]

The above definitions focus on the primacy of Scripture in the theological task. Systematizing Scripture's teaching concerning an issue forms a necessary part in the overall theological method, but not the only step. As Phillips and Okholm state, "Interpretation cannot be escaped by just repeating Scripture."[46] Even a mere arranging of Scripture includes an interpretative component. One's tradition, culture, and personal experience shape his theology and should do so carefully and intentionally. Hence simply ordering verses into a coherent whole helps, but it falls short of the task of systematic theology.

Systematizing Doctrines

Others describe the task of systematic theology as showing the relationships between areas of doctrine. Charles Hodge's definition of systematic theology illustrates systematizing doctrines drawn from the Bible. Hodge asserts,

> So the Bible contains the truths which the theologian has to collect, authenticate, arrange, and exhibit in their internal relation to each other. This constitutes the difference between biblical and systematic theology. The office of the former is to ascertain and state the facts of Scripture. The office of the latter is to take those facts, determine their relation to each other and to other

---

42. Ryrie, *Basic Theology*, 15.

43. Grudem gives John Frame credit for teaching him this method. Grudem, *Systematic Theology*, 21. See also Evans, *Theology*, 17.

44. Grudem, *Systematic Theology*, 21.

45. Ibid., 22.

46. Phillips and Okholm, *Welcome to the Family*, 55.

> cognate truths, as well as to vindicate them and show their harmony and consistency.⁴⁷

What does Hodge mean by "other cognate truths?" It is admittedly ambiguous as to whether the phrase references truths outside of Scripture or other truths within Scripture. I understand him to refer to the latter for two reasons. First, the immediate context suggests one begins with isolated biblical facts, then arrange these isolated facts into doctrines, and finally determine the interrelationship between doctrines. Second, his statements regarding the Bible's use in theology warrant this interpretation. He states, "He [God] gives us in the Bible the truths which, properly understood and arranged, constitute the science of theology."⁴⁸ Hodge's method, therefore, consists of explaining the "internal relation of facts, one to another, and each to all."⁴⁹

In chapter two I point out the pervasive influence of Hodge's method among evangelical theologians. Some explicitly follow his systematizing doctrine approach. For example, Williams writes, "the word *system* points up the interlocking and interdependent character of all the doctrines that make up theology."⁵⁰ Likewise, Rolland McCune unambiguously explains that systematic theology "is the doctrine(s) of the Bible set forth according to plan or order."⁵¹ He further explains that systematic theology "is the correlation of the various teachings or doctrines found in the Bible."⁵² Similarly, Michael Horton "seeks to offer a summary of Christian doctrine in its systematic relations" because "systematic theology pulls together these insights in a formal dogma and relates [for example] the Trinity to other doctrines in Scripture."⁵³

These explanations of systematic theology emphasize the interconnectedness of doctrines. Stress on the interrelatedness of doctrines does not necessitate a "Bible only" approach to systematic theology. However, Hodge, Williams, McCune, and Horton mention that these doctrines develop out of Scripture. They do not refer to extra-biblical truths in their methodology. In this regard, they differ little from the "Bible only" approach to systematic theology explained above. Identifying systematic theology as systematizing doctrines faces the same limitations as systematizing the Bible.

---

47. Hodge, *Systematic Theology*, 1:1–2.
48. Ibid., 3.
49. Hart, "Systematic Theology at Old Princeton Seminary," 8.
50. Williams, *Renewal Theology*, 1:17; emphasis added.
51. McCune, *Systematic Theology*, 1:3.
52. Ibid., 5.
53. Horton, *Christian Faith*, 29.

Systematizing All Truth

Some evangelicals define the task of systematic theology as systematizing all truth from any and every source. This group knows the importance of Scripture in systematic theology. However, they also realize the need to collect and arrange truth from the created order as well. The proposed method draws from both Scripture and the created order as forms of divine revelation.

Lewis Chafer asserts, "Systematic Theology may be defined as the collecting, scientifically arranging, comparing, exhibiting, and defending of all facts from any and every source concerning God and His works."[54] Material for systematic theology comes from any and every source.[55] Benjamin Warfield states, "It is with no reserve that we accept all these sources of knowledge of God—nature, providence, Christian experience—as true and valid sources, the well-authenticated data yielded by which are to be received by us as revelations of God, and as such to be placed alongside of the revelations in the written Word and wrought with them into one system. As a matter of fact, theologians have always so dealt with them; and doubtless they always will so deal with them."[56] Warfield observes that theologians have always used sources outside of Scripture in their construction of theology. This is not a new idea.

Gerhard Hasel differentiates Biblical theology from systematic theology: "Systematic theology which takes the Bible as its authoritative source has the function of engaging in a constructive presentation the meaning of biblical and Christian faith with full usage of information available beyond Scriptural revelation such as history, psychology, sociology, philosophy, and so forth, as long as such information is subject to the norms of biblical revelation and its truth claims."[57] He favors integrating the Bible with other fields of study in systematic theology. Similarly, Norman Geisler states, "Systematic theology is an attempt to construct a comprehensive and consistent whole out of *all* revelation from God, whether special (biblical) or general (natural)."[58]

These theologians understand systematic theology as systematizing general and special revelation or the created order and the Bible, respectively.

---

54. Chafer, *Systematic Theology*, 1: 6; emphasis removed.
55. Ibid., 5.
56. Warfield, *Studies in Theology*, 58.
57. Hasel, "Biblical Theology and Systematic Theology," 127. See also Gamertsfelder, *Systematic Theology*, 16, 19.
58. Geisler, *Systematic Theology*, 1:16. See also Towns, *Theology*, 8, 15.

They also give priority to the teaching of Scripture.[59] Finally, as both Warfield and Chafer state, the theologian must take into account all revelation. In fact, "Theology . . . is concerned with God and other things as they relate to God, potentially everything, in other words."[60]

Stott also offers important insight. He understands Christian theology as "a response to divine revelation," and notes that "divine revelation . . . is not mediated only through Christ and the biblical witness to Christ, but also through the created order."[61] Similarly, Phillips and Okholm affirm, "A fuller definition of theology would be: 'a human response to the revelation of God done within and for the Christian church that engages in critical reflection for responsible talk about God.'"[62] This description highlights the theologian's response to all of God's revelation both within and for the Christian community. I simply add to their "talk about God" the following "and all creation as related to God."

Integration

People use the term "integration" in a number of contexts (integrated life, integrated learning, integrated curriculum), and speak of the various levels of integration (presuppositions, methods, applications). As Badley points out, integration is a complex topic. The reader must always ask the following: (1) what do the authors intend to integrate? For example, does the author seek to integrate her faith with a particular field of study or with one's life; or does the author seek to integrate two different fields of study? (2) At what level does integration occur? For example, does it occur within an individual professor or student, does it occur in dialogue between people, or does it occur at the level of the curriculum within a school system? (3)

---

59. By "teaching of Scripture," I refer to the canon in its entirety which includes not only direct propositional statements, but also that which people learn from all genres in Scripture (narrative, prophecy, poetry, etc.).

60. Williams, "Systematic Theology," 46.

61. Stott, "Theology: A Multidimensional Discipline," 4, 5. Unfortunately, Stott's continued explanation keeps theology and science as very distinct disciplines with similar approaches to different content. In brief, he limits theology to "what God has revealed in Christ and in Scripture" (5). See my discussion of Stott under "Content of Revelation" below in chapter five.

62. Phillips and Okholm, *Welcome to the Family*, 292. The community of faith (across time and space) plays an essential role in interpreting Scripture, formulating, and applying theology.

Does "integration" refer to a process or a product? (4) What does the author intend to fuse, incorporate, dialogue, or transform?[63]

I sympathize with the statement of Stokes and Lewis: "Unfortunately, since the term integration has become the watchword for an entire movement lasting four decades, we are hard-pressed to put forth a widely accepted alternative."[64] The longstanding use of the term requires its appearance here, however with a nuanced explanation.

Some explain the task of integration as putting back together that which others divided. Those speaking of the integration of faith and learning may describe integration as "merg[ing] the world of facts and the world of values."[65] Those attempting to integrate the findings in academic disciplines might describe integration as "drawing together two data bases."[66] Gaebelein defines integration as "the bringing together of parts into the whole."[67] These descriptions stress the work of people putting back together a fundamentally divided reality or restoring to original unity reality divided by humanity. This split between "studying solely created realities in science and studying distinctly Christian realities in theology . . . . [results] in the unhelpful and false radical bifurcation of the world into a study of the secular and of the sacred, of science divorced from theology and vice versa."[68]

However, the focus, like that of Scripture, resides in the fundamental unity of all things in Christ (Col 1: 16–17). The metaphysical distinction found in the Bible is "not between sacred and secular but between God and his creation."[69] Wilhoit emphasizes that people simply explore the unity that already exists. Instead of "attempting to integrate or harmonize two separate or differing spheres of understanding or truth" we should "demonstrate[e] the *unity* of truth whose author is God and whose stewards we are."[70] We do this by studying all of reality in the Spirit."[71] Gangel emphasizes the need to "enable the student to see the unity of natural and special revelation."[72] As with Wilhoit and Gangel, integration means seeing the unity that already exists.

63. Badley, "Locus of Faith-Learning Integration," 286–95.
64. Stokes and Lewis, *Integration of Behavioral Sciences and Theology*, 3.
65. Van Dyke et al., "Integration and the Christian College," 93.
66. Berry, "Integration of the Social Sciences," 34.
67. Gaebelein, *Pattern of God's Truth*, 7.
68. Coe and Hall, "Transformational Psychology View," 207.
69. Holmes, *Truth*, 28.
70. Wilhoit, "Faith and Learning Reconsidered," 81.
71. Coe and Hall, "Transformational Psychology View," 207.
72. Gangel, "Preface," viii.

One aspect of integration consists of seeing the unity between Christian belief and fields of academic inquiry. Harris highlights the hard work of seeing the interconnectedness of Christian belief and academic disciplines. He writes, "Integration involves the development of interconnections, relationships, and mutual clarifications between Christian truth and academic content. We might call integration the construction—or discovery—of the wholeness and coherence of all knowledge."[73] Integration includes not only an integration of one's faith with his specific field of study but also the necessary inclusion of other fields of study.

Additionally, a faith response to divine revelation includes studying the created order. DeVries highlights the important aspect of integration as a human response to divine revelation. He describes, "In the primary sense I would like to define integration as a process of revelation and faith-response. In a second sense . . . the focus is upon achieving unity and consistency in our scientific knowledge, especially between psychology and theology."[74] Similarly, Farnsworth explains integration as "the process of *discovering* God's truth through theology and psychology, *verifying* the accuracy of the findings, *relating* them, and *applying* them in one's life. That is, truth is revealed and must be received and then responded to."[75]

Synthesizing key aspects of the above descriptions, I define integration as the exploration of the interrelationship of God's revelation through the Bible and through the created order. Integration requires the active and intentional involvement of those variously gifted in the body of Christ (theologian, scientist, artist, for example). Integration involves the critical examination and selective incorporation of insights given by God through common grace to unbelievers. The written Word and the world come together to create a fuller picture of God, the world, and the relationship between the two. Scripture and the created order mutually relate to one another. In brief, I focus on the integration of all truth.

Some may question the mutual integration proposed above. However, Scripture assumes prior knowledge of things such as "the difference in quantities" and "the link between cause and effect" even literary structure and the interpretation of poetry versus narrative for interpretation.[76] Therefore, Scripture itself sets the precedence for mutual integration.

---

73. Harris, *Integration of Faith and Learning*, 24.
74. DeVries, "Conduct of Integration," 323.
75. Farnsworth, "Conduct of Integration," 310.
76. Budziszewski, *Evangelicals in the Public Square*, 31–33.

Additionally, many theologians affirm mutual integration as the proper task of the Christian. Bavinck serves as an example of one who sees a mutual reinforcement between general and special revelation. He states,

> But as a disclosure of the greatness of God's heart, special revelation far surpasses general revelation, which makes known to us the power of his mind. General revelation leads to special, special revelation points back to general. The one calls for the other, and without it remains imperfect and unintelligible. Together they proclaim the manifold wisdom which God has displayed in creation and redemption.[77]

Similarly, Erickson writes, "Since both creation and the gospel are intelligible and coherent revelations of God, there is harmony between the two and mutual reinforcement of one by the other. The biblical revelation is not totally distinct from what is known of the natural realm."[78] Finally, Geisler proposes the mutual engagement of theology with other disciplines as well.

> In theology the interaction between biblical studies and other disciplines should always be a two-way street. No one provides a monologue for the other; all engage in a continual dialogue. Although the Bible is infallible in whatever it addresses, it does not speak to every issue. Furthermore, as we have seen, while the Bible is infallible, our interpretations of it are not. Thus, those in biblical studies must listen to as well as speak to the other disciplines. Only in this way can a complete and correct systematic worldview be constructed.[79]

Scripture and the created order reveal God, creation, and the relationship between the two. While Scripture informs the created order, the created order also informs Scripture. Both forms of revelation taken together create a more complete picture of reality.

Created Order

The created order encompasses everything created by God as well as that which his image bearers create. The created order, therefore, entails human beings and animals as well as non-living things such as the solar system. The created order includes the expressive creativity of those created in God's image as they fulfill the creation mandate to fill and subdue the earth (Gen 1:28). The goodness of creation extends to "the full range of human cultures

---

77. Bavinck, *Philosophy of Revelation*, 28.
78. Erickson, *Introducing Christian Doctrine*, 42.
79. Geisler, *Systematic Theology*, 1:79.

that emerge when humans act according to God's design."⁸⁰ The task of dominion (or stewardship) of the earth means "discover[ing] the character of other creatures and . . . assist[ing] these creatures to act in character."⁸¹ Therefore, the created order encompasses culture. Culture, describes Crouch, "*is what we make of the world.* Culture is, first of all, the name for our relentless, restless human effort to take the world as it's given to us and make something else."⁸² The created order includes God's recreation in part now and in fullness in the eternal state. The created order therefore consists of the direct creation of God, the creation of those made in his image, and his re-creation. Use of "created order" instead of "nature" or other such terms is intentional. The terminology separates God from his creation. The term also reminds the reader of the fact that God created all that exists. Additionally, "order" emphasizes the plan, sovereignty, and providence of God.

Need for the Study

The theology of revelation, a core epistemological concept for Christians, receives a paucity of attention in proportion to its importance.⁸³ Latourelle observes, "Revelation is the first fact, the first mystery, and the first category of Christianity. But, this reality is not a much studied subject."⁸⁴ Even when people study revelation, they often focus on a narrow examination of one form of revelation. Latourelle continues, "The twentieth century, more conscious of the complexity of the activity of revelation and the multiplicity of the aspects of revelation, oscillates from one aspect to the other, always in danger of stressing one element to the detriment of the other."⁸⁵

If revelation as a whole receives little attention, revelation through the creation receives even less thought. Tozer observes, "The idea that God

---

80. Plantinga, *Engaging God's World*, xv.

81. Ibid., 31.

82. Crouch, *Culture Making*, 23.

83. Similarly, Moore wants Christians to "take seriously the revelation of God in creation." He views the neglect of the created order as revelation as "a significant lacuna" in the theological study and spiritual growth of Christians. Moore, *Consider the Lilies*, 14.

84. Latourelle, *Theology of Revelation*, 14. Revelation is a primary concept within epistemology. God's revelation confronts humans with his existence. Only by his grace does anyone respond positively to this gift. So, God exists, he reveals, and he enables fallen people to respond properly to his revelation of his existence.

85. Latourelle continues, "[R]evelation is at once activity, event, history, knowledge, testimony, encounter, doctrine, immutable deposit, inner word." Latourelle, *Theology of Revelation*, 244.

reveals Himself in the creation is not held with much vigor by modern Christians; but it is, nevertheless, set forth in the inspired Word, especially in the writings of David and Isaiah in the Old Testament and in Paul's Epistle to the Romans in the New."[86] More recently, Johnston observes, "There have been in the last fifty years relatively few monographs written on 'general revelation.'"[87] He attributes this to "[t]heology's bias toward the redemptive over the creational, and toward the propositional over the narrative."[88]

Even more, the relationship between general and special revelation requires continued thought with particular attention given to general revelation.[89] As Bavinck states, "In former times Christian theology drew the distinction between special and general revelation. But it never wholly thought through this distinction, nor fully made clear its rich significance for the whole of human life."[90] Likewise Budziszewski asserts, "The reality of general revelation changes the whole meaning of how to take revelation seriously."[91]

However, since the Reformation a shift from the two books of God (Word and world) to Scripture alone took place and is seen most acutely in evangelicalism. Dyrness observes a shift from two books to a focus on one book. He writes, "Little by little what had been widely understood as two books, revelation in Scripture and in nature, was reduced to God's voice in Scripture alone. And it was in the evangelical movement in particular where this reduction became most evident."[92] Demarest also observes the tendency to depreciate general revelation among some evangelicals:

86. Tozer, *Knowledge of the Holy*, 13–14.

87. Johnston, "Discerning the Spirit in Culture," 54. See also Johnston, *God's Wider Presence*, 8.

88. Johnston, *God's Wider Presence*, 8

89. Evangelicals tend to use the categories of "general" and "special" revelation in reference to revelation. Some other categories used throughout church history are: Word and world; book of nature, book of Scripture and book of the cross (Bonaventure); knowledge of God as Creator and knowledge of God as Redeemer (Calvin); legal knowledge of God and saving knowledge of God (Charnack); glasse of the creature, glasse of the Holy Scriptures, and glasse of Jesus Christ (Zanchi); light of nature and light of revelation (Edwards). Some other contemporary categories include: revelation and discovery (Litfin, Gaebelein); knowledge of covenant keepers and knowledge of covenant breakers (Van Til); supernatural and natural (Saucy); special grace and common grace; events, words, and persons (Frame); and faith in God and faith in reason (Van Dyke). Calvin, *Institutes*; Litfin, *Conceiving the Christian College*; Saucy, "Divine Revelation;" Van Til, *Christian Apologetics*; Van Dyke et al., "Integration and the Christian College," 89–96; and Frame, *Doctrine of the Word of God*, 72.

90. Bavinck, *Philosophy of Revelation*, 26.

91. Budziszewski, *Evangelicals in the Public Square*, 33.

92. Dyrness, "Evangelical Theology and Culture," 146.

> Throughout history, theological liberalism by various means has inflated the value of general revelation, thereby reducing special revelation to but one aspect of God's universal providence. On the other hand, fundamentalism has tended to depreciate the value of general revelation, arguing that the only things worth knowing about God are supernaturally revealed in the Bible.[93]

Erickson notices the same trend: "Some Christians, noting the excesses to which natural theology has gone in constructing a theology quite apart from the Bible, have overreacted to the point of ignoring the general revelation."[94]

Budziszewski observes and articulates the specific problem within evangelicalism. He notes their inconsistency between affirmation and practice regarding the created order as revelation. He observes that evangelicals rightly ground political thought (his area of concern) in the Bible, but miss the fact that revelation exists outside the Bible. The Bible, though fully true, does not contain all truth.[95] Yet, as Budziszewski comments, "Evangelical theologians are somewhat reluctant to say much about it [general revelation], not because they think it isn't real . . . but because they fear that saying much about it might detract from the more perfect revelation of the Bible."[96] He points out that "[t]his is a strange fear" because Scripture itself testifies of God's general communication.[97] He suggests, "the greater danger lies in *not* talking about general revelation."[98]

Budziszewski offers basic examples to make this important point regarding evangelicals and general revelation. In studying the political theories of four influential Christians (Henry, Kuyper, Schaeffer and Yoder), he concludes all four exemplify an ambivalent attitude toward general revelation. He critiques,

> All four thinkers are ambivalent about the enduring structures of creation and about the reality of general revelation. Although Henry vigorously affirms general revelation, he undermines it just as vigorously. Although Kuyper unfolds his theory mainly from the order observable in creation, he insists on hiding this fact from himself, regarding his theory of creational spheres as a direct inference from Scripture. Although Schaeffer acknowledges the importance of general revelation, he makes little use

---

93. Demarest, *General Revelation*, 15.
94. Erickson, *Christian Theology*, 75.
95. Budziszewski, *Evangelicals in the Public Square*, 30.
96. Ibid., 31.
97. Ibid.
98. Ibid.

of any part of it except the principle of non-contradiction. No sooner does Yoder affirm God's good creation than he declares that we have no access to it.[99]

Evangelicals all too often fall into the same pattern of affirming creation as revelation, but then neglecting it.

Bouma agrees that Christians are "ambivalent . . . regarding creation as a source of revelation about God."[100] He states, "Scripture and creation are acknowledged as two books of revelation, special and general, respectively; but creation is relegated to secondary status."[101] He clarifies what he means, "Nature is confirmatory and not revelatory" for Christians and particularly "that branch of Christian theology considered to be conservative and evangelical."[102] As Bouma observes, for these people, "creation itself is not truly revelatory, but only signatory."[103] Creation serves as confirmation of theological beliefs; in other words, "I told you so," or signifies whereby creation "point[s] to God without making substantial contribution to our knowledge of the Divine."[104]

In another work, Wolters, interacting with evangelicals in a Counterpoints book observes, "It is telling that none of the four authors [Walter Kaiser Jr., Daniel Doriani, Kevin Vanhoozer, William Webb] refers to it [general revelation], even though it is part of standard Protestant theology. Instead, they discuss special revelation as contained in the Bible. The only kind of normativity that they want to acknowledge is that which comes from the Bible."[105]

J. P. Moreland believes evangelicals neglect the created order because of a myopic focus on Scripture. He writes, "[I]n the actual practice of the Evangelical community in North America, there is an over-commitment to Scripture in a way that is false, irrational, and harmful to the cause of Christ."[106] Moreland describes this over-commitment to Scripture as both "ubiquitous and harmful" and then states, "the Bible is the *sole* source of

---

99. Ibid., 120. Budziszewski's words indicate that "ambivalence" is too soft. Evangelicals actually undermine their affirmation of general revelation just as strongly as they affirm it.

100. Bouma, "Creation's Persistent Voice," 1.

101. Ibid., 2.

102. Ibid.

103. Ibid., 1.

104. Ibid., 5.

105. Wolters, "A Reflection by Al Wolters," 317. The authors examine and critique four models of how people move beyond the Bible to theology with the intent of addressing significant contemporary issues.

106. Moreland, "Over-Committed."

knowledge of God, morality, and a host of related important items" for evangelicals.[107] Granted, neglect of other forms of revelation does not *necessarily* mean that evangelicals are over-committed to the Bible, as Moreland asserts. Nonetheless, the point of his message is worthy of thoughtful examination. Moreland reminds the reader that while evangelicals use Scripture as the "sole authority," the long standing belief by Christians is that Scripture is instead the "ultimate authority."[108]

As Moreland articulates, "By and large, Evangelicals responded during this shift [secularization and fact-value divide] by withdrawing from the broader world of ideas, developing a view of faith that was detached from knowledge and reason, and limiting truth and belief about God, theology and morality to the inerrant Word of God, the Bible."[109] Moreland views the retreat from the intellectual as evidence of an unhealthy over commitment to the Bible.[110]

---

107. Ibid.

108. Ibid. It must be acknowledged that while a lineage of the Christian tradition makes this affirmation, there have always existed questions regarding the use of sources outside of Scripture. While there is no single universal response or one God-ordained way to understand this complex issue, there is certainly room for critical thought on approaches and adjustments to be made as Christians continue to wrestle with theological issues in light of changing cultural contexts.

109. Ibid.

110. Ibid. Undermining other forms of revelation does not necessarily mean one is overly committed to Scripture. However, within evangelical circles still influenced by fundamentalism, the two occur together. Moreland's comments raise an important issue which is the unhealthy idea that "sola Scripture" means "only Scripture." More recently, Christian Smith wrote on the prevalence of biblicism among evangelicals. He observes that evangelicals use the Bible as handbook that deals with all of life's issues (5). As such the Bible directly addresses every question a person may ask and no other source of knowledge on the topic is needed. Smith argues that the reality of interpretive pluralism proves the inadequacy of biblicism (3–54). He suggests that "biblicism demeans scripture" (93). Smith makes some important observations and suggestions that evangelicals must take seriously as we explore the relationship between Scripture and the created order. He then proposes a Christo-centric reading of Scripture that takes into account the complexity of human interpretation. (Smith, *Bible Made Impossible*). Moreland and Smith notices the continued effects of the debate between modernists and fundamentalist. The debated resulted in a polarization of general and special revelation that carries over into some sectors of evangelicalism. Some want to correct this (Noll's *The Scandal of the Evangelical Mind*), however, more work is needed. I believe Scripture retains a position of privilege in relation to other forms of revelation, but this does not require rejecting, undermining or insufficiently attending to other forms of revelation and in particular the created order. The relationship between Scripture and other forms of revelation is complex and requires additional thought.

David Diehl blames "an underdevelopment in their doctrine of general revelation" for evangelical problems in integration.[111] His analysis grows more specific: "Evangelicals, especially in America, have concentrated on special revelation and inspiration and have highly developed views in these areas. But they have not written nearly as much on general revelation."[112] Therefore, Diehl suggests, "presenting a full-orbed, consistently Biblical doctrine of general and special revelation is largely the inherited task of Evangelical theologians."[113] We still await this work, but the current dissertation begins to address the issue. Let us now look at the thesis.

Thesis of the Study

Evangelicals affirm the created order as revelation, but tend to neglect it in systematic theology. The same inconsistency is evident in efforts to integrate faith and learning. As such, I propose a theology of revelation intended to overcome the inconsistency between evangelicalism's confession and practice. The theology emphasizes similarities between the forms while maintaining the distinctness of each form.

I propose the following theology of revelation: Revelation is divine communication.[114] Though God uses numerous forms of revelation, three chief forms include the created order (world), Scripture (written Word), and the Incarnation (Word who came into the world created through him). Revelation, regardless of form, comes from God and retains his character.

---

111. Diehl, "Evangelicalism and General Revelation," 441.

112. Diehl later states that if revelation undergirds all human knowledge then more thought must be given to the implications of general and special revelation. Ibid., 442–43.

113. Ibid., 442.

114. The term "communication" seems ubiquitous when discussing revelation. Some use "communication" in reference to special revelation, but not general revelation. Ryrie, *Basic Theology*, 31, 71; Chafer, *Systematic Theology*, 1: 48. Others view revelation as communication without differentiating the form of revelation. Bavinck, *Reformed Dogmatics*, 1:283; Olson, *Mosaic of Christian Belief*, 72; Lightner, *Evangelical Theology*, 10–11; Moore, "Natural Revelation," 106; and Packer, *Knowing Christianity*, 11. Noll uses "communication" in reference to "revelation in nature, in Scripture, [and] in Jesus Christ." Noll, *Life of the Mind*, 106. Furthermore, Michael Horton uses a theory of communication to explain divine revelation. He uses speech act theory as a way to overcome Dulles' models of revelation and to describe revelation. Horton, *Christian Faith*, 117–22. On one hand, failure to use a theory of communication to understand revelation is understandable since, as Fortner observes, no single comprehensive definition of communication exists. Fortner, *Communication, Media, and Identity*, 15. On the other hand, not seeing the similarities between human communication and divine revelation demonstrates blindness to the created order as revelation.

In brief, adjectives such as true, authoritative, sufficient, contextualized, progressive, and interpreted characterize revelation.[115] The recipients of divine communication include all created beings. However, those created in God's image (unredeemed as well as redeemed) uniquely receive and respond to God's revelation. In a post-fall world, people suppress and twist revelation instead of responding with thanksgiving and praise. Therefore, people depend (intentionally or unintentionally) on the Spirit's work of illumination and redemption to respond rightly. The content of revelation includes knowledge of God, his relationship to creation, as well as creation itself. The effects of revelation range from knowing God, redemption of man, sharing the gospel, worshipping God, and finally rejection of it leads to condemnation.

Method of the Study

I begin by demonstrating the evangelical tendency to affirm the reality that God reveals through the created order but then neglect its usefulness. One can discern this tendency in evangelical systematic theologies. I examine roughly eighty evangelical systematic theologies on the basis of their description of theology, discussion of revelation, and use of revelation.[116] Evangelicals tend to describe systematic theology in three ways (systematizing verses, systematizing doctrine, and systematizing all truth). Only one of these three ways intentionally suggests the inclusion of the created order as divine revelation. I organize this chapter, then, around these three categories. Then within each section, I list the theologies in chronological order. I then note ways in which each theologian uses the created order. Evangelical theologians' usage of this revelation fits into roughly six discernable categories: opposition, proofs, application, illustration or analogy, contribution, and integration.

Since no comprehensive list of evangelical systematic theologies exists, I begin with those known in my own tradition and those listed by Grudem and Elwell.[117] The list largely reflects works by North Atlantic evangelicals because Majority World evangelicals write books on specific issues of great

---

115. Van Til provides an excellent explanation of the necessity, authority, sufficiency and perspicuity of both natural and special revelation. While both retain these qualities they are for different purposes, to different extents and in different ways. Van Til, *Christian Apologetics*, 55–82. Van Til asserts, "God speaks with authority wherever and whenever he speaks." Ibid., 73.

116. See Bibliography, "Systematic Theologies."

117. Grudem, *Systematic Theology*, 1224–30; and Elwell, *Evangelical Theologians*.

concern not systematic theologies.[118] The reader may question some on the list and wish others were included. The list reflects how I defined evangelicalism above. Therefore, works from the Reformed tradition to Pentecostalism find inclusion. Those listed adhere to the Bible as the "supreme authority for faith and practice" and the "centrality of the redeeming work of Christ."[119] The works include some discussion of standard doctrines found in systematic theologies.

The tendency of evangelicals toward neglecting the created order as a form of revelation also appears in efforts at the integration of faith and learning. Evangelicals hold to four presuppositions that suggest mutual integration between Scripture and the created order. They believe in the unity of reality, that all truth is God's truth, that God reveals through both Scripture and the created order, and that Scripture maintains a special place. However, evangelicals approach the task of integration in four discernable ways. Evangelicals take a "Bible only" approach, a uni-directional approach, a leaning toward Scripture approach, or a mutually informing approach to integration. The last approach alone seeks to use the created order as a complementary form of revelation with Scripture.

I then examine how evangelical definitions and categorizations of revelation contribute to utilizing Scripture to the neglect of the created order. I observe how evangelicals explain the relationship between reason and revelation and how they use the categories of general and special revelation. Insights here guide the construction of my own theology of revelation.

Finally, my theology of revelation results from synthesizing teachings of Scripture, tradition and contemporary thinkers regarding the following aspects of revelation: source, form, characteristics, recipients, content and function. Akin to Latourelle's method in *Theology of Revelation*, Scripture, tradition and contemporary thought build my understanding of revelation. The goal is to "sum up the reflections which spring from the very contemplation of the object of faith, collected and systematized; a reflection faithful to revealed truth, taking account of the theological activity of past centuries,

---

118. Scott Horrell made this observation. Resultantly, Majority World evangelicals do not compose systematic theologies covering a range of doctrine as North Atlantic evangelicals do. The author only finds two works outside North America and Europe. One does not reflect a true systematic theology, but covers pertinent issues of prolegomena. Gnanakan, *Biblical Theology in Asia*. The other represents a South American systematic theology, but one greatly shaped by North Atlantic thinking. Myatt and Ferreira, *Teologia sistemática*. J. Scott Horrell, informal conversation, July 9, 2010.

119. Bingham, *Pocket History*, 162.

in all its best elements, and also taking account of the aspirations and orientations of present-day research."[120]

Conclusion

The created order is true, valid, and real revelation with the potential of pointing humanity back to and more significantly revealing God. The created order can open our eyes to seeing God and his creation in new and more intense ways. Evangelicals affirm the reality of revelation given through the created order, but tend to neglect this revelation in systematic theologies and efforts at integration. One book cannot correct the inconsistency between affirmation and practice. However, the current work highlights the tendency and offers a theology of revelation intended to overcome the issue.

In the chapters to follow, I demonstrate the evangelical tendency to argue for the existence of the created order as revelation, but then to neglect it. In chapter two, I demonstrate this tendency in systematic theologies. In chapter three, I explore the same tendency in evangelical works discussing integration. In chapter four, I explain some complications with current evangelical definitions and categorizations of revelation. These insights lead to the creation of the evangelical theology of revelation proposed in chapter five.

---

120. Latourelle, *Theology of Revelation*, 313.

2

Review of Systematic Theologies

Introduction

The moderator of a regional Evangelical Theological Society meeting asked, "What is the most significant challenge facing evangelical theological method?"[1] Three of the four respondents mentioned a need to include the created order.[2] Their responses highlight evangelicalism's neglect of this form of revelation. Although evangelicals argue that the created order reveals God, they make little use of it. Systematic theologies provide a place to observe this inconsistency between words and practice.

As I review evangelical systematic theologies, I look for the author's teaching regarding the created order as revelation, his explanation of systematic theology, and his use of the created order in his theology. Why examine how each theologian describes systematic theology? Evangelicals explain "systematic theology" in one of three ways. Some identify systematic

---

1. Panel Discussion, "Evangelical Theological Method."
2. Robert Stewart said evangelicals fail to take general revelation seriously. He clarified that taking general revelation seriously meant either studying science or at least entering into serious dialogue with those who do. Stewart referred to the integration of theology and science as an important theological issue. In the same discussion, Craig Blaising mentioned that evangelicals need to engage the social sciences. Additionally, Glenn Kreider pointed out the need to look at any and every source, but understand that we do so as finite creatures. We, therefore, depend upon the Spirit's work through others (redeemed and unredeemed) as we study both books (Scripture and nature). Panel Discussion, "Evangelical Theological Method."

theology as a systematization of verses on specified topics. Others describe systematic theology as systematizing doctrines whereby the author demonstrates the relationship between doctrines. Still others describe systematic theology as a systematization of all truth (or Scripture and the created order). A theologian's stated methodology either includes the created order or it excludes such revelation.

Regardless of how evangelicals describe systematic theology, a unified method undergirds the great variety of perspectives across denominations. Grenz and Franke observe:

> The rationalist approach that typifies evangelical theology is characterized by a commitment to the Bible as the source book of information for systematic theology. As such, it is viewed as a rather loose and disorganized collection of factual, propositional statements. The task of theology in turn becomes that of collecting and arranging these varied statements in such a way as to bring their underlying unity into relief and reveal the eternal system of timeless truths to which they point. This "concordance" or "rationalist loci" conception of theology looks back to Charles Hodge, arguably the most influential American theologian for evangelicals, and his view that the task of theology "is to systematize the facts of the Bible, and ascertain the principles or general truths which those facts involve."[3]

The theologies evaluated below unearth the pervasive influence of Charles Hodge's description of the theological task.[4] The idea of mining Scripture to find the data of theology marks evangelicalism's tendency. However, confusion and complexity abound. On one hand, those limiting systematic theology to the Bible generally use tradition and the created order in some measure.[5] On the other hand, those who speak of a complementary role for Scripture and the created order mostly systematize Scripture. What role, then, does the created order play in evangelical systematic theologies?

The created order does appear in systematic theologies in six discernible ways.[6] First, the theologian mentions views *opposed* to his own. One

---

3. Grenz and Franke, *Beyond Foundationalism*, 13–14. Carl Henry serves as one example. He writes, "The task of Christian theology is to exhibit the content of biblical revelation as an orderly whole." Henry, *God, Revelation and Authority*, 1: 215.

4. Hodge follows the Baconian method of scientific investigation. The individual interprets the data of Scripture and collects them to form a theological system. Pearcey, *Total Truth*, 299.

5. At the very least everyone uses logic in their *systematic* theology.

6. People cannot escape the world in which they live. As such, philosophy (even common sense philosophy), tradition, and reason find their way into the works of men

generally finds the oppositional use of the created order in chapters on creation. Second, the reader notices an explanation of the classic *proofs* for God. Third, many evangelical theologians include a section of *application*. Sometimes the writer proposes ways to apply theology to life. Other times application questions encourage the reader to think about the implications of a doctrine for life. Fourth, the created order provides *illustrations or analogies* by which the author seeks to clarify his explanation of the doctrine. Fifth, some authors use the created order as a piece of *evidence* (verification) that contributes to the doctrine described. Finally, sometimes one finds an evangelical systematic theology where the writer seeks to *integrate* the created order with the Bible in forming a doctrine or part of a doctrine.[7] We can now look at how evangelical theologians use the created order.

Systematizing Verses

Evangelicals from Pieper (1917–1924) to Evans (2008) explain the task of systematic theology as simply systematizing verses of Scripture.[8] Each acknowledges the created order as revelation, but they do not include it in their stated methodology. These "Bible only" theologians seek to follow strictly the approach set out by Hodge. They mine Scripture for data and then organize that which they collect. However, their practice includes use of sources in addition to Scripture; namely, tradition, reason, and some nominal use of the created order.

Francis Pieper recognizes that the created order reveals God. He favorably cites Luther, "The natural knowledge of God . . . enables us to know

---

intent on only systematizing the biblical text. However, my acknowledgement of the pervasiveness of philosophy, reason, and one's tradition on theological methodology does not detract from the overall point. These simply represent the air breathed by evangelicals. Generally, evangelicals overlook or neglect the *intentional and purposeful* use of philosophy, tradition, reason, other academic disciplines, contemporary culture, and experience of the creation (intellectual or merely lived) in their theologies.

7. Categories like "oppositional" or "applicational" stretch the idea of utilizing creation as a source since the authors do not actually *use* the created order in a positive way. However, even in my efforts toward generosity, I find little use of the created order in evangelical systematic theologies. The fifth and sixth categories reflect a positive and intentional use of the created order in systematic theologies.

8. Cornelius Van Til suggests a "Bible only" method. Since he limits his work to prolegomena, I mention his description of systematic theology here instead of in the text. Van Til writes that "Systematic theology seeks to offer an ordered presentation of what the Bible teaches about God." He consistently holds that theologians systematize verses found throughout the entire canon of Scripture: "[S]ystematics alone seeks to offer the truth about God as revealed in Scriptures as a *whole*, as a unified system." Van Til, *Systematic Theology*, 15, 17.

God, as it were, from without, from his works, just as we learn something of the character of the builder from the quality of the house he builds."[9] However, he emphatically explains a "Bible only" approach to systematic theology. He believes that theologians simply restate or re-present the doctrine taught in Word of God. He describes theology thusly:

> The theological aptitude includes the ability of the theologian to *confine himself in his teaching entirely to God's Word*; he must be able to *suppress his own thoughts* about God and divine matters and *put aside the thoughts of other men, deriving the doctrine exclusively from the Word of God*, from Holy Scripture. The theologian who refuses to do this is, in the words of St. Paul, a bloated ignoramous . . . Scripture thus declares all those to be theologically incompetent and disqualified for the Christian ministry who are not willing to take their doctrine *exclusively from Holy Scripture*.[10]

Pieper here rejects all but Scripture in a response of fear to those wrongly elevating other sources.

Later Pieper asserts that theology "is nothing more and nothing less than the *presentation in oral and written form of the doctrine presented in Holy Scripture*. The Christian doctrine is *not produced by the theologian*;" instead the theologian "compiles the doctrinal statements contained in Scripture (in the text and context), groups them under their proper heads, and arranges these doctrines in the order of their relationship."[11] Pieper limits exegetical theology to Scripture alone, as well. Scripture provides all the historical background necessary for the correct understanding of Scripture.[12]

However, Pieper builds his own position with "biblical and confessional references."[13] He not only collects the data of Scripture, he also relies upon Luther and human reason. In one place, he mentions that "the Lutheran theologians are agreed" that the image of God "is lacking in man after the fall," but they differ on whether "a divine image is still ascribed to man after the Fall." He then cites various Lutheran theologians and concludes, "[T]

---

9. Pieper, *Dogmatics*, 1:377. Pieper cites: "Luther XII: 629ff." Pieper's "English translation of his *Christliche dogmatik* still sets the tone in large part for the theology of the Lutheran Church-Missouri Synod." Scaer, "Francis Pieper," 40.

10. Pieper, *Dogmatics*, 1:48; emphasis added.

11. Ibid., 52; emphasis added.

12. Ibid., 101. No extra-biblical material, philological or historical, may determine the exegesis.

13. Scaer, "Francis Pieper," 45.

he interpretation of Luther is to be preferred."[14] Pieper does not follow his own "Bible only" approach to theology, but the reader does find a consistent refrain throughout his work, "Scripture teaches" or "Scripture shows."[15] He then follows this with either a listing of references or a quotation of a verse or verses.

Following Pieper, Lutheran theologian John Mueller states that the task of the theologian "consists only in presenting the several divine truths given in Holy Scripture under their proper heads. Mueller derives these truths from the proof-passages (*sedes doctrinae*), that is, from the clear and unmistakable passages in which particular doctrines are set forth."[16] Contrary to Charles Hodge, Mueller rejects the notion that one can liken theology to other disciplines.[17] Instead, theology's "subject-matter is the divine truth, set forth in Holy Scripture; its source, the Holy Bible; its method (*medium cognoscendi*), faith; its purpose, the salvation of sinners."[18] For Mueller, theology simply requires the Bible and faith.

Mueller's work consists largely of his *reasoning* about citations of Scripture. The reader notices occasional quotes from other theologians to assist in explaining a point or as examples of opposing positions. Mueller does observe that the created order verifies the teaching of Scripture regarding the unity of man. He states, "With this doctrine agree also the conclusions of outstanding anthropologists, who, on grounds *apart from divine revelation*, have affirmed the unity of the human race."[19] However, the affirmation means little to Mueller since he believes in the unity of man "on the basis of Scripture" alone.[20] Likewise, Mueller agrees that people can discern the providence of God from the created order, but he limits the source of this doctrine to Scripture as well.[21] Although Mueller cannot deny the

---

14. Pieper, *Dogmatics*, 1:519.

15. Pieper, *Dogmatics*, 2:3, 2:27, 2:468, 2:541, 2:335.

16. Mueller, *Christian Dogmatics*, 88.

17. Hodge argues, "The Bible is to the theologian what nature is to the man of science. It is his store-house of facts; and his method of ascertaining what the Bible teaches, is the same as that which the natural philosopher adopts to ascertain what nature teaches." Hodge, *Systematic Theology*, 1:10. Mueller asserts, "Christian theology is not a science in the same sense as, for instance, geology, psychology, biology, etc., are sciences. It differs from these sciences not only in subject matter, but also in source, method, and purpose." Mueller, *Christian Dogmatics*, 68.

18. Mueller, *Christian Dogmatics*, 68.

19. Ibid., 185; emphasis added. Anthropologists may know apart from Scripture, but not apart from divine revelation. God reveals through the created order.

20. Ibid.

21. Ibid., 189.

affirmations of Scripture regarding God's revelation through the created order, he does decide to neglect any significance of such teaching for theology.

Reformed theologian P. B. Fitzwater begins with Scripture as his sole source of theology. He describes theology as "the science of God's essential being and His relationship to the universe as set forth in the Holy Scriptures."[22] However, as he continues, he accepts the importance of knowledge from other sciences "[s]ince God is immanent in the universe and is a transcendent personality above the universe, every branch of true science makes its contributions to theology. The wider, therefore, the knowledge of the sciences, the fuller and clearer will be one's comprehension of theology."[23] Fitzwater uses the Bible as his standard, but he does not believe this requires a rejection of revelation through the created order.

In practice, Fitzwater heavily relies on the Bible throughout. He rarely quotes other conservative theologians. However, the reader does spot occasional usage of the created order. For instance, Fitzwater briefly explains the traditional proofs for God.[24] He cites the changed lives of those who believe in the Bible as verification for the inspiration of Scripture.[25] Additionally, the biblical doctrine of the unity of man is *corroborated* by history and science. Fitzwater provides a paragraph explanation from history, philology, physiology, and psychology to demonstrate each field's contribution to the unity of man. However, he offers no sources or quotes.[26] Fitzwater, contrary to his stated method, does make limited use of the created order.

Dispensationalist Henry Thiessen follows Hodge's explanation of theology. Theologians systematize the biblical text: "The Bible is to the theologian what nature is to the scientist, —a body of unorganized or only partly organized facts. God has not seen fit to write the Bible in the form of a Systematic Theology; it remains for us, therefore, to gather together the scattered facts and to build them up into a logical system."[27] Unlike Pieper, Thiessen admits the "importance of reason, intuition, the creeds and confessions of the Church," but insists "they are not really sources for theol-

---

22. Fitzwater, *Christian Theology*, 19. Another example from the Reformed perspective comes from Timothy Phillips and Dennis Okholm. In their popular level theology they equate revelation with the Bible yet teach the created order reveals God. The authors utilize the created order as illustrations (positive or negative) of points made by Scripture. They also use the created order to help people apply Scripture within their current context. Phillips and Okholm, *Welcome to the Family*, 42–52, 56–57.

23. Fitzwater, *Christian Theology*, 19.

24. Ibid., 72–74.

25. Ibid., 39.

26. Ibid., 307.

27. Thiessen, *Systematic Theology*, 28.

ogy, but helps in the understanding of the revelation of God, particularly as contained in the Scriptures."[28]

Accordingly, Thiessen builds a case for revelation through the created order based on Scripture. He includes the testimony of believers in other fields of study who see God's revelation in the created order. He observes:

> But men in general have always seen in nature a revelation of God. The more gifted of them have often expressed their convictions in language similar to that of Psalmists, Prophets and Apostles (Ps. 8:1, 3; 19:1, 2; Isa. 40:12-14, 26; Acts 14: 15-17; Rom. 1:19, 20) . . . Many outstanding men in the field of the natural and biological sciences have testified to the conviction that nature reveals God. They have pointed to the universe as a manifestation of the power, glory, divinity, and goodness of God.[29]

The created order, therefore, verifies the teaching of Scripture regarding its identity as revelation.

In practice, the reader finds some references to an extra-biblical source in Thiessen's theology. For example, in discussing the work of Satan, Thiessen states, ". . . in harmony with Milton's *Paradise Lost*, the Word of God represents him [Satan] as having power (*dunamis*), a throne (*thronos*), and great authority (*exousia*) (Rev. 13:2; Matt. 4:8, 9)."[30] Here Thiessen not only refers to an extra-biblical text but also harmonizes the Bible with Milton instead of the reverse. Thiessen also points out that "the universe everywhere exhibits evidence of intelligence and control" as evidence for God's providence *prior to the teaching of Scripture* on divine providence.[31] Despite his stated methodology Thiessen finds limited use for the created order.

Charles Ryrie, author of a popular level dispensational theology, teaches that God reveals through the created order.[32] Yet he limits systematic theology to "correlat[ing] the data of biblical revelation as a whole in order to exhibit systematically the total picture of God's self-revelation."[33] Throughout his work Ryrie quotes and cites Scripture, as well as other theologians and biblical scholars. Aside from a short chapter on evolution, anything one might consider general revelation is missing.[34] Ryrie limits his use of the

---

28. Ibid., 118.
29. Ibid., 32-33.
30. Ibid., 210.
31. Ibid., 178; emphasis added.
32. Ryrie, *Basic Theology*, 31.
33. Ibid., 15.
34. For example, Ryrie misses an opportunity to reference the created order when

created order to proofs for God, "General revelation provides evidences for the existence of God."[35] Like Pieper, Ryrie largely follows a biblical theology, plus historical theology equals systematic theology methodology.[36]

Baptist theologian Wayne Grudem adopts the methodology proposed by Hodge.[37] Grudem explains, "Systematic theology is any study that answers the question, 'What does the whole Bible teach us today?' about any given topic."[38] Yet he acknowledges the reality of revelation through the created order.[39] Grudem does leave some room for tradition, philosophy, and apologetics. However, these largely give structure to the act of systematization. They do not integrate to form the content of theology.

In practice, Grudem's few uses of the created order include verification when he argues that seasons, food, and gladness reveal that the Creator "is a God of mercy, of love, and even joy."[40] In his section on creation, Grudem explains other views in opposition to the teaching of Scripture.[41] And he refers to the faith of Newton, Galileo, and Kepler to illustrate the importance of evangelicals studying creation.[42] Grudem includes hymns and application questions throughout his work. So, although Grudem proposes a "Bible only" theology, like many other evangelicals he includes limited use of the created order in his systematic theology.

---

discussing attributes such as love, grace, or mercy. He cites Scripture, but does not reference the created order for illustrations. The reader may question the fairness of such a critique until he realizes that Charnock uses both Scripture and the created order in his work on God's attributes. Charnock, *Attributes of God*.

35. Ryrie, *Basic Theology*, 31.
36. Ibid., 15.
37. Grenz and Franke, *Beyond Foundationalism*, 14.
38. Grudem, *Systematic Theology*, 21; emphasis removed. Tony Evans, writing for a lay audience, follows Grudem's method much more closely than Grudem himself. Evans identifies that "[t]he challenge then is to organize those truths in a way that communicates a clear understanding of the Bible's teaching on any subject it addresses. This organizing process is called *systematic theology*." Evans, *Theology*, 17. Evans' work follows his description. Endnotes and footnotes do not exist. The reader finds an occasional quote to illustrate a point. However, he mostly cites passage of Scripture after passage of Scripture. Resultantly, he provides the best example of a "Bible only" theology. However, even he cannot escape the influence of his training, his cultural context, and his own experience. Furthermore, he, too, affirms the reality that God reveals through the created order, though he uses it only as illustration and application. Evans believes that "God's revelation of Himself in creation is powerful and profound" but severely limited since it does not save sinners. Ibid., 1065.

39. Grudem, *Systematic Theology*, 122.
40. Ibid., 121.
41. Ibid., 271.
42. Ibid., 273.

J. Kenneth Grider, like Hodge, likens theology to other scientific disciplines and believes the data of Scripture must be systematized. Grider writes, "Just as people observe nature and build physical and biological sciences from it, so theologians come to the spread-out revelation of God in Scripture, sort through it, order it, systematize it, and often use its raw material to build theological sciences that are useful to the Church in its worship, its faith, its hope, its love, its evangelism."[43] Resultantly, "Christian doctrine and practice should be founded only upon what is taught in Scripture."[44] For Grider, Scripture becomes the only source of theology. The Bible informs life and practice in a uni-directional way.

Grider, a representative of the Wesleyan-Holiness tradition, does not use the categorizations of general and special revelation, but he mentions that God reveals himself through nature.[45] The created order illustrates and provides examples of specific topics. For instance, in his chapter on evil Grider quotes Shakespeare's *Hamlet* and *Othello* along with a section from James Thomson's poem, *City of Dreadful Night* as examples of pessimism.[46] However, in a chapter on the doctrine of creation Grider depends heavily on conservative theologians regarding the age of the earth with minimal citation of conservative Christian scientists.[47] Grider intersperses examples and illustrations from the created order but generally cites a plurality of passages of Scripture and quotes other theologians from his tradition to support or help explain his theology. In sum, knowledge of the created order enables people to apply their theology within their current context.

Like Grider, Robert Reymond focuses on the teaching of the Bible and intersperses this with theologians and exegetes primarily from his (Reformed) tradition. He does not mention tradition when he defines theology as the "intelligent effort to understand and explicate the whole Bible viewed as revealed truth."[48] Instead, theologians merely systematize verses of the Bible. He asserts:

> Systematic theology is the methodological study of the Bible that views the Holy Scripture as a *completed* revelation . . .

---

43. Grider, *Theology*, 100. However, contrary to the objective and timeless theology sought by Hodge and others, Grider understands the historical situatedness of the theological task. The continued work of the Spirit and new scientific developments provide new ways to apply theology. Ibid., 32–34.
44. Ibid., 100.
45. Ibid., 42–45.
46. Ibid., 193.
47. Ibid., 172.
48. Reymond, *Systematic Theology*, xxv.

Accordingly, the systematic theologian, viewing the Scriptures as a completed revelation, seeks to understand holistically the plan, purpose, and didactic intention of the divine mind revealed in Holy Scripture, and to arrange that plan, purpose, and didactic intention in orderly and coherent fashion as articles of the Christian faith.[49]

Following the stated method, in some places Reymond simply quotes passages of Scripture without comment.[50] He acknowledges that the created order reveals God, but sees no need of it in theology.[51]

Pentecostal theologian Larry Hart understands systematic theology in terms of systematizing verses of Scripture. He, like Grider, believes that theology addresses the current cultural context. Hart initially defines systematic theology as "*a coherent and comprehensive explication of the teachings of the canonical Scriptures (the Bible) in relation to contemporary questions and knowledge.*"[52] Later he includes historical and contemporary theology in his explanation of the task of systematic theology. Systematic theology "has the audacious challenge of utilizing the results of all these disciplines [Biblical theology, Historical theology and Contemporary theology] and then taking the further step of providing a comprehensive presentation of the Christian faith for contemporary society."[53] The created order, then, helps inform the theologian of what questions to address in his theology as he mines Scripture for answers.

Hart teaches that the created order reveals God.[54] He mentions general revelation when discussing God's wisdom. However, he uses Scripture alone to make the point that people see God's wisdom in creation. Hart concludes,

---

49. Ibid., xxv–xxvi.

50. For example, regarding the body of Christ, Reymond simply lists verses that speak of the "accomplishments of Christ's 'body'" without explanation or commentary. Ibid., 625.

51. Ibid., 5.

52. Hart, *Truth Aflame*, 18. One work produced by Asian evangelicals states the need for contextualization. Chow writing on issues in theological method acknowledges that some speak of "formative factors" such as "experience, revelation, Scripture, tradition, culture and reason," but critiques this approach for making "no clear commitment to the Bible as the normative source." Chow, "Evangelical Theology," 112–13. He proposes a method very similar to Grudem's. Chow writes "we must first understand what the Bible says as a whole about particular subjects and then obey and apply it to the present context." Ibid., 115. Furthermore, even though God reveals through history and the Christ event "evangelicals accept only the Bible as the source of theology, because it is the written Word of God." Ibid., 112.

53. Hart, *Truth Aflame*, 19.

54. Ibid., 43–45.

"*The evidence is abundant both in Scripture and in the universe itself* that God's wisdom permeates his creation (Prov. 3:19; 8:22–31; Jer. 10:12)."[55] He misses an opportunity to point the reader to examples directly from the created order as well as pointing the reader to the Bible's teaching. Hart defends the usefulness of the created order as revelation, but mainly uses Scripture and tradition in forming his systematic theology.

Daniel Akin serves as editor of a Baptist theology in which Gregory Thornbury addresses issues of prolegomena. Thornbury explains that systematic theology, "the intellectual support mechanism of the Christian truth claim, therefore, becomes a project of explaining precisely *how* God's sovereignty applies in every domain of knowledge. The way to do this is to move in a coherent fashion throughout the text of Scripture and distill the doctrine therein in propositionally coherent language."[56] Thornbury's description follows Hodge's methodology.[57] Every chapter in this multi-author theology "is organized around four main questions, the order of which is significant: (1) What does the Bible say? (2) What has the church believed? (3) How does it all fit together? and (4) What is the significance of the doctrine for the church today?"[58] Resultantly, Scripture serves as the source for theology and tradition appears as a background "to help God's people see how we arrived where we are today."[59]

In the same work, Russell Moore builds a case for and explains the created order as revelation.[60] He identifies a number of applicational benefits of general revelation; such as fulfilling the creational mandate and leading people to worship God.[61] In another chapter, Timothy George cites a poem by St. Patrick, stanzas of hymns, and a soliloque from Augustine as he explains God's nature.[62] Another contributor, Stanton Norman uses the created order as an illustration. Norman begins his chapter on harmartiology with an overview of M. Night Shyamalan's *The Village*.[63] Finally, Russell Moore includes use of the created order as application in his chapter on eschatology. Applications include bodily integrity (affirming the impor-

---

55. Ibid., 100; emphasis added.

56. Thornbury, "Prolegomena," 55.

57. Thornbury quotes Hodge's description of systematic theological method. Ibid., 54.

58. Akin, "Preface," vii.

59. Ibid., viii.

60. Moore, "Natural Revelation," 109–16.

61. Ibid., 114, 116.

62. George, "The Nature of God," 182, 188, 193, 197.

63. Norman, "Human Sinfulness," 409–10.

tance of our body without being ruled by our appetites), and vocation (joy in work, whatever it is, since work will be part of eternal state).[64] This final systematic theology not only spends the most time discussing general revelation it also contains the most uses of the created order, though largely as illustration or application.

In summation, all of the above theologians believe that God reveals through the created order. However, their stated methodology (systematizing verses) leaves no room for this revelation as a source of theology. One might question why they defend the existence of general *revelation* but then do not use it. If systematic theologians simply repeated Scripture then there would be one systematic theology. Instead, the above theologies differ in many areas which result in Lutheran, Wesleyan, Dispensational, and Reformed theologies.[65] Each author's tradition shapes his theology and many explicitly quote other theologians. All use logic, reason, and the scientific method in their theology. Furthermore, many use the created order (proofs, illustrations, opposition, and application), but few use it as verification or in an integrative way with Scripture. Those who use the created order as verification of the Bible do so sparingly (Fitzwater and Thiessen). Since our "Bible only" theologians in fact use more than the Bible and argue that the created order reveals God, then how might evangelicals use the created order in systematic theology? Next, we look at evangelicals who systematize doctrine.

Systematizing Doctrines

From Hodge (1871–1873) to Horton (2011), some evangelicals describe systematic theology as systematizing doctrine. In other words, the theologian demonstrates the inter-relationships between doctrines. Such an explanation does not necessarily limit the data of systematic theology to Scripture alone. However, many theologians limit the source of their doctrines to the biblical text. The difference, then, between these and the previous systematic theologies primarily resides in focus. The theologies that follow concern themselves with how one doctrine relates to others. For example, Horton relates all other doctrines to his doctrine of the Trinity.

Reformed theologian Charles Hodge represents the "systematizing doctrine" methodology. For Hodge, systematic theology consists of mining the Bible for data and compiling that data into a system. The theologian then explains how the texts within a particular doctrine relate to one

---

64. Moore, "Personal and Cosmic Eschatology," 920–21.
65. Sawyer, *Survivor's Guide to Theology*, 111.

another as well as how one doctrine relates to another doctrine. Hodge explains, "The Bible contains the truths which the theologian has to collect, authenticate, arrange, and exhibit in their internal relation to each other . . . [Systematic theology] determine[s] their relation to each other and to other cognate truths, as well as to vindicate them and show their harmony and consistency."[66] The Bible serves as the sole source of systematic theology.

However, Hodge like other evangelicals believes that God reveals through the created order.[67] He even mentions the great value of the laws of nature and religious experience.[68] Yet, he minimizes the importance of the created order because Scripture more clearly teaches the same things.[69] When Hodge does use the created order it is generally to explain views that oppose his own.[70] Occasionally, Hodge uses the created order to illustrate a doctrine. For example, people attribute inability to see to blindness. Likewise, if someone cannot see "the glory of God in the face of Jesus Christ" it is "because the god of this world has blinded his eyes."[71] Last, Hodge borrows his theological method from accepted scientific investigation.[72] The fact that Hodge and other *evangelicals apply the scientific method to* Scripture is the greatest and most overlooked use of the created order.[73]

Arminian theologian William Pope explains that systematic theology "takes the system of doctrine as its basis, but illustrates it from history, and verifies it by Scripture. It has this peculiarity that while every work on systematic theology more or less bears the impress of one confessional stamp."[74] Instead of coming to Scripture as a *tabula rasa*, Pope asserts that people begin within a system of doctrine because all theologians write from a particular confessional standpoint. He describes theology as "the systematic arrangement of the truths pertaining to the revelation of God."[75] This

---

66. Hodge, *Systematic Theology*, 1:1–2. See "Systematic Theology" in chapter one for an explanation of my interpretation of Hodge's method.

67. Ibid., 11.

68. Ibid., 10, 16.

69. Ibid., 11, 15, 19, 21.

70. Hodge, *Systematic Theology*, 3:195–203.

71. Ibid., 74.

72. Hodge, *Systematic Theology*, 1:10. His theology "is generally derived from the scholasticism characteristic of post-Reformation Protestant orthodoxy and its emphasis on rationalism." Grenz and Franke, *Beyond Foundationalism*, 14.

73. In fact, contemporary theologians who include discussions of prolegomena in their works (for example, Erickson, Demarest, and Geisler) derive their methodology from the created order not Scripture.

74. Pope, *Christian Theology*, 1:27.

75. Ibid., 24.

statement appears as though Pope includes all forms of revelation. However, Pope explicitly equates revelation with the Bible, "The Bible means all revelation and all revelation means the Bible."[76] In the end, Pope, like Hodge, seeks to show the relationships between doctrines that the theologian derives from Scripture alone.

Nonetheless, Pope, like many evangelicals, affirms the reality that God reveals through the created order, but minimizes its importance in light of Scripture.[77] However, unlike many evangelicals, Pope sees the benefit for *both* the created order and Scripture to form theology. He asserts, "With the progress of human culture theology progresses. In its relation to science, philosophy, learning, and civilization generally, it gives and receives."[78] For example, the fields of psychology and ethics study aspects of humanity which could "throw much light upon the doctrines of the Fall and conversion and regeneration and sanctification."[79] Pope also uses the created order as secondary verification for the unity of God.[80] In practice, Pope mostly cites Scripture as he expounds upon various doctrines. However, he does include historical theology and occasional references to the created order.

Reformed theologian William Shedd also describes systematic theology as the systematizing of doctrine. He articulates, "When the individual doctrines have been deduced, constructed, and defended by the exegetico-rational method, they are to be systematized. Systematic theology aims to exhibit the logical order and connection of the truths of revelation."[81] Shedd believes that God reveals through the created order. He equates general revelation with unwritten revelation and includes within it all human knowledge.[82]

How, then, does Shedd use this revelation? Shedd observes that Scripture incorporates knowledge gained outside of Scripture. He points out that Scripture offers no formal argument for the existence of God. Instead, "The evidence relied upon in the Scriptures for divine existence is derived from the immediate and universal consciousness of the human soul, as this is

---

76. Ibid., 41. Similarly, H. Orton Wiley also states that the created order reveals God, but then equates revelation with the Bible. Wiley, *Christian Theology*, 1:18, 1:37, 1:52. Wiley also explains systematic theology in terms of systematizing doctrine. Ibid., 27.

77. Pope, *Christian Theology*, 1:36.

78. Ibid., 24.

79. Pope, *Christian Theology*, 3:170.

80. Pope, *Christian Theology*, 1:258–59.

81. Shedd, *Dogmatic Theology*, 50.

82. Ibid., 85, 87.

awakened and developed by the works of creation and providence."[83] So Shedd uses the created order as verification of the teaching of Scripture. He begins a section on "arguments from pagan philosophers for an innate knowledge of God" with the statement, "The teaching of St. Paul respecting the innate idea is confirmed by that of the pagan philosophers themselves."[84] Shedd also employs both Scripture and the created order to propose a case for monotheism. Shedd states that the original form of religion was monotheism not polytheism or pantheism. He asserts, "This is proved by the Bible and the earliest secular records . . . The earlier Greek poetry is more monotheistic than the later."[85] He, therefore, utilizes the created order to both verify and integrate with the teaching of Scripture to a greater extent than many other evangelicals.

Shedd draws on the created order in a variety of ways. In his chapter on creation he includes a sub-section "harmony of the Biblical creation account with physical science."[86] Shedd uses the created order to illustrate.[87] In some cases, Shedd limits himself to the Bible alone or the Bible plus other theologians.[88] Overall, Shedd makes room for the created order without neglecting the importance of Scripture. However, his use of the created order typically occurs in distinct sub-sections. For example, he begins with the teaching of Scripture on an issue in one section, the next section he covers key thoughts of other theologians, then in a third section he explains the teaching that stems from the created order. The sections exist side by side not in a fully integrated fashion.

W. T. Purkiser, a follower of Pope and Wiley, does not include a section on prolegomena or discussion of general revelation in his multi-authored theology. He intends "to provide an introduction to evangelical Wesleyan Christianity as understood in churches conventionally described as part of the holiness movement."[89] I include his theology here because of his use of the created order. Pope mentioned the potential significance of integrating Scripture and the created order, but Purkiser begins to carry this out.

---

83. Ibid., 186.

84. Ibid., 188.

85. Ibid., 196.

86. Ibid., 374–79. Shedd mentions that the created order corroborates with the teaching of Scripture.

87. Ibid., 470. Shedd provides three illustrations of unity and individuality as he proposes physiological arguments for traducianism. He argues on the basis of Scripture, church history, and the created order in favor of traducianism.

88. Ibid., 803–6, 867–73, and 550–602, 793–800, respectively.

89. Purkiser, ed., *Exploring Our Christian Faith*, 8.

Purkiser includes proofs for God in this theology. He also directly quotes people who hold the specific view instead of citing secondary sources such as other systematic theologies. For instance, in his explanation of the cosmological argument, Purkiser refers to Jeans, "The significance of this is explained by Sir James Jeans, the noted Cambridge physicist, astronomer, and mathematician."[90] He then includes a lengthy paragraph from Jeans' *The Mysterious Universe*. Purkiser employs the created order as verification of the teaching of Scripture. For example, he believes the scientific method evidences "the existence of a Supreme Being."[91] He allots four pages to the "empirical evidence" for God, which is the testimony or experience of those who encounter God.[92] In the same work, Sanner points out that the created order reveals God's attributes. For example, "The discovery of the almost incredible extent of our universe, where distances are measured in light-years, has given us a new understanding of the omnipotence of God, as well as of His other attributes."[93]

Most other contributors to the work rationally explicate the biblical text. They generally present "the biblical position" in contrast to positions held by those outside the Christian community. For instance, phraseology such as "the biblical understanding of God"[94] or "[i]t falls far short of the biblical position"[95] and "the biblical doctrine of sanctification,"[96] reoccurs across chapters. However, like Shedd, Purkiser provides glimpses of how the created order and Scripture mutually inform one another.

J. Rodman Williams' systematic theology represents "the first published from an explicitly charismatic perspective."[97] He describes systematic theology as a systematization of doctrines. He defines theology as the "contents of the Christian faith as set forth in orderly exposition by the Christian community."[98] Williams clarifies that "the word *system* points up the interlocking and interdependent character of all the doctrines that make up theology."[99] His definition does not necessarily limit systematic theology

---

90. Ibid., 36. In a three page explanation of the teleological argument Purkiser quotes no less than six different scientists (37–39).

91. Ibid., 43.

92. Ibid., 46–50.

93. Ibid., 120.

94. Ibid., 131.

95. Ibid., 115.

96. Ibid., 328.

97. Grudem, *Systematic Theology*, 1230.

98. Williams, *Renewal Theology*, 1:15.

99. Ibid., 17; emphasis added.

to Scripture. However, in practice Williams constructs his theology from Scripture with occasional citation of other theologians for support or clarity.

Williams briefly explains seven views of man (materialistic, biological, psychological, economic, sociological, philosophical, and existentialist) in his theology.[100] He acknowledges that "[d]oubtless, there is truth in many of the things said about man."[101] However, in the remainder of the chapter he turns to "view man in light of *divine revelation*," which means Scripture with an occasional quote from another theologian.[102] He does not explore what truths these other views might contribute to his anthropology. This inclusion of the created order is an isolated case in Williams' work. In spite of the fact that Williams believes "it is important to observe that there is a general revelation of God."[103]

Baptist theologians Gordon Lewis and Bruce Demarest understand systematic theology as systematizing doctrine. They propose an integrative theology which follows a verification method whereby the theologian "defines a major topic, surveys influential alternative answers in the church [historical theology], amasses relevant biblical data in their chronological development [biblical theology], formulates a comprehensive conclusion [systematic theology], defends it against competing alternatives [apologetics], and exhibits its relevance for life and ministry [practical theology]."[104] The very description of their theology informs the reader that they limit the construction of systematic theology to church history and Scripture.[105] They do this in spite of the fact that they argue that God reveals himself through the created order.[106] They apply their theology in apologetics and everyday

100. Ibid., 197–98.
101. Ibid., 198.
102. Ibid., 95.
103. Ibid., 33.

104. Lewis and Demarest, *Integrative Theology*, 1:25. Similarly, Bray explains that theology "is essentially no more than the teaching of Holy Scripture set out in a coherent way." Bray, *God is Love*, 88. He largely uses the created order in an applicational sense. For example, he includes a section on "our responsibility for the fallen material world." Ibid., 504. He does include a chapter on world religions under the broader heading of the rejection of God's love whereby he points out similarities between the religions and Christianity, though not because he explains these as divine revelation through the created order. Ibid., 427–38.

105. Michael Bird does the same in his work. He holds that "there is a symbiotic relationship between Scripture and tradition" in theological method. He acknowledges that God reveals himself through creation. However, he states nature is "a *stimulus* for theology" and culture is "more of an embedded context in which theology takes place," neither of which does he count as sources of theology. Bird, *Evangelical Theology*, 65, 72, 76. For another recent example, see Sproul, *Everyone's a Theologian*.

106. Lewis and Demarest, *Integrative Theology*, 1:61–91.

life and ministry. Their definition of systematic theology further limits its content to Scripture. Lewis and Demarest write, "*Systematic theology* not only derives coherent doctrines from the entirety of written revelation but also systematically relates them to each other in developing a comprehensive world view and way of life."[107] Systematic theology stems from Scripture. The created order helps people apply the theology derived from Scripture.

Lewis and Demarest use the created order in their theology in a few ways. They use the created order to illustrate. For instance, in their discussion of the problem of evil, they use the illustration that Henry Ford "is the final cause of all Ford cars" and "who could well have envisioned misuses of his automobiles," but decided to invent them anyway.[108] The authors use the created order in an oppositional fashion. Their interaction with those in other fields of study comes not in their systematization of anthropology, but in their apologetic interaction.[109] Lewis and Demarest also use the created order as application. For example, they include a section entitled "Relevance for life and ministry," in which they offer ways to apply a specific doctrine to life.[110] Although they begin each chapter with a survey of major teachings throughout church history, they state: "To determine which historical perspective on Scripture is closest to the Bible's view of itself, we need to survey the relevant biblical materials in the context of progressive revelation."[111] In the end, their "integrative theology" resembles the methodology of a "Bible only" theology.

Another prominent Baptist theologian, Millard Erickson, defines theology as "that discipline which strives to give a coherent statement of the doctrines of the Christian faith, based primarily on the Scriptures, placed in the context of culture in general, worded in a contemporary idiom, and related to issues of life."[112] More succinctly, theology is "[t]he discipline that concerns itself with describing, analyzing, criticizing, and organizing the doctrines."[113] The doctrines primarily come from Scripture. The theologian forms them into a coherent whole. Erickson understands that systematic theology occurs within time and space. He also leaves room for the use of the created order in his description of systematic theology.

---

107. Ibid., 23.

108. Ibid., 322.

109. Lewis and Demarest, *Integrative Theology*, 2:142–71.

110. Ibid., 113–19; 357–65; 490–95. Even here the authors tie many of these ideas back to a particular passage of Scripture.

111. Lewis and Demarest, *Integrative Theology*, 1:322.

112. Erickson, *Christian Theology*, 23.

113. Ibid., 21.

Erickson not only asserts the reality of revelation given through creation, he writes of its value.[114] He supports a *minor role* for the created order in systematic theology. He cautions, "While philosophy, along with other disciplines of knowledge, may also contribute something from general revelation to the understanding of theological conceptions, this contribution is minor compared to the special revelation we have in the Bible."[115] Accordingly, Erickson largely uses Scripture, thoughts from exegetes, and other theologians throughout his work. For instance, his chapter on sanctification makes no mention of contribution from revelation given through the created order.[116] However, he does occasionally use the created order to illustrate a point.[117] He also includes opposing views of humanity (machine, animal, sexual being, economic being, pawn in the universe, free being, and a social being) to alert the reader to non-Christian understandings. He desires to enable the reader to dialogue intelligently with people holding these views. Erickson derives his anthropology from Scripture alone, though.[118] Erickson leaves room for and only allots a minor role to the created order in his systematic theology.

Rolland McCune, another representative of Baptist theology, defines systematic theology as systematizing doctrines. Systematic theology is "the doctrine(s) of the Bible set forth according to plan or order."[119] McCune acknowledges that many authors in the Bible affirm that "God has plainly disclosed Himself in creation."[120] However, systematic theology comes from Scripture alone. He asserts, "Of the various channels of God's self-disclosure (e.g., miracles, nature, etc.), there is only one with which the theologian can work in his construction of doctrine—*Scripture*."[121] He reasons: "[I]t is impossible to construct an authoritative theology on material that is not propositional in content *and* form."[122] Therefore, the created order is an "illegitimate source for systematic theology."[123] He even explicitly rejects

---

114. Ibid., 198–99.
115. Ibid., 29.
116. Ibid., 979–95.
117. Ibid., 283–84, 556.
118. Ibid., 486–93.
119. McCune, *Systematic Theology*, 1:3. The doctrines, though, come from the Bible alone. Systematic theology "is the correlation of the various teachings or doctrines found in the Bible." Ibid., 5.
120. Ibid., 174.
121. Ibid., 171.
122. Ibid., 18.
123. Ibid., 19.

tradition as a source of theology.[124] However, McCune himself uses conservative theologians to help him make his point. For example, his seven channels of revelation are "taken from Alva J. McClain."[125] So, like others, McCune falls short of his "Bible only" methodology.

As with the above theologians, Michael Horton explains the task of systematic theology as systematizing doctrine. Systematic theology "pulls together these insights [themes drawn from Biblical theology] in a formal dogma and relates the Trinity to other doctrines in Scripture."[126] He continues, systematic theology "point[s] out the logical connection between various doctrines spread throughout Scripture."[127] Horton affirms that "God is knowable because he has revealed himself to us."[128] Therefore, we "know God according to his works," but Horton limits our knowledge to Scripture as he continues, "the history of God's action—revealed and interpreted in Scripture—is our only access."[129] So, though Horton argues that God reveals through the created order, he finds only revelation given in Scripture as useful for constructing systematic theology.

In practice, Horton relates every area of theology to the covenantal relationship between God and creation. He reads Scripture through the lens of covenantal theology (his tradition) and explicitly relates each doctrine to his doctrine of the Trinity. In regard to revelation given through the created order Horton makes use of it in an oppositional sense. However, in his chapter on creation he does point out that "the idea that our cosmos came into being at a definite point in time . . . is now affirmed generally by the sciences."[130] He also observes the "growing overlap between Christian theology and the sciences" among issues like temporality and relationality.[131] Horton, however, generally builds his doctrines from Scripture and tradition.

In summary, the above evangelicals explain systematic theology as a systematization of doctrines. Such an explanation does not necessarily limit the source of their theology to Scripture. However, many of the above theologians provide additional explanation that narrows the source of theology to Scripture alone (Hodge, Pope, Lewis and Demarest, McCune, and Horton).

---

124. Ibid., 25.
125. Ibid., 173.
126. Horton, *Christian Faith*, 29.
127. Ibid.
128. Ibid., 35.
129. Ibid., 61.
130. Ibid., 341.
131. Ibid., 343.

Yet even these theologians teach the reality that God reveals through the created order. They also utilize tradition in addition to Scripture in their theology. Many do employ the created order in some way (proofs for God, illustrations of doctrine, and including opposing views).

Others in this group, like Pope and Erickson, express potential benefit of including the created order in the formation of theology. Purkiser and Shedd either use the created order to verify the teaching of Scripture or they integrate Scripture and the created order. Since theologians that systematize doctrine in fact use more than the Bible and argue that the created order reveals God, then how might evangelicals use the created order in systematic theology? Next, we look at evangelicals who explain systematic theology as systematizing all truth.[132]

Systematizing All Truth

Evangelical theologians from Strong (1886) to Plantinga, Thompson, and Lundberg (2010) explain that systematic theology consists of correlating Scripture and the created order. The reader therefore assumes that each theologian integrates Scripture and the created order. Surprisingly, many fail to follow through with their stated method. Instead, like those in the categories above, they largely cite Scripture, occasionally make reference to the created order, and sparingly integrate Scripture and the created order.

Baptist theologian Augustus Strong proposes that the theologian integrates the created order and Scripture. For Strong, theology "is therefore a summary and *explanation of the content of God's self-revelations*. These are, first, the *revelation of God in nature*; secondly and supremely, the revelation of God in the Scriptures."[133] He recommends a mutual relationship between these forms of revelation, "Science and Scripture *throw light upon each other*" as enabled by the Spirit.[134]

In practice, Strong identifies the philosophical proofs for God (cosmological, teleological, anthropological and ontological) as corroborative evidences for God.[135] He integrates the created order and Scripture, on oc-

---

132. "Systematizing all truth" is a misnomer. Finite people cannot know "all truth" therefore *literally* systematizing *all truth* is impossible. However, the idea of observing how the created order and Scripture cohere as two forms of divine revelation is possible. The authors who follow seek to integrate or correlate truth from across forms of revelation. They do not propose to arrange in systematic fashion everything that is true.

133. Strong, *Systematic Theology*, 25; emphasis added. The created order reveals God.

134. Ibid., 27; emphasis added.

135. Ibid., 71–89.

casion. For example, Strong points out that Scripture (Gen 1:27) does not tell us the method of man's creation. However, psychology "comes in to help our interpretation of Scripture."[136] Strong uses both psychology and comparative physiology to build a case for mediate creation.[137] When discussing the unity of mankind, Strong builds his argument from Scripture, human history, language, psychology, and physiology.[138] However, through most of the work Strong heavily cites and quotes Scripture and references and quotes historical and contemporary theologians. He makes relatively little use of the created order as revelation. Though in contrast to other evangelicals, Strong does make at least some positive use of God's revelation given through the created order.

Like Strong, Arminian theologian John Miley claims that doctrinal truth stems from *both* Scripture and the created order. He explains, "So must systematic theology study the elements of doctrinal truth, *whether furnished in the book of nature or the book of revelation, and in a scientific mode combine them* in doctrines."[139] He argues for the significance of *both* nature and revelation as sources of theology. Rejection of revelation (Scripture) "maintains that whatever we need to know of God and his will and of our duty and destiny may be discovered in the light of nature"; rejection of nature (created order) maintains "that nature makes no revelation of God and duty, and, at most, can only respond to the disclosures of the divine revelation.[140] Therefore, Scripture and the created order integrate to form doctrines. For example, "Out of the facts respecting God, as *manifest in nature and revealed in Scripture, we may construct a doctrine of God.*"[141]

In practice, Miley's theology looks similar to those who use Scripture as their only source. He primarily cites and quotes Scripture. He uses other conservative theologians to support his logical argumentation. He does use the created order as he covers the proofs for God's existence.[142] He also includes description of the philosophies which he opposes.[143]

---

136. Ibid., 466.

137. Ibid., 470–72. Strong argues, "The radical differences between man's soul and the principle of intelligence in the lower animals, especially man's possession of self-consciousness, general ideas, the moral sense, and the power of self-determination, show that that which chiefly constitutes him man could not have been derived, by any natural process of development, from the inferior creatures."

138. Strong, *Systematic Theology*, 476–82.

139. Miley, *Systematic Theology*, 1:5; emphasis added.

140. Ibid., 7–8.

141. Ibid., 47; emphasis added.

142. Ibid., 73–109.

143. Ibid., 110–36.

Samuel Gamertsfelder differentiates biblical theology "which is properly limited to the Bible for its source," and systematic theology for which the entire "world is open as a field of research."[144] The created order reveals God. Gamertsfelder writes, "Facts that throw much light on the being of God and His relation to the works of His hand are discovered in all parts of the universe."[145] Therefore, "The unbiased theologian will make room for the fully verified conclusions of science in his body of divinity."[146] Thus, Scripture and the created order integrate to form doctrine.

In practice, Gamertsfelder uses the created order to illustrate how a carnal and a divine nature (moral nature not material substance) co-exist in the redeemed. He writes, "It is a common occurrence in the physical world that two natures are found in the same organism. One branch of a tree may be dead while others are living."[147] On this basis, Gamertsfelder argues the same happens in the moral realm. He then states, "This appeal, however, is valid in theology only if it is in accord with the teaching of God's Word. The Word of God is our ultimate authority."[148] He then references New Testament passages that exhort believers to "put away the remains of the carnal nature."[149] Similarly, he begins the chapter on eschatology stating that reason alone cannot prove immortality. Only special revelation can prove the doctrine, but "a number of cogent arguments on this precious doctrine are available."[150] He then explains arguments for immortality based on reason.[151] He largely uses Scripture with an occasional reference to other theologians.

Benjamin Warfield, a Reformed theologian, did not produce a systematic theology. However, he did write on theological method. I include him here because of his prominence as well as his discussion of theological method. Warfield writes, "[T]he sole source of theology is revelation."[152] He continues, "[W]e distribute the one source of theology, revelation, into the various methods of revelation, each of which brings us true knowledge of God, and all of which must be taken into account of in building our

---

144. Gamertsfelder, *Systematic Theology*, 16.
145. Ibid., 17.
146. Ibid., 19.
147. Ibid., 532–33.
148. Ibid., 534.
149. Ibid.
150. Ibid., 578.
151. Ibid., 578–81.
152. Warfield, *Studies in Theology*, 58.

knowledge into one all-comprehending system."[153] Warfield explains that systematic theology is systematization of data from nature and Scripture. He explains,

> It is with *no reserve* that we accept all these sources of knowledge of God—nature, providence, Christian experience—as true and valid sources, the well-authenticated data yielded by which are to be received by us as revelations of God, and as such to be *placed alongside of the revelations in the written Word* and wrought with them into one system. As a matter of fact, theologians have always so dealt with them; and doubtless they always will so deal with them.[154]

However, he later responds, "the theologian must yet *refuse to give these sources of knowledge a place alongside of the written Word*, in any other sense than that he gladly admits that they, alike with it, but in unspeakably lower measure do tell us of God."[155] Warfield illustrates common confusion among evangelicals. At first he states evangelicals use the created order in theology, but later he refuses to use the created order in theological method.

Lewis Chafer, a prominent dispensational theologian, describes systematic theology as "[a] science which follows a humanly devised scheme or order of doctrinal development and which purports to incorporate into its *system all the truth about God and His universe from any and every source*."[156] Chafer explicitly rejects systematic theology as merely "the scientific treatment of those truths which are found in the Bible" because systematic theology "while drawing the majority portion of its material from the Scriptures, does, nevertheless, draw its material from any and every source."[157] Chafer points out the inadequacy of Hodge's method. He writes, "Systematic Theology has been defined as the orderly arrangement of Christian doctrine; but as Christianity represents only a mere fraction of the whole field

---

153. Ibid., 59.
154. Ibid., emphasis added.
155. Ibid., 61; emphasis added.
156. Chafer, *Systematic Theology*, 1: 5; emphasis added. See also Robert Lightner, who uses Chafer's definition of systematic theology Lightner, *Evangelical Theology*, 2. Lightner heavily cites Scripture. The reader finds little use of general revelation. Lightner explains that his work is "a survey and review, not a systematic theology per se." Ibid., 2–3. In his section on the existence of God, Lightner moves from tradition (36–42), to the philosophical proofs (42–43), then to biblical justification (44–45), and ends with "God's revelation of himself in His world" (45–46).
157. Chafer, *Systematic Theology*, 1:5.

of truth relative to the Person of God and His universe, this definition is inadequate."[158] Chafer thereby rejects a "Bible only" definition of systematic theology.

However, Chafer changes his description from systematizing truth "from any and every source" to systematizing "the truth contained in the Bible" something he previously rejected as inadequate.[159] In practice, he quotes or cites Scripture throughout. Additionally, he finds use for quotations from other conservative theologians and exegetes, creeds, and major historical figures. In some chapters he provides brief descriptions of other positions, but even then much of this comes from other theologians. Chafer's awareness of the breadth of theology ends up tempered by his actual practice where little contribution is made by anything outside of Scripture.

Ultra-dispensationalist Charles Baker's initial explanation of theology suggests he intends to systematize all truth. Theology "in the broadest sense of the word is the study, not only of God, but also of all of His works."[160] Sources of revelation include, "Intuition, Tradition, Science, and Revelation. Theology makes use of knowledge from all four sources, although Revelation is the chief and only authoritative source."[161] Theology, then, can include a relationship "between God and His universe" however the method can be limited to "a systematizing of the teachings of the Bible."[162]

Baker points to experience and archeology as evidence for the authenticity of the Bible.[163] He concludes, "Archeological proofs are perhaps the most objective type of evidence for the genuineness of the Scriptures."[164] Baker also explains the traditional philosophical arguments for the existence of God.[165] He includes, for example, radioactivity, the second law of thermodynamics and the expanding universe theory as pointing to a created not eternal universe under the cosmological argument.[166] Finally, when discussing God's work of preservation, Baker begins by quoting Scripture, but then turns to "the testimony of science," speaking of electrical charges that repel and attract as evidence of God's work.[167] However, as with other

---

158. Ibid.

159. Ibid., 21.

160. Baker, *Dispensational Theology*, 8. Ultra-dispensationalists hold that the church begins in Acts 13 not Acts 2.

161. Ibid., 17.

162. Ibid., 13.

163. Ibid., 58–59, 60–61.

164. Ibid., 61.

165. Ibid., 110–24.

166. Ibid.

167. Baker, *Dispensational Theology*, 232.

evangelicals, Baker largely quotes Scripture and other theologians throughout his theology.

The Wesleyan theology edited by Charles Carter represents a systematic theology that retains a high view of Scripture, but also integrates Scripture and the created order. Systematic theology is "the contemplative, analytical, and holistic study of the God concept as set forth in Scripture, variously interpreted by the church throughout history, experienced in the community of faith, and critically reviewed in light of contemporary concerns both pastoral and societal."[168] Chapters such as "Social Involvement" and "Psychology" alert the reader to its uniqueness among theologies. Duane Thompson writes the chapter on social involvement. He begins with an examination of biblical foundations. Then, he looks at the teaching and practice of Wesley. Last, he turns to "contemporary principles and issues" whereby he seeks to work toward a "Christian moral/social order" which in fact is distinctly Wesleyan.[169] He concludes the chapter stating that "[o]ne significant step has been taken: a major theological work from the Wesleyan perspective has realized the crucially relevant nature of social involvement in theological writings. It is to be hoped that this is not the end of the story but the wave of the future."[170]

James Ridgway, author of the chapter on psychology, includes a justification of relating theology and psychology. His chapter includes an examination of how psychology impacts Christian thought, how Wesley and other Wesleyans view psychology, tensions between psychology and theology, and using both disciplines on specific issues.[171] Ridgway covers a number of issues where both Scripture and psychology speak to an issue, but does so in great brevity.[172] Though these chapters offer a beginning at integrating Scripture and the created order, much of the rest of the work consists of the teachings of Scripture and Wesley (or the Wesleyan tradition) on the doctrine.

Post-foundational Baptist theologian Stanley Grenz asserts that "if theology is to be truly systematic and meaningful, theologians must take into consideration the discoveries and insights of the various disciplines of human learning and seek to show the relevance of Christian faith for the human quest for truth."[173] He identifies the Bible, "the flow of church

---

168. Stafford, "Frontiers in Contemporary Theology," 46.
169. Thompson, "Social Involvement," 712.
170. Ibid., 725.
171. Ridgway, "Psychology," 877.
172. Ibid., 888–928.
173. Grenz, *Theology for the Community*, 25. The reader finds Grenz's treatment of

history," and the "thought-forms of contemporary culture" or "*kerygma*, heritage, and culture" as the three norms or sources of theology.[174] He emphasizes that "the primary norm for theology is the biblical message."[175] The heritage of the church then is of "secondary importance" to the extent it "is instructive in our quest for a relevant theology" and so "must be tested by the Scriptures and by their applicability to our cultural situation."[176] Finally, the "thought-forms of contemporary culture" serve as the "tertiary source" of theology.[177] Culture provides the language by which theologians communicate doctrinal beliefs.

Grenz includes the philosophical proofs for God in a chapter on "The God Who Is." He explains each with reference to its major proponent.[178] He demonstrates an awareness of contemporary issues and concludes that "only Christian living on this plane can confirm our testimony that we know God and therefore the God is."[179] In other words, Grenz affirms the importance of the created order as revelation. God reveals himself through his church to the outside world. Grenz relies heavily on the early church as well as Scripture in his chapter on "The Triune God." He also uses the created order in an applicational way as he points out implications of the doctrine of the Trinity. He helps the reader begin to understand that the doctrine of the Trinity impacts "the way we pray" as well as "the way we act."[180] Throughout his theology, the reader sees the importance of the historical community and Scripture as two sources of theology. Yet, much of Grenz's use of the created order comes through as he applies theology to the current context.[181]

Elmer Towns draws from both Strong and Chafer as he explains systematic theology in terms of correlating Scripture and the created order.[182] He defines systematic theology as, "an effort to draw truth from any and every source concerning God and His universe and to express this truth

---

general revelation in his chapter on anthropology. Ibid., 132–39. He identifies the nature of general revelation by contrasting it with special revelation. In his final contrast he states, "general revelation is 'noetic' rather than 'salvific.' " Ibid., 133.

174. Ibid., 21–26
175. Ibid., 21.
176. Ibid., 24.
177. Ibid., 25.
178. Ibid., 33–43.
179. Ibid., 52.
180. Ibid., 76.
181. For example, Grenz concludes his chapter on "The Significance of Eschatology" with "eschatology as insight for living." Ibid., 655–59.
182. Towns, *Theology*, 10, 901.

simply in a comprehensive and complete system."[183] He clarifies, "theology may draw its source, method or proof from any and all sources of truth (logic, arithmetic, biology, history, etc.), because all truth (both special revelation and general revelation) comes from God."[184]

In spite of his description of the theological task, Towns exemplifies what Grenz and Franke call the "concordance" approach to theology. Throughout most of his work he lists not one but a multitude of passages of Scripture on a topic.[185] While mostly using Scripture through his theology, Towns includes use of the created order in a number of ways. Towns explains proofs for God,[186] gives evidence of doctrine[187], and cites oppositional views.[188] The created order provides evidence for God.[189] For example, "The power of God keeps the comets in their path and the planets in their orbit. The power of God keeps the atom from exploding into unlimited nuclear fission. The omnipotent God preserves the world as He created it in the beginning and is the greatest evidence of the Person of God."[190] Towns rarely cites truths revealed through the created order.

Like Towns, Norman Geisler understands systematic theology as systematizing all revelation. He asserts, "Systematic theology is an attempt to construct a comprehensive and consistent whole out of *all* revelation from God, whether special (biblical) or general (natural)."[191] Geisler executes his theological method in his section on bibliology. Outside his chapter on prolegomena he generally uses Scripture alone.

Geisler occasionally uses the created order to verify the teaching of Scripture. He includes a section where he cites some scientific evidence for the Bible. For example, science's understanding of evaporation verifies Gen 2:6–7.[192] Similarly, Geisler points out that no archaeological find has refuted the Bible.[193] Instead of integrating material from Scripture, tradition, and

---

183. Ibid., 15.

184. Ibid., 8.

185. A quarter of one page lists verses from the Gospels where Jesus recognizes the Mosaic authorship of the Pentateuch. Ibid., 66.

186. Ibid., 46–51. On page 898, he directly links general revelation with the traditional arguments for God's existence.

187. Ibid., 48–52. Towns points to fulfilled prophecy and the testimony of changed lives as evidences that the Bible "is a message of God" (52).

188. Ibid., 447–48, 510–11, 513–16, 561–62.

189. Ibid., 142.

190. Ibid., 122. Unfortunately, Towns provides the reader with few examples.

191. Geisler, *Systematic Theology*, 1:16.

192. Ibid., 546.

193. Ibid., 557.

science into one section on the doctrine of Scripture, Geisler classifies these under distinct sections which serve to make his final point. He concludes,

> The testimony of science that demonstrates it, of the scrolls that transmit it, the scribes who wrote it, the supernatural that confirms it, the structure that manifests it, the stones that support it, the Savior who verified it, the Spirit that witnesses to it, and the saved who have been transformed by it. These combined testimonies confirm that the Bible is what it claims to be—the divinely inspired, infallible, and inerrant Word of God.[194]

Unfortunately the rest of his work fails to demonstrate the same level of commitment to various forms of revelation. Other chapters consist of a biblical basis, theological basis, and historical basis for the doctrine. He briefly explains objections and his response to them. In a discussion of divine providence, Geisler provides a single paragraph explanation of other worldviews (neotheism, deism, finite godism and atheism, polytheism, pantheism, and panentheism) and lists a prominent proponent in parenthesis.[195] He offers no footnotes or interaction with the position, simply a very brief description. He then turns to "the biblical basis of God's providence."[196] He posits a logical-theological argument for God's providence before rooting his doctrine in tradition.[197] Only in his final section where he addresses objections to God's providence does Geisler use the created order as an example and verification.[198] However, Geisler fails to include the arts, which he specifically affirms as forms of God's revelation in his chapter on revelation.[199]

Finally, Richard Plantinga, Thomas Thompson, and Matthew Lundberg see the systematization of all truth as the task of systematic theology. They explain,

> This text is a work in *systematic theology*. Systematic theology endeavors to orchestrate these three branches of theology [biblical, historical and philosophical] and their respective sources [Bible, tradition, philosophy], in order to articulate in the most comprehensive, ordered, and coherent way what may be known

---

194. Ibid., 560.
195. Geisler, *Systematic Theology*, 2:565–68.
196. Ibid., 568–77.
197. Ibid., 577–79, 579–90.
198. Ibid., 591. He uses the fact that the carbon dioxide people exhale "randomly mixes in the air" to become oxygen needed for breathe as an example of divine providence demonstrated through randomness. He also quotes "agnostic Robert Jastrow" as stating that the anthropic principle is proof of a created universe.
199. Geisler, *Systematic Theology*, 1:68.

about the triune God, creation and their relation—and, importantly, how we are to live in light of this knowledge.[200]

Each chapter of the work begins with an introduction to the issue. The chapters continue with biblical materials, historical developments, and systematic considerations. The authors integrate the data from the Bible and tradition in the last part of each chapter. They also explore contemporary applications at the end of every chapter. So, the authors use the Bible, tradition, and philosophy to build their theology. The authors occasionally use the created order in terms of application, as well. For example, they "endorse the social view as the most orthodox and coherent model of the Trinity," and then they provide three "practical advantages of the social model."[201]

In summary, a number of evangelical theologians describe systematic theology as systematizing all truth. In other words, they specifically emphasize the need to integrate Scripture and the created order. As with the first two categories, the theologians in this group largely systematize verses and use other theologians to build their doctrine. When they use the created order, it differs little from the other two groups (evidence, proofs, illustration, and application). The theology edited by Carter offers some examples of integrating Scripture and the created order. How might evangelicals use the created order in systematic theology?

Theoretical Proposal

The above sections illustrate the confusion that abounds among evangelicals. On one hand "all [evangelicals] acknowledge that in several clear scriptural statements God has spoken of the revelation of Himself in nature (Ps 19; Rom 1; Acts 14:15–17; 17:22–34)."[202] However, only one group proposes a methodology that includes this revelation. And yet, the theologies of this group differ little from the theologies that limit their method to the Bible alone. Furthermore, the theologians proposing a "Bible only" theology include tradition and some use of the created order in their theologies. As Stackhouse observes, "Many evangelicals, however, have been slow to take stock of just what role should be played, and in fact is played, by reason,

---

200. Plantinga, et al., *Christian Theology*, 16. The authors cover general revelation in roughly two pages of a seventeen page chapter titled, "Revelation and Knowledge of God."

201. Ibid., 142–45.

202. Lightner, *Evangelical Theology*, 45.

experience, and tradition in their theologies."²⁰³ What role does the created order play in an evangelical systematic theology, then?

Theology is not "solely the construction of truth by appeal to the Bible alone."²⁰⁴ As Kelsey argues, theology is generally much more complex than a simple translation of a text to a theological argument.²⁰⁵ Every theology examined above exemplifies the complexity Kelsey explains. For example, Pieper most strongly insists on a "Bible only" approach, but cannot escape his Lutheran tradition. Furthermore, Hodge and all who follow him employ the scientific method as they interpret and arrange passages of Scripture to form doctrines. They use reason as they seek to demonstrate the relationship between doctrines. Moreover, theologians "cannot simply divest ourselves of our environment; we are always children of our time, the products of our background."²⁰⁶ So, although Scripture "must remain the primary norm for theological statements, contextualization demands that we take seriously thought-forms and mindset of the culture in which our theologizing transpires."²⁰⁷ In the end, the task of systematic theology always entails use of more than the Bible alone. In light of this fact, the third proposed method (systematizing all truth) remains preferred.

In reality each of the theologians reviewed above use the created order in his systematic theology. They teach that God reveals through both Scripture and the created order. Furthermore, they also use the created order in some way in their theology. Shedd points out that sometimes Scripture relies upon knowledge through the created order. And as Warfield explains, historically theologians use sources outside of the Bible in theology. Therefore, the chosen method is systematizing all truth or intentionally integrating Scripture and the created order.

I find company among other theologians who suggest that the created order and Scripture mutually inform one another.²⁰⁸ Grenz and Stackhouse include the created order in constructing systematic theology. In an essay

---

203. Stackhouse, *Evangelical Landscapes*, 53.

204. Grenz, *Theology for the Community*, 19. Systematic theology by its very nature precludes a "Bible only" approach.

205. Kelsey, *Proving Doctrine*, 122.

206. Bavinck, *Reformed Dogmatics*, 1:82.

207. Grenz, *Theology for the Community*, 19.

208. The process is never linear whereby theologians begin with the divinely inspired written Word. People always begin with their own context, beliefs, and questions. No one can sterilely and objectively proceed in a linear fashion as described. Instead of a line, or a circle, or even spiral, perhaps a web most adequately illustrates the complexity of life and modification of belief over time. Grenz suggests that a web or mosaic serve as good analogies. Grenz, *Renewing the Center*, 205.

on methodology, Grenz envisions the mutually informing written Word interpreting the world, which interprets the written Word, as a method of theology. He affirmatively cites Pannenberg,

> the discoveries and insights of the various disciplines of human learning—informs our theological construction. For example, theories about addictions and addictive behavior can provide insight into the biblical teaching about sin . . . Our theological reflections can draw from the so-called secular sciences, because ultimately no discipline is in fact purely secular. Above all, because God is the ground of truth . . . all truth ultimately comes together in God. Theology therefore looks to all human knowledge, for in so doing it demonstrates the unity of truth in God.[209]

Similarly, Bacote and Spencer assert that systematic theology draws from other disciplines, "such as history, philosophy, literature, science, sociology, anthropology, and the arts, among others."[210] They also believe that Scripture "is not God's only revelation . . . so it must not be read in isolation from the created order or the history and cultural life of humanity."[211] This being the case, Stackhouse reaffirms, "Indeed, truly evangelical thinking about any subject will always privilege scriptural interpretation and never willfully contradict what the Scripture at least *seems* to say—however much tension we must live with while we try to sort out apparent contradictions."[212] The created order and Scripture together enable people to know God.

Stackhouse supports the same mutually interpreting methodology and highlights the importance of the created order as an aid to interpreting Scripture. Theologians interpretations of the Bible "may well need to be adjusted in the light of our interpretations of God's other means of revelation, whether science, history, tradition, spiritual experience, and so on—just as, nonetheless, our interpretations of those phenomena also ought to be in respectful dialogue with our understanding of Scripture."[213] The created order enables people to understand Scripture as well as the reverse. Simply reading Scripture requires knowledge of a particular language, its grammar, and the distinct function of different genres.[214] Some basic understanding of

---

209. Pannenberg, *Systematic Theology*, 1:59–60, quoted in Grenz, "Articulating the Christian Belief-Mosaic," 127–28.

210. Bacote and Spencer, "Theological Implications," 62.

211. Ibid.

212. Stackhouse, "Evangelical Theology," 47.

213. Ibid.

214. Readers interpret prophecy (e.g., Dan 2) differently than narrative (e.g., Judg

shepherds, pastures, and water enables people to interpret Ps 23:1–3. People cannot interpret Scripture without prior understanding of certain things. God reveals this knowledge through the created order.

The future of systematic theology must include insights gained from other academic disciplines. McGrath states that natural theology "is a matter that must involve theologians, philosophers, mathematicians, physicists, biologists, psychologists, artists, and the literary community."[215] Sawyer also includes the academic disciplines in systematic theology as secondary sources. These sources, for Sawyer, include the hard and soft sciences (psychology, sociology, sociology of knowledge, cross-cultural anthropology, linguistics, and communications theory). He asserts that "[c]ontemporary evangelical theologians can no longer ignore these disciplines but must see them as supplementing the traditional concerns for philosophy and natural theology. Any theological-hermeneutical method must account for the data that arise from the sciences, both hard and soft."[216] Using the created order means accounting for knowledge gained through other fields of study.

One final example comes from Williams. He charges, "Evangelical theologians probably spend proportionately too much time talking to each other or to non-evangelical theologians and too little talking to Christian artists, scientists, political thinkers, and activists."[217] He then offers a strong suggestion, "It would be no idle ambition if a squad of theologians sought to team up with a number of Christian thinkers in different subject areas to work out a contemporary theological anthropology that adumbrates the Christian understanding of the human person right across the spectrum of academic disciplines."[218] Not only must theologians begin to integrate Scripture and the created order in systematic theology, they first need to learn from specialists in other fields of study. Such dialogue might address medical and ethical issues not resolved by concordances. At least applying theology requires that "we have to get interdisciplinary. And still less is the study the place, and the concordance the tool, that will enable us to think through those things that constitute all the business of life. Here we need the fellowship. Here we engage in theology together, just as we worship and pray together."[219] Dialogue with specialists in other fields must occur.

---

1) or didactic (e.g., Gal 5) portions of Scripture.

215. McGrath, *Open Secret*, 20.

216. Sawyer, *Survivor's Guide to Theology*, 62.

217. Williams, "Theological Task," 164. Noll identifies this as a problem as well. He suggests it occurs because theologians do their work in seminaries not universities. Noll, *Scandal*, 19.

218. Williams, "Theological Task," 164.

219. Ibid., 163.

Conclusion

Systematic theology means systematizing all truth from any and every source. The task requires integrating two forms of revelation; namely Scripture and the created order. The suggestions above highlight first steps toward such an approach. Dialogue between theologians and specialists in other fields on topics of mutual interest must occur. As the theologians at the ETS meeting stated, and those quoted above exhort, the key issue in theological method is using the created order in theology. At the end of chapter five, the reader will find an explanation of how Jonathan Edwards exemplifies this methodology. However, before evangelicals set out to create a systematic theology that follows this methodology, they must begin with a comprehensive examination of revelation. A theology of revelation that explores the commonalities and differences between the created order and Scripture provides both impetus and guidance for the task of systematizing all truth.

Before proposing a theology of revelation, I examine one other area where evangelicals should use the created order, but too often neglect it. The issues of faith and learning integration and the integration of all truth arose among evangelicals. In many ways, the integration of truth overlaps with systematizing all truth. As such, in the next chapter, I look at how evangelicals explain and carry out the task of integration.

3

Review of Integration Practices

Introduction

Evangelicalism gave shape to the term "integration" as it pertains to faith and learning.[1] Frank Gaebelein proposed "integration" as a solution to the problems of secularization and fragmentation in education on one side and fundamentalisms' retreat from intellectual involvement on the other.[2] He explains that "all truth is God's truth."[3] Therefore, evangelicals suffering from *aletheiaphobia* or fear of "some newly apprehended scientific truth" need not fear because all truth comes from God and "*builds into a coherent whole.*"[4] Integration aims to "rebuild" the coherent whole of which Gaebelein speaks. Therefore, integration deals with the relationship between what evangelicals call general and special revelation or the created order and Scripture, respectively.[5] As such, works on integration provide second-

---

1. Badley credits Gaebelein as "the first evangelical to make frequent use of 'integration.'" Badley, "Integration," 188.

2. Gaebelein, "Nature of a Christian Philosophy of Education," 3–11. Gaebelein does not create something new. Christians throughout the centuries have wrestled with the relationship between God's world and his written word. Gaebelein simply calls the task of bringing these truths back together "integration." Gaebelein, *Pattern of God's Truth*, vii.

3. Gaebelein, *Varied Harvest*, 77.

4. Gaebelein, "Need and Nature," 9.

5. Gangel states that integration "refers to the teaching of all subjects as a part of the total truth of God thereby enabling the student to see the unity of natural and special

ary sources where people can observe how evangelicals use the created order as revelation.

Since Gaebelein, literature exploring the relationship between Scripture and the created order arose among evangelical educators and professors in various fields of study.[6] In this chapter, I examine works on integration to assess how evangelicals use the created order as revelation. Four presuppositions inherent in evangelical understandings of integration suggest a complementary relationship between Scripture and the created order.

The evangelical tendency to affirm the created order as revelation, but then fail to use it as such appears in works on integration. As Coe proposes, "[T]heology is not exempt from needing to be informed by the natural disciplines as is often implied in discussions on meta-integration."[7] He observes uni-directional integration between theology and other fields of study. He writes, "Whereas a number of efforts have been made by the natural disciplines [to learn from and be informed by theology], there is less evidence of serious work having been done [to learn from and be informed by natural disciplines] by theologians, particularly within contemporary Protestant evangelical circles."[8] So, how do evangelicals use the

---

revelation." Gangel, "Integrating Faith and Learning," 100; italics removed. See also Green, "Theological and Philosophical Foundations, 74.

6. For example, Holmes, *Idea of a Christian College*; Gangel, "Integrating Faith," 99–108; Gangel, *Toward a Harmony of Faith and Learning*; Badley, "Faith-Learning Integration,"105–18; Dockery and Thornbury, *Shaping a Christian Worldview*; MacArthur, *Think Biblically!*; Claerbaut, *Faith and Learning on the Edge*; Dockery, *Faith and Learning*; and Smith and Smith, *Teaching and Christian Practices*.

7. Coe, "Interdependent Model of Integration," 112. Coe's article addresses interdisciplinary integration. He speaks here of integration between the field of theology with other academic fields of study. However, since evangelicals equate theology with studying Scripture (see previous chapter), then his words fit the current context as well.

8. Coe, "Interdependent Model of Integration," 122. Coe attributes this to a misunderstanding of theology as queen of the sciences. He holds that the label "Queen of the Disciplines" meant that the other disciplines "served to inform theology and provide it with a fuller view of God's world than the Bible provided on its own." He believes contemporary evangelical theologians interpret this to mean that theology now informs the other disciplines. He points to Charles Hodge and Milliard Erickson as examples. Ibid.," 122, 136. My own research verifies Coe's findings. People in other disciplines seek to figure out how theology or at least their faith informs their field of study. Theologians are conspicuously absent in such discussions. For example, see the articles published in the *Journal of Psychology and Theology* in 1981 and 2010. No professional theologian contributes to a journal with the term "theology" in the title on the relationship between theology and psychology. For the most recent example see Porter, "Theology as Queen and Psychology as Handmaid," 3–14; Porter, "A Reply to the Respondents," 33–40; and Entwistle and Preston, "Epistemic Rights vs. Epistemic Duties," 27–32; Sandage and Brown, "Monarchy or Democracy in Relation Integration," 20–26.

created order? Evangelical tendencies fall within Niebuhr's categories found in *Christ and Culture*.[9] They approach integration in four ways: (1) people need the *Bible only* to understand the creation, (2) *uni-directional* integration whereby Scripture (theology or their Christian worldview) informs a field of study, (3) all else being equal they *lean toward Scripture*, or (4) a *mutually informing relationship* between the created order and Scripture.

Relating Scripture and the Created Order

The expectation of mutual integration stems from four presuppositions that combine to form the concept of integration.[10] First, evangelicals teach a *unified* view of creation based on Gen 1 and Col 1. In other words, the metaphysical distinction found in the Bible is "not between sacred and secular but between God and his creation."[11] Gaebelein writes, "Christian education . . . must renounce once and for all the false separation between sacred and secular truth. It must see that truth in science, and history, in mathematics, art, literature, and music belongs just as much to God as truth in religion."[12] Hasker states, "There is not a secular world and a sacred world, but a single world created by God and a single, unitary, truth which is known to God."[13] Or as Yancey states, "The biblical view is at once more subtle and more connected. It presents reality as a seamless whole, with no neat division between

---

9. Niebuhr, *Christ and Culture*. Carter and Narramore explain four models of integrating psychology and theology (against, of, parallels and integrates). They observe that these "follow in a general way" Niebuhr's *Christ and Culture*. Carter and Narramore, *Integration of Psychology and Theology*, 72. Hasker describes three strategies of integration (compatibilist, tranformationist, and reconstructionist) which he likens to select types from Niebuhr's *Christ and Culture*. Hasker, "Faith-learning Integration," 239–40. Cosgrove highlights four models (sole authority, separate authority, equal authority and foundational authority). Cosgrove, *Foundations of Christian Thought*, 54–59. See also Johnson, *Psychology and Christianity* and Carter, *Rethinking* Christ and Culture. I strongly suggest Carson's work on the topic. He acknowledges the benefits of identifying the various ways in which Scripture speaks of the relationship(s) between Christ and culture. He exhorts his reader toward flexibility and away from reductionistic tendencies whereby only one model is used. Carson, *Christ and Culture Revisited*.

10. Recall from chapter one that I am primarily concerned about the integration of truth.

11. Holmes, *Truth*, 28. See also Guthrie, "The Authority of Scripture," 37. Van Dyke et al. reject the fact-value divide and state, "Integration merges the world of facts with the world of values." Van Dyke et al., "Integration and the Christian College," 93.

12. Gaebelein, "Major Premise of Christian Education," 13.

13. Hasker, "Faith-learning Integration," 238.

sacred and profane or between natural and supernatural. There is only God's world, a sacred world, which has been profaned by human rebellion."[14]

Since no sacred-secular divide exists, then truth from Scripture does not contradict with truth in creation. Therefore, the mantra "*all truth is God's truth*" is a second idea that underpins integration.[15] In essence, all truth comes from God no matter where "found" or who "discovers" it.[16] The Bible is true, but "there are areas of truth not fully explicated in Scripture and that these, too, are part of God's truth."[17] Or as Holmes states,

> To say that all truth is God's truth, moreover, does not mean that all truth is either contained in the Bible or deducible from what we find there. Historic Christianity has believed in the truthfulness of Scripture, yet not as an *exhaustive* revelation of everything men can know or want to know as true, but rather as a *sufficient* rule for faith and conduct.[18]

That which is true comes from God and he reveals through his inspired Word, incarnate word and created world. In other words, "Whatever the truth is, we want to know it, because it tells us about God, the author of truth."[19] Fischer explains that "[t]ruth, whether in a Spielberg film, a John Irving novel, a stunning sunset, or a James Taylor song, always leads me back to its source;" namely God.[20]

A third essential presupposition is that God *reveals* truth. Scripture and the created order exists as two primary forms of revelation.[21] As Green writes, general revelation "is still *revelation*," which means "there is a coherence and complementary relationship between 'general' and 'special' revelation."[22] Therefore, as Van Dyke exhorts, "We must come to grips with the relationship between general and special revelation, for it is the linchpin

---

14. Yancey, *Rumors of Another World*, 188.

15. Holmes, *Truth*, 1; Green, "Theological and Philosophical Foundations," 79; Dockery, *Renewing Minds*, 84; Litfin, *Conceiving the Christian College*, 94–95; and Harris, *Integration of Faith and Learning*, 4. Oden points to the historicity of this view citing Justin Martyr, Clement of Alexandria, and Augustine. Oden, *Systematic Theology*, 7.

16. Gangel, "Integrating Faith," 101.

17. Gaebelein, *Pattern of God's Truth*, 21. The reader will find an expanded discussion of truth in chapter five.

18. Holmes, *Truth*, 8. See "sufficiency" in chapter five.

19. Harris, *Integration of Faith and Learning*, 32.

20. Fischer, *Finding God*, 75.

21. Ryrie, *Basic Theology*, 31. See chapter five for an expanded explanation.

22. Green, "Theological and Philosophical Foundations," 74.

of all subsequent efforts at integration."[23] Curtis suggests that a correspondence relationship between Scripture and the created order results from the unity of truth and God as its source. He asserts, "Our recognition of the unity of truth in the world created by God requires that ultimately there be correspondence between the data of general and special revelation."[24]

The *primacy of Scripture* forms the fourth presupposition of integration.[25] Scripture retains a special place in integration. Evangelicals view Scripture as "the more important and more reliable source of knowledge and, in any apparent conflict between the two [special and general revelation], to be the decisive voice."[26] Therefore, the "Word of God is normative in all disciplines," and resultantly "it becomes the center around which all disciplines can and must be integrated."[27] Resultantly, "Christian integration is based on a 'Biblical framework of reality.' "[28] Scripture does include propositional statements (God is one) as well as the meta-narrative of Christianity which informs central doctrines (creation, fall, redemption). Therefore, Scripture serves as "our normative framework of interpretation."[29]

The above core beliefs suggest that integration of Scripture and the created order mutually inform one another. The fourth presupposition maintains the uniqueness of Scripture in the relationship. Therefore, both Scripture and the created order together paint a fuller picture of God, the world, and the relationship between the two. However, Scripture, like the painter's pallet, defines the colors the artist uses. The result of mutual integration, suggests Coe, is a "depend[ence] upon one another for completing their respective tasks of exploring God and His world in order to provide the fullest possible picture of them."[30] Next we observe evangelical tendencies in works on integration.

---

23. Van Dyke et al., "Integration and the Christian College," 95. The article represents an example of interdisciplinary integrative dialogue. The three authors represent different fields of study (science, Greek and Bible, and teacher education; respectively).

24. Curtis, "Philosophy of Education," 101.

25. For example, Gangel, "Integrating Faith," 101; Litfin, *Conceiving the Christian College*, 206; Curtis, "Philosophy of Education," 97; and Johnson, "Between Two Wor(l)ds," 77.

26. Van Dyke et al., "Integration and the Christian College," 91.

27. Beck, *Opening the American Mind*, 17.

28. Harris, *Integration of Faith and Learning*, 4.

29. Vanhoozer, "Everyday Theology," 44.

30. Coe, "Interdependent Model of Integration,"111; emphasis removed.

Evangelical Methods and Practices

The very nature of integration suggests that both Scripture and the created order play an important role. However, here, as with systematic theology, evangelicals tend to neglect or minimize the importance of the created order as revelation. We observe this in three of the four ways evangelicals handle the integrative task ("Bible only," uni-directional, and leaning toward Scripture). The first group consists of those who use the Bible alone. They may affirm the reality of the created order as revelation, but believe it merely teaches the same things explained more reliably in Scripture. A second group identifies a role for the created order, but Scripture not only has priority, the integration is uni-directional. In other words, Scripture informs the created order, but the created order does not inform Scripture. A third group gives more weight to the created order in the integrative process. In the final analysis, Scripture retains a higher authority even when all else is equal. The fourth and final group represents evangelicals who articulate a mutually integrative approach.

Bible Only

Some evangelicals take a "Bible only" approach assuming the Bible directly and specifically addresses all necessary issues. In essence, the study of creation offers nothing new. For example, David Weeks observes the "Bible only" approach taken by evangelicals in the realm of politics and social involvement. Evangelicals returned to politics "[i]n the waning decades of the twentieth century," after years of withdrawal from political engagement.[31] Though involved in politics, Weeks perceives "evangelicals have never developed a coherent and compelling political philosophy. Instead, they have relied on the moral authority and perspicuity of the Bible as a foundation for their social activism."[32] He later states, "From the outset, the reawakened evangelical social conscience had little direction in navigating difficult political waters; their newly found enthusiasm for politics needed guidance from a political philosophy. Consequently, evangelicals have relied upon the resources at their disposal: the Bible and their intuition."[33]

Douglas Bookman rejects integration: "Frankly, it is my persuasion that the impulse [integration of psychology and theology] is, in fact, both

---

31. Weeks, "Uneasy Politics of Modern Evangelicalism," 403.
32. Ibid.
33. Ibid., 407.

foolish and wicked."[34] His understanding of the sufficiency of Scripture precludes him from valuing insights from the discipline of psychology. Bookman states, "By the same token, if the proposition to be considered by the believing community is that the integration of Christian theology and secular psychology should be done, then the case must be made that there is some intrinsic inadequacy or imperfection in the Scriptures demanding that insights be gleaned from secular psychology that will redress those deficiencies and enable Christian counselors to more effectively help hurting people."[35] Citing 2 Tim 3:15–17 and 2 Pet 1:3, Bookman concludes, "Scriptures make explicit claim to sufficiency."[36] Although he affirms the reality of general revelation and allows for the *possibility* of a "rule-book" approach whereby all human reasoning "is subjected to the Word of God," in the end he rejects the integration impulse.[37] Bookman only needs the Bible for counseling.

Like Bookman, Robert Thomas rejects the impetus to integrate Scripture and the created order. He explains the problems caused in biblical interpretation by those seeking to integrate other fields of study with New Testament interpretation.[38] Then he concludes, "what is or what is alleged to be general revelation should have no effect on rules for interpreting the Bible, because the moment it does so, it distorts those rules and hinders a quest for true meaning through grammatical-historical principles."[39]

Theoretically, Jay Adams agrees with the exploration of the created order. For example, findings in the field of psychology might "fill out" biblical principles "concerning the Bible and its care" but "this 'filling out' function, however, is not necessary to counseling, but it may be found useful."[40] Due to the sufficiency of Scripture, "nothing else is needed."[41] Therefore, any

---

34. Bookman, "Scriptures and Biblical Counseling," 93.

35. Ibid.

36. Ibid.

37. Ibid., 90–91.

38. Thomas, "General Revelation," 15–22.

39. Ibid., 23. He does not see the impact of general revelation on his own hermeneutical method.

40. Adams, *How to Help People Change*, 39.

41. Ibid., 36. John Street holds to a similar view of the sufficiency of Scripture. He posits: "If it is true that the Word of God is greater in bringing about the glory of God in man than is general revelation, then why would Christians want to return to the simpler and more fundamental truths of general revelation when they have a far greater life-transforming truth at their disposal?" Street, "Biblical Counseling," 217. Street not only neglects the benefits of revelation given through the created order, he also fails to mention the *necessary work of the Spirit* for both justification and sanctification. He writes, Word of God "*alone* transforms the heart of man." Ibid., 219. See "Sufficiency"

truth "necessary to counseling," Adams believes, "will be found already *in a purer form* in the Bible."[42] He assumes Scripture contains all necessary knowledge for counseling. In essence, Adams takes a "Bible only" approach to counseling.

Finally, Fred Van Dyke et al. greatly affirm the importance of the created order as revelation based on Ps 19. However, as they describe general revelation they sound like "Bible only" integrationist. They illustrate evangelical insistence on the importance of revelation given through the created order and then the minimization of this same revelation. They look forward to the day when "all the streams of truth will run together, and God will be revealed in nature as He is now revealed only in Scripture."[43] They uphold the value of students "drawing both from biblical revelation and the general revelation of related academic disciplines" in order to "see the unity of truth to which both general and special revelation testify."[44] In these statements they greatly value a place for the created order in integration.

However, they limit the value of the created order merely to *illustrating* what Scripture clearly teaches. They write, "Nature can provide powerful illustrations of that which Scripture teaches as concept, but, by itself, nature can teach precisely nothing."[45] As a matter of fact, "natural revelation is itself, even if perfectly observed and interpreted, an inadequate data source for our understanding of God."[46] So, general revelation "may become, then, a kind of idol which can show some characteristics of God, but omits or distorts others, and so, in fact, *dishonors God*."[47] If the created order only illustrates what Scripture clearly teaches, then it serves no true integrative purpose.

---

in chapter five for a different perspective.

42. Adams, *How to Help People Change*, 39–40.

43. Van Dyke et al., "Integration and the Christian College," 92. They confuse revelation with human responses to revelation. As I will point out in chapter five, God's revelation in both forms is quite clear. Fallen humans misinterpret both forms of revelation, which causes problems.

44. Ibid., 94.

45. Ibid., 91–92.

46. Ibid., 91.

47. Ibid., 91–92, emphasis added. Revelation, if given by God, cannot "dishonor God." This quote highlights not only a common evangelical understanding of general revelation, but also the need for a carefully researched and articulated understanding of revelation.

Uni-directional

Some evangelicals believe in the revelatory nature of the created order, but articulate a uni-directional model of integration whereby Scripture informs a field of study. For example, Antonio Chiareli sees Scripture providing an interpretive framework from which to read and understand human social phenomena.[48] He affirms a Word-world dialogue, but tends toward a uni-directional approach. In regard to violent shootings in American schools, "The 'Word-world' approach can also help us to think truthfully. . . . By infusing our classroom discussions with God's principles of justice, compassion, righteousness, etc., and by developing their applicability to social issues" showing God's Word relevant to their world.[49] Scripture informs issues of justice, compassion, and righteousness. He does not mention how the created order also informs our practices in areas of social justice.

Eloise Meneses notices that since few Christians work in the field of anthropology then "Christians have done little to challenge or reconstruct the philosophical foundations of anthropology as a discipline."[50] She rejects a mutual integration model because such "give[s] equal weight to each [faith and science]."[51] Such an approach fails to retain the primacy of Scripture and core theological beliefs. Instead, she supports a transformational approach to integration whereby Scripture informs the field of anthropology. Her article demonstrates this approach. Her uni-directional model "allows the theology of anthropology to construct and inform the science of anthropology."[52] Theology informs the field of anthropology, but the reverse does not occur.[53] Nor does she mention the value of both fields (theology and anthropology) coming together to address a particular issue.

Similarly, Mark Eckel explains integration as a uni-directional activity whereby special revelation (Bible) informs general revelation in order to obtain "God's perspective on the world."[54] Eckel holds we must begin "with God's thoughts about His world and we interpret our teaching from his perspective."[55] The overview given by Eckel begins with a passage of Scripture, which then is expressed in a principle, which leads to a plan that

---

48. Chiareli, "Christian Worldview and the Social Sciences," 244.
49. Ibid., 259.
50. Meneses, "No Other Foundation, "535.
51. Ibid., 532.
52. Ibid., 549.
53. Ibid., 533.
54. Eckel, *Whole Truth: Classroom*, 87.
55. Ibid.

makes a point and which is reiterated through a project.⁵⁶ Scripture drives study in various disciplines. The following sub-title of a chapter illustrates uni-directional integration, "Writing curriculum that discovers biblical truth in each discipline."⁵⁷ This assumes that no new information comes through the created order than that which is found in Scripture. Eckel limits truth to the Bible.

Last, Grant Horner exemplifies the uni-directional position whereby Scripture informs one's study of culture. He begins by proposing a theology of culture derived from both Scripture and observations of nature.⁵⁸ Although both Scripture and the created order reveal, "Scripture *guides* interpretation of nature, while nature *reinforces* Scripture."⁵⁹ Horner insists that the importance of truths outside of Scripture "lies in their *demonstration* that what Scripture says about man is true and valid."⁶⁰ Nature merely *reinforces* or *demonstrates* the teaching of Scripture. In essence, nature simply says the same thing one can learn more clearly through the written Word.

The researcher gains no new knowledge nor does nature enable people to interpret Scripture. In the final analysis, Horner equates revelation with Scripture alone, "Scripture is *the* revelation of God, and it is absolutely complete, without error, perfect, and *the only true way to learn of God.*"⁶¹ And yet, Horner does acknowledge that Scripture "does not deal with every conceivable topic directly" and that even "mature believers" fallibly interpret Scripture.⁶²

Horner provides good reasons for interacting with culture, but leaves out the revelatory nature of "culture creating" and overlooks the relationship between this Scripture.⁶³ The reason for this neglect becomes plain. Horner believes creating culture is fallen humanity's attempt to find meaning without God. He argues on the basis of Romans 1 that "culture is what

56. Ibid., 88–100.
57. Ibid., 84.
58. Horner, *Meaning at the Movies*, 12–13, back cover.
59. Ibid., 10, emphasis added.
60. Ibid., 29, emphasis altered.
61. Ibid., 28, emphasis added.
62. Ibid.
63. Horner offers three reasons, drawn from Scripture, for Christians to interact with culture, namely, growth in thankfulness of "God's grace toward us," to observe the veracity of Scripture regarding fallen humanity and as a bridge for interaction with unbelievers. In Horner's words, "to use wise and prudent interaction with that culture to help us grow in our appreciation of God's grace toward us, to see what God says about fallen mankind is in fact absolutely accurate (even as found in pagan works), and to better equip us for interaction with the many human beings who do not yet know him." Horner, *Meaning at the Movies*, 26.

we produce in our futile attempts to understand the world."[64] He, then, asserts, "I believe that human culture in all its forms is inextricably linked with man's fallen state."[65] For Horner, human culture is not reflective of our creation in God's image, it is not an effect of finitude, nor is it an effort to carry out the creation mandate to rule over and subdue the creation, though as fallen people.

Horner's view of culture thereby impacts his study of films. For example, in his evaluation of *The Matrix*, Horner concludes, "not only is the film *not* Christian, it is about as far from Christianity as it can be. Having affinities with Christian images and ideas means nothing more than just that: it has similarities and resonances with Christian symbols."[66] According to Horner's critique, any time one sees the theme of creation, fall, and redemption in film the person views mere similarities to Christianity. Such does not reveal truth about God and creation. Horner asserts, "Some of these responses are almost frightening in their foolishness and lack of biblical knowledge and worldview understanding. This is a direct result of not asking 'who believes what about what and why?' from an informed and biblically grounded position."[67] In essence, culture does not reveal God, nor does it teach truth. Therefore, he limits studying of culture to either critique or finding points of contact with unbelievers.

Scriptural Leanings

Other evangelicals state that all else being equal they favor the interpretation of Scripture over an interpretation of the created order. Steve Porter, as one example, gives greater potential value to the created order than the evangelicals in the above sections. He believes that psychology remains a handmaiden to theology. He explains that sometimes psychology challenges an initial interpretation of a text and thereby requires a closer analysis of

---

64. Ibid., 39.

65. Ibid. Crouch provides a helpful alternative to Horner's view of culture. Crouch explains that "Culture is what we make of the world," which began before the fall as the first man and women begin working. He ties culture to the creation mandate. More pointedly, Crouch states that "culture begins, just as human beings begin, in the realm of created blessing. The beginning of culture and the beginning of humanity are one and the same because culture is what we were made to do." Therefore, we cannot escape culture and "that's a good thing." Crouch, *Culture Making*, 23, 36. See also, Plantinga, *Engaging God's World*, 28–33.

66. Horner, *Meaning at the Movies*, 56.

67. Ibid., 63.

the text.⁶⁸ However, he insists that if reconciliation between interpretations of Scripture and interpretations of the created order conflict the interpretation of the Bible retains greater authority.⁶⁹ Porter argues that a theologian's interpretations of Scripture retain higher authority because Scripture comes directly from God.⁷⁰ In other words, since theology comes from Scripture, then it wields greater authority when conflicting interpretations arise.

Porter does not give a specific example, but he makes it abundantly clear that he does not refer to differing presuppositions or truth claims not well grounded. He focuses on "when all else is equal and the findings appear to conflict."⁷¹ He clarifies, "[T]he idea is that theological methodology, rightly understood, yields claims that have greater authority than the claims psychological method yields. The claims in question are not just any old theological or psychological claims, but rather, *well-grounded* claims."⁷² Instead of holding well grounded truth claims in tension, he leans toward the interpretation of Scripture.

In another case, Crabb leans in favor of interpretations of Scripture. He rejects the two book approach to integration as espoused by Ellens.⁷³ He also denies the epistemological humility approach by Guy.⁷⁴ Crabb, in his final critique of both models states, "For all practical purposes, the Bible is eliminated as the ultimate yardstick of truth. Only humble guesses based on our study of nature and the Bible are permitted in our pursuit of truth about psychology."⁷⁵

68. Porter, "Theology," 10.

69. Ibid., 12, 13.

70. Ibid., 3-14.

71. Porter, "Theology," 5. If all else is truly equal and the claims are "well grounded" then why not hold the findings in tension? Such a stance understands the perspectival nature of knowledge and values the reality of revelation given through the created order.

72. Ibid., 5.

73. Crabb, "Biblical Authority," 307. Ellens does not hold to inerrancy, which I believe fuels the dialogue between him and Crabb. In a "pastoral" response to Crabb, Ellens concludes, "Dr. Crabb has resorted, for the sake of more objectivity and authority, to the inerrancy-of-Scripture hypothesis. That of course then becomes his arbitrary faith assumption (blind faith, it seems to me) that lands him in a new kind of positivist foundationalism, one which can only be called a bastardized rational-empiricism." Ellens, "Biblical Authority," 324.

74. Crabb, "Biblical Authority," 309. In fairness, Guy is likely the victim of slippery slope argumentation. He affirms the noetic effect of sin reaches to our interpretation of Scripture as well as nature. He simply concludes that "we are unable to fully know truth since our knowledge is partial, at best." He rejects the notion that diversity necessarily equals error and therefore should be rejected. Instead, he sees diversity as the natural state of affairs as finite and fallen people seek truth. Guy, "Search for Truth," 30.

75. Crabb, "Biblical Authority," 311.

Crabb, then, calls the field of Christian psychology back to biblical authority as its epistemological foundation.

Yet, Crabb exhorts evangelicals to study the created order. He encourages evangelicals to "acknowledge freely and non-defensively that for some questions the revelation of God in nature provides data far more relevant than the revelation of God in Scripture."[76] He testifies that regarding knowledge, Scripture is not exhaustive. Crabb believes that truth comes from two sources; namely, the Bible and nature.

When Crabb addresses the issue of authority the reader becomes more confused. He asks the question: "What source of data—the Bible or nature—has greater authority?"[77] He affirms the unity of truth and continues, "To ask whether truth found in biblical revelation can claim greater authority to truth found in natural revelation is of course an absurd question. No truth is more truthful than another truth. Truths may differ in importance or relevance but not in authority."[78] If revelation comes from God then it is true, and if true, then in some way authoritative.[79]

He now reframes the question: "The problem, however, is that conclusions reached through biblical study may differ from the conclusions reached through empirical research. Which conclusions will guide our thinking? Which will we regard as true?"[80] He admits that both the scientist and the biblical scholar might misinterpret the created order or Scripture, respectively.[81] Yet, Crabb, like Porter, gives Scripture higher authority. He concludes, "the written revelation of Scripture speaks with more authority than the illustrative revelation of nature because it speaks in propositions and because it therefore speaks with greater clarity than nature in whatever it addresses."[82] Instead of holding in tension two interpretations, Crabb immediately favors the interpretation of the Bible over the interpretation over nature all the while acknowledging that either or both may be wrong. And conversely, either may actually be correct.

Crabb, then raises the issue of relevancy; namely, "the *relevance* of each data source to specific subjects." Crabb definitively states, "It would be a serious mistake to set the study of natural revelation in opposition to the study of special revelation and to then measure orthodoxy by one's

---

76. Ibid., 306.
77. Ibid.
78. Ibid.
79. See sections on "truth" and "authority" in chapter five.
80. Crabb, "Biblical Authority," 306–7.
81. Ibid., 308.
82. Ibid.

insistence that biblical revelation comprehensively speaks to every question which psychologist might ask. Differing vehicles of revelation must be seen as complementary, not contradictory."[83] However, Crabb does not create a model based on this assertion. He instead ends with the epistemological foundation of people's interpretation of the Bible. Similar to Porter, Crabb wrestles with the proper relationship between Scripture and the created order, but ends leaning in the direction of Scripture.

Mutually Informing

Some evangelicals espouse a mutually informing model of integration whereby both Scripture and the created order come to bear on an issue. By way of example, Norman Geisler identifies special revelation with the Bible and general revelation with nature, human nature, history, art, and music.[84] Geisler affirms mutual integration on the basis of divine revelation. Since God reveals some truth through the Bible and other truth through the arts and sciences, then, "the arts and sciences both complement the content of Scripture and are complemented by it."[85] Later Geisler reiterates that "Biblical studies and arts and sciences enrich each other."[86] Yet, "The Bible is the inspired Word of God and, as such, it is the last word on all the topics it covers, including the arts and sciences."[87] Geisler gives Scripture a privileged position, but emphasizes the necessity of both forms of revelation.

Coe and Hall promote a transformational model based on a unified understanding of reality.[88] In this model, "One must be willing to rigorously and painstakingly observe and reflect on whatever is relevant from (1) Scripture, (2) creation, particularly the study of persons, and (3) preexisting psychological/scientific/theological reflections and theories."[89] Their methodology begins with the spirituality of the learner. They emphasize the importance of the transformative work of the Spirit in the process of integration.[90] They then move to the methodologies of studying both the created order and Scripture (observation, reflection, and interaction).[91] The

---

83. Ibid., 307.
84. Geisler, "Biblical Studies," 35–38.
85. Ibid., 25.
86. Ibid., 44.
87. Ibid., 26.
88. Coe and Hall, "Transformational Psychology View," 199–226.
89. Ibid., 207–8.
90. Ibid., 221.
91. Ibid., 222. For example, the student makes "observation[s] on creation and the

researcher then develops theories of knowledge based on her study of the created order and Scripture. This leads to the application of that knowledge, which in the university in turn leads to training others beginning at the first level "Transformation of psychologists by spiritual-epistemological disciplines and virtues for doing psychology and science in the Spirit."[92] Coe and Hall present a cyclical process whereby the integration of the created order and Scripture take place in each level. They understand that the "very acts of doing science, making theories and practically applying them for neighbor-love all serve the final end of transforming the scientist in the love of God."[93]

A practical example of mutual integration comes from William Struthers who brings both his understanding of Scripture as well as his study of the human brain, hormones, and culture together in exploring the issue of pornography. The result extends beyond mere quoting of Scripture or an uncritical embrace of psychological findings. Instead he comes to a fuller understanding of cultural teachings of masculinity and sexuality, the chemical make-up of the male brain, the relationship between the external world and inner bio-chemical responses, the difference between true and false intimacy, and what renewing the mind means.[94]

Struthers sees recovery as a holistic event. Recovery "takes place in community and is rooted in changing your embodied nature" which requires rewiring the brain.[95] He continues, the rewiring "must be informed by the mandates of Scripture and the wisdom found in the body of Christ. This must be empowered by the Holy Spirit. This empowering, however, might be a little less mystical and more embodied than most of us think it is."[96] Actual, physical, changes in the human brain occur over time. Therefore, the process of sanctification "is not just a spiritual one, but involves the way that his brain is neurologically wired."[97] Struthers exemplifies mutual integration.

Charles Kraft also illustrates mutual integration. Contrary to Meneses, Kraft proposes that the field of anthropology informs theology. Though antagonism exists between anthropologists and theologians, Kraft points out that evangelical theology might benefit from the insights of anthropologists in how to interpret Scripture in "cross-culturally valid" ways instead

---

Word in the love of God."
- 92. Ibid.
- 93. Ibid., 224.
- 94. Struthers, *Wired for Intimacy.*
- 95. Ibid., 188.
- 96. Ibid.
- 97. Ibid., 189.

of ethnocentric ways.⁹⁸ Anthropologists more clearly see the implications of finitude on interpretation and can therefore help theologians see the impact of their own culture on their theology.⁹⁹ Additionally, anthropology can help evangelical theologians better understand culture.¹⁰⁰ Evangelical theologians can also learn from anthropologists "concerning the outworking of evil in sociocultural systems."¹⁰¹ Kraft differentiates between underlying assumptions of the cause of evil where theologians and anthropologists rightly disagree, but emphasizes the present manifestations of the fall where theologians can learn from anthropologists. Kraft concludes, that complementarity instead of polarization should mark the two disciplines as they explore a multitude of issues of mutual interest.¹⁰²

Other evangelicals make statements in favor of a mutual integration method. David Claerbaut explains the mutuality of integration when he states, "As certainly as Scripture illuminates one's understanding in these academic disciplines, these disciplines can deepen our understanding of Scripture."¹⁰³ Similarly, Cosgrove views integration as a "two-way growth process" stating "that faith should affect learning *and* that learning should affect faith."¹⁰⁴

The presuppositions underlying integration suggest that Scripture and the created order come together in a mutually informing way. However, in practice three of the four methods prescribed by evangelicals betray a neglect of the created order. Evangelicals that take a "Bible only" approach do not acknowledge the possibility of the created order offering beneficial truth or insight. Evangelicals that represent a uni-directional approach find some impetus to study the created order. However, the Bible informs presuppositions, methodologies, content, and application. The approach leaves little room for insight from revelation given through the created order. The evangelicals that lean toward Scripture not only affirm a mutually integrative role, they practice it in part. However, Scripture retains priority when the interpreters do not understand the relationship between competing truth claims. Finally, some evangelicals encourage and practice mutual integration whereby both Scripture and the created order speak to an issue or serve in mutually integrative roles.

98. Kraft, "Can Anthropological Insight Assist Evangelical Theology?" 72.
99. Ibid.
100. Ibid.
101. Ibid.
102. Ibid.
103. Claerbaut, *Faith and Learning on the Edge*, 109.
104. Cosgrove, *Foundations of Christian Thought*, 61.

God reveals through both Scripture and the created order. Descriptions as well as practices of integration stem from how evangelicals understand the relationship between Scripture and the created order. Therefore, evangelicals need a thorough theology of revelation that explores the similarities and differences between these forms of revelation. Diehl substantiates this need. The problems with evangelical integration stem from "underdevelopment in their doctrine of general revelation."[105] The reader will find my proposed theology of revelation in chapter five. In the meantime, I provide a theoretical proposal for mutual integration.

Theoretical Proposal

What is integration? I understand integration as the exploration and understanding of the interrelationship of God's revelation through the Bible and through the created order. Integration requires the active and intentional participation of those variously gifted in the body of Christ (theologian, scientist, artist, for example). Integration involves the critical examination and selective incorporation of insights given by God through common grace to unbelievers. The work of integration is not uni-directional (the written Word informs or interprets the world), but rather the written Word and the world come together to create a fuller picture of God, the world, and the relationship between the two.

The complexity of integration does not allow for a single prescribed method. As Agee and Henry point out,

> there is no clear-cut, universally agreed upon way of being responsive as Christian academics to our different disciplines. There is no creed that tells us how points of tension should be understood or resolved. The nuances of Scripture, the profundity of the faith, and the complexity of the world render formulaic prescriptions for integrating faith and learning trite at best, and misleading at worst.[106]

As such, I do not provide a method here. Instead I highlight general principles that address integration of fields of study. The same points apply, though perhaps in a nuanced way, to integrating one's faith into all aspects of one's life. They can also serve as guidepost for integration across the entire curriculum.

---

105. Diehl, "Evangelicalism and General Revelation," 441.
106. Agee and Henry, "Introduction," x.

First, integration begins with the well verified assumption that God reveals through both the written Word and the created order (see "forms" in chapter five). Therefore, the individual and community read both Scripture and the created order asking God for enablement to read both forms of revelation rightly. Sometimes the created order provides the impetus for the study of a specific topic. Other times Scripture begins the journey of exploration. Often the two converge to frame an issue. Resultantly, the individual or community may begin with either form of revelation then proceed to examine both forms.

Second, integration occurs in dialogue before it begins to take root in an individual. The conversation occurs between those representing different fields of study or those with varying perspectives.[107] Coe proposes examples of how interdisciplinary integration could occur in a university setting. He suggests that every field includes specialist who concentrate on their field of study and develop it. These fields also contain those who share interest or training with those in other fields of study. The people in this group learn from the specialist in their own field, but also dialogue with and learn from second level specialist in other fields. They dialogue about areas of overlap between fields of inquiry and then inform the first order specialist of their integrative findings.[108]

Third, integration does not mean unanimity of understanding. As a twist on Gadamer, to the extent at which we understand, we understand differently.[109] Core theological beliefs, such as the finitude and fallenness of mankind, lead to an expectation that people do not see or understand the same thing in the same way.[110] Gadamer understands this reality and suggests the need for a dialogic structure of understanding.[111] Warnke explains the process as

---

107. For example, Beck suggests that theologians and biblical scholars should partner with psychologists in thinking through a more balanced effort to integrate the two fields. Beck, "Integration of Psychology and Theology," 20–29.

108. Coe, "Interdependent Model of Integration."

109. Warnke, *Gadamer*, 96.

110. Diversity of perspective stems from finitude. As Kuyper writes, "one can assume only that apart from sin, a rich variety of opinion and conviction would have existed." Therefore, just as the "colors that exist when the beam of light shines through the prism are multiform, but together they constitute a harmonious ray," in like manner a multiformity of understanding leads to a more harmonious understanding of truth. Kuyper, *Wisdom and Wonder*, 85. Sin also leads to diverse interpretations. The Spirit must guide the community of God toward accepting true diversity of perspective from faulty interpretations.

111. Warnke, *Gadamer*, 100.

... one of integration and appropriation. This does not mean either that the participants give up their positions or that they use those of others simply to buttress their own. Rather it means that each participant takes account of the other opinions, attempts to show what is wrong and right with them as well as with his or her own position and thereby formulates, in concert with the others, a view that each recognizes to be closer to the truth than any of the original positions.[112]

At times, this means talking with the unredeemed in the same field of study or in other fields of study that examine a similar area. However, much of the time, the conversation occurs between the redeemed specializing in various fields.

Fourth, integration means approaching a field of study from an unapologetically Christian perspective (thinking Christianly). This means Scripture reserves a privileged place as it provides a meta-narrative by which to guide all of life. Therefore, the core beliefs of the Christian faith inform all aspects of integration (presuppositions, methods, content, and application). Thinking Christianly may entail asking different questions, using different methods, interpreting the results in a nuanced way, or applying conclusions differently.[113] Sometimes one's Christian perspective requires the person to neglect certain questions that concern the academy. At other times it means addressing questions ignored by the academy.

Fifth, a goal of integration is constructing a more complete picture of God, the world, and the relationship between the two. Some parts of the picture reflect Scripture alone, some the created order alone, most reflect both forms of revelation. At times integration extends to issues of interpretation. When it does, the written Word interprets the world, which in turn interprets the written world (that is if reality allows for a linear process).

Finally, one form of revelation does not "dominate to the exclusion or lessoning of the other's contribution."[114] So, the "process of doing science as a Christian is *not* primarily an act of employing naturalistic methodology of investigation to which is added a second act of glorifying and loving

---

112. Ibid., 101.

113. Plantinga suggests that the redeemed do not always need to follow the issues and methods used by the unredeemed. Sometimes Christians must explore areas of unique interests to them and in ways faithful with their beliefs. Plantinga, "Advice to Christian Philosophers," 253–71. Kuyper also concluded that Christians must "begin pursuing science independently on the basis of their own principles, leading them to strive for a university life that honors the mystery of all wisdom and all science in Christ." Science here represents all areas of scientific inquiry. Kuyper, *Wisdom and Wonder*, 104.

114. Coe and Hall, "Transformational Psychology View," 208.

God from the doing of science. Rather, the very act of doing science and psychology was meant by God to be done in the love of God, contemplating and open to all relevant reality while contemplating and loving God."[115]

Conclusion

Evangelicals describe integration as a way to understand the relationship between Scripture and the created order. Therefore, it is one place whereby one can observe evangelical understanding of the created order as revelation. As with works on systematic theology, evangelicals speaking of integration often neglect the created order in favor of Scripture. Three of the four ways in which evangelicals treat the relationship between Scripture and the created order demonstrate this tendency ("Bible only," uni-directional, and leaning toward the Bible). Evangelicals must develop an evangelical theology of revelation that takes into consideration the similarities as well as the differences between forms of revelation (and in particular Scripture and the created order). Then, this theology of revelation should inform further conversations and practices regarding integration. The theoretical proposal above serves as a primer for this dialogue. At the end of chapter five I present Herman Bavinck as a positive example of one who integrates truth claims using both Scripture and the created order. First things first, a theology of revelation must be offered prior to suggesting examples worth following. Before we can construct a theology of revelation designed to anchor integrative efforts we must look at two key issues. Current definitions of revelation and categorizations of revelation cause problems for systematizing or integrating all truth. In the next chapter, we look at these definitions and categorizations of revelation to help us see more clearly current problems that a theology of revelation needs to address.

---

115. Ibid.

4

Problems with Current Definitions and Categorizations

Introduction

As shown in the previous chapters, evangelicals tend to affirm the created order as revelation, but then neglect its usefulness. I propose that a theology of revelation will enable evangelicals to overcome this inconsistency. Yet, before offering a potential solution, an examination of existing descriptions of revelation alert us to problems to address. Two problems with current evangelical explanations of revelation contribute to the neglect of the created order as revelation: (1) the dichotomy between revelation and reason, in other words, the notion that God reveals some things to humanity, but people discover other things, and (2) confusion arising from the categorization of revelation as "general" and "special."

The first problem, the dichotomy between revelation and reason, could stem from brevity of definitions. Some evangelical definitions of "revelation" focus on the act of revealing and do not allow room to call the product of this activity "revelation," as well. The problem increases when evangelicals move beyond a simple definition of "revelation" and explicitly link the act of revealing with one form of revelation (Bible) and the act of discovery (use of reason) with other forms of revelation (created order). Resultantly, they assert that people know some things by divine revelation and others by human discovery. These understandings of revelation make neglect of the creation as a form of revelation easy since revelation comes from God, but humans discover the created order. The former retains the character of God, the latter the character of man. These assumptions oversimplify the complex issue of divine revelation and human interpretation.

The second problem stems from confusion that arises when evangelicals categorize revelation as "general" and "special." Evangelicals by and large categorize revelation based on its distribution. In essence, God reveals to all people at all times, which they call "general revelation." Yet, God reveals specific things to specific people at specific times, which they label "special revelation." However, not all agree on the finer details when providing further explanations of these forms of revelation. Additionally, some evangelicals force other aspects of revelation to fit under the category of distribution (general and special) and overlook the commonalities between forms of revelation.

Both problems, simplistic definitions and confusing categorizations, contribute to the neglect of the creation as revelation. The next chapter will attempt to provide a theology of revelation designed to overcome these problems. But first, we must examine current definitions of "revelation" and problems that arise.

Definitions

Simple definitions of revelation help as far as they go. However, such definitions often focus on the act of revealing and not the product revealed. Such a treatment often results in a faulty epistemology that emphasizes two ways of knowing: revelation and reason. The former comes immediately from God which makes it more trustworthy than the later. Some who do speak of revelation as a product also maintain that special revelation comes directly from God, but people know general revelation by use of human reason alone.

Some evangelicals describe revelation as the "*making known* of something previously unknown."[1] The definition links revelation with an activity. In emphasizing the verb "revelation" the definition does not help people understand the noun form of the same word. For instance, the above definition tells the reader nothing about the content, source, or recipients of revelation. What is made known? Who makes it known? Who knows it? Answers to these questions help people begin to understand similarities and differences between Scripture and the created order as forms of revelation.

---

1. Henry, "Revelation, Special," 946; and Dockery, "Revelation of God," 1181; emphasis mine.

Problems with Current Definitions and Categorizations 81

The absence of answers to the above questions limits the usefulness of the definition.

Many evangelicals define revelation as "*making known* something that man could not otherwise know" or "*divine disclosure* of divine truth."[2] The first definition continues to emphasize the action of revealing, but identifies the recipients; namely humanity. What, though, could man not otherwise know? Does this content differ substantially from what man can know otherwise? The second definition continues to maintain the active nature of revelation. The definition also alerts the reader that God reveals (discloses) and the content of this disclosure belongs to him. Though accurate, one must ask, "What is the scope of divine disclosure?" or "To what extent do people rely on God's disclosure for not only knowledge of God, but also creation and the relationship between the two?" Granted, answers to such questions lie beyond the scope of a definition, which by nature requires brevity not detail. However, all three definitions confine revelation to activity, thereby, neglecting the possibility of revelation as a product of divine activity. The definitions remain limited in their utility. One wonders, "Do they allow room for the creation as a form of revelation?"

Within all three definitions the reader notices the possibility of setting revelation in contrast to some other way of knowing. The first definition (making known of something previously unknown) either suggests all knowledge is revealed or more likely that we know some things by means of something other than revelation. The second definition (making known something that man could not otherwise know) more clearly delineates revealed knowledge from that which people could know in other ways. The third definition (divine disclosure of divine truth) could imply that God reveals all truth. However, one could interpret it as pointing to some uniquely divine truth revealed by God, while other truth comes from other ways of human knowing. The definitions entail the potentiality of two ways of knowing. As evangelicals offer additional clarity, the possibility of two ways of knowing turns to reality.

Evangelicals expanding on such definitions explicitly place revelation in opposition to discovery or human rationality as two ways of knowing. Revelation provides believers with God's perspective.[3] Conversely, limits

---

2. Evans, *Theology*, 1075–76; Lightner, *Evangelical Theology*, 10; Baker, *Dispensational Theology*, 18, 31; Chafer, *Systematic Theology*, 1: 48; Earle, "Revelation and Inspiration," 287; Milne, *Know the Truth*, 25; Towns, *Theology*, 30; and Wiley, *Christian Theology*, 1:127, emphasis mine.

3. Use of "divine perspective" insinuates that God, like humanity, only sees in part, but not the whole. Finite beings know only in part and therefore have a perspective. However, the divine attribute of omniscience belongs to God alone.

of finitude, fallenness, and limited usefulness (focus on the present life instead of eternity) mark human discovery. God does the former, but people carry out the later. Evangelicals tie the former means of knowing to special revelation whereas the later they call general revelation.

Litfin serves as an example of one who emphasizes two ways of knowing. He writes, "Human knowledge of reality stems from two prime sources:[4] special revelation and discovery."[5] Litfin uses 2 Cor 4:18 as the basis upon which he distinguishes between these two forms of knowledge. Litfin states that "[b]y the seen he [Paul] means all that is for humans *independently discoverable, all that we can learn on our own through application of our own faculties.*"[6] What does Paul mean by unseen, then? Litfin answers that anything we cannot discover we know by revelation alone. He equates the unseen with "special revelation, the testimony of God. The world of the unseen represents all we know is the case because God has told us it is so."[7] For Litfin, revelation gives people "a God's eye view of things," and the "revealed worldview."[8] In fact, "gaining a God's eye view of things is precisely what a historical Christian concept of revelation promises. It certainly is what the Apostle Paul believed it offered."[9] Litfin creates a dichotomy between that

---

4. I find two key issues with Litfin's terminology here. First, the term "sources" seems misapplied to both special revelation and discovery. Ultimately, all knowledge comes from God (see "source" in "Theology of Revelation"). Second, the categorizations of "special revelation" and "discovery" cause problems. While "special revelation" designates a certain type of revelation, it seems odd to use "discovery" as a similar way to classify knowledge. "Discovery" seems best used as a way to obtain knowledge. Also, why call revelation "special" which implies that another classification of revelation exists? Litfin does not speak of "general revelation" as most evangelicals do.

5. Litfin, *Conceiving the Christian College*, 91. Litfin does not stand alone as one hesitant to use the designation of "revelation" in relation to the created order. In a discussion panel on evangelical theological method, Glenn Kreider queried, "What is the role of non-canonical sources in your theological method?" Daniel Treier responded that evangelicals should not use the term "revelation" in evangelical prolegomena. He reasons that Scripture does not use the term as such, so theologians should not use it. Additionally, the term comes from philosophical circles that view revelation and reason as competing epistemological sources. He stated the "two books" terminology as his preferential wording. Panel Discussion, "Evangelical Theological Method."

6. Litfin, *Conceiving the Christian College*, 182, emphasis added. Notice that Litfin uses reason to understand Scripture. In practice, he blurs the lines between his two ways of knowing. If God simply gave revelation to man in a non-mediated fashion and people rightly understood this revelation, then everyone would agree with Litfin's understanding of this passage.

7. Ibid.

8. Ibid., 183, 203. He does state an important caveat that God communicates "his perspective" in human language.

9. Ibid., 184. Can finite and fallen people truly have a "God's eye view?" I suggest

which humans discover by use of autonomous reason and that which God reveals to them.[10]

Unlike Litfin, Pope uses the terminology of general and special revelation. Yet like Litfin he equates knowledge through the creation with human discovery. Pope realizes that "[t]here are secrets gradually unveiled in the worlds of mind and matter," but believes they are "the aim and reward of human science" so we do not "call their discovery revelation."[11] He then equates revelation with the Bible. He concludes, "The Bible means all revelation and all revelation means the Bible."[12]

Further examples come from Miley and McCune who agree that people know some things by revelation and other things by reason. They add to the revelation-reason distinction the idea of the immediacy of revelation, but the mediated nature of truth gained through reason. Miley begins by affirming that in one sense "all knowledge is from God."[13] However, he writes, "As between nature and revelation there is still the profound difference in the modes of knowledge: in the one case its acquisition in the use of human faculties, in the other its immediate communication by the divine agency."[14] McCune agrees with the differentiation between mediated and unmediated truth. Truth mediated or "arrived at by human investigation" is truth, but "it is not revelation."[15] Discovery therefore is mediated by our own faculties, but God immediately and supernaturally gives revelation. Adding the immediate-mediated distinction further affirms the significance of the former and the suspect nature of the later.

Plantinga, Thompson, and Lundberg, Thorsen, and Waltke and Yu retain the terminology "general revelation" and use "revelation" as a noun

---

that we cannot. We can, though, know and express transcendent truth in a finite way. For example, our understanding of "trinity" differs from this truth as God knows it. However, the term serves as a way finite and fallen people attempt to express the transcendent truth that the Father, Son, and Spirit exists eternally as distinct *prosopon* (persons), but *homoousias* (same substance/essence).

10. Litfin does affirm the necessary use of reason to interpret revelation. He also acknowledges the mutually interpreting functions of Scripture and the created order. On one hand, Litfin understands the complexity of the relationship between reason and revelation and between Scripture and creation. Yet, on the other hand, he continues to use problematic language that diminishes the importance of the created order as revelation. Litfin illustrates the difficulty of carefully examining and articulating a theology of revelation that includes the created order. Ibid., 206.

11. Pope, *Christian Theology*, 1:37.

12. Ibid., 1:41.

13. Miley, *Systematic Theology*, 1:8.

14. Ibid., 8–9.

15. McCune, *Systematic Theology*, 1:172.

not a verb. However, Plantinga, Thompson, and Lundberg link reason with general revelation and faith with special revelation. People apprehend general revelation "by human reason, intuition, or conscience" but special revelation is "a revealed knowledge of God . . . apprehended by faith."[16] These authors isolate two distinct ways people comprehend revelation. Thorsen differentiates between general and special revelation in a similar way. In a chart, he succinctly states that God intends general revelation "for all people; they may discover it for themselves," but special revelation "for all people; they must somehow be told."[17] Waltke and Yu also emphasize that special revelation (Scripture) "is not available by natural reason and cannot be discovered by the scientific method" implying that people know general revelation through "natural reason."[18] The statements of each of these men affirm that people depend on God for special revelation, but discover general revelation themselves.

A more detailed and extreme example comes from Shedd who explains that only certain portions of Scripture qualify as revelation. He begins with an acknowledgement of humanity's dependency on God for all knowledge, "Revelation in its general and wide signification is any species of knowledge which God is the ultimate source and cause. In this sense, all that man knows intuitively is revealed to him; for even his axiomatic knowledge does not originate from himself independently and apart from his Creator."[19] However, he later limits revelation to Scripture: "In the common use of the term, revelation is employed in the restricted signification and signifies the written word of God."[20] Or to state the case more accurately, Shedd confines revelation to selective passages of Scripture.

Shedd continues by narrowing his explanation of revelation to parts of Scripture. He identifies revelation as "the communication of truth or facts hitherto unknown to man and incapable of being deduced from the structure of the human intellect or derived through the ordinary channels of human information."[21] He uses the prophecy in 2 Thess 2:3 as an example of revelation. Shedd writes, "Paul could not have obtained the knowledge from any human source."[22] Shedd, therefore, considers 2 Thess 2:3 as both

---

16. Plantinga, et al., *Christian Theology*, 52–53.

17. Thorsen, *Christian Theology*, 28. He equates general revelation with "things we can discover for ourselves" in a question at the end of his chapter on revelation (24).

18. Waltke and Yu, *Old Testament Theology*, 31.

19. Shedd, *Dogmatic Theology*, 85. I believe Shedd is correct on this point and should have stopped here.

20. Ibid., 88.

21. Ibid., 94.

22. Ibid. Shedd lists additional examples: 1 Cor 15:35–55, 15:24–28; Rom 11:25;

revealed and inspired. He considers prophecy recorded in Scripture as revelation. However, Shedd does not count observable history; even that recorded in Scripture, as revelation. For example, "the history of the exodus of the Israelites and similar histories in Scripture" are "inspired but not revealed" because people observed and recorded the event of the exodus.[23]

Shedd uses the doctrine of the Trinity as another example to make his point. Since the "doctrine of the Trinity is a truth not deducible by rational reflection" Shedd labels it "a revelation."[24] However, the doctrine of the unity of God "is capable of being inferred by the human intellect . . . from a contemplation of the works of creation outwardly and the operations of the human soul inwardly."[25] Therefore, Shedd concludes "The Trinity is a part of written revelation; but the divine unity is a truth of natural religion or unwritten revelation. The doctrine of the Trinity as stated in the Bible is both revealed and inspired; the doctrine of divine unity as stated in the Bible is inspired but not revealed."[26] Shedd not only differentiates between reason and revelation as ways of knowing he also limits revelation to specific propositional truths.

Like Shedd, other evangelicals narrowly limit revelation to propositions. Dulles finds this characteristic among fundamentalists who "insisted that the Bible alone is revelation, that it is to be interpreted in its obvious literal sense, and that it is totally inerrant."[27] He summarizes the evangelical doctrine of revelation, "Revelation, for these orthodox Evangelicals, is thus equated with the meaning of the Bible, taken as a set of propositional statements, each expressing a divine affirmation, valid always and everywhere."[28] Dulles uses J. I. Packer and Carl F. H. Henry as examples of evangelicals who limit revelation to Scripture. Packer affirms that "God reveals Himself to men both by exercising power for them and by teaching truth to them," and that "[t]he two activities are not antithetical, but complementary." However, Packer maintains, "the biblical position is that the mighty acts of God are

---

and Gen 1.

23. Ibid., 95.

24. Ibid.

25. Ibid.

26. Ibid. Is Shedd contradicting himself? Did he not just call it "unwritten revelation?"

27. Dulles, *Models of Revelation*, 22.

28. Ibid., 39. Dulles's models of revelation prove helpful to the extent people use them as talking points concerning how various communities tend to understand revelation. However, such categorizations can easily lead to overstating the differences, overlooking commonalities, and assuming that extreme examples adequately represent the entire community.

not revelation to man at all, except in so far as they are accompanied by words of God to explain them."[29] In sum, he equates revelation with propositional content.

Similarly, Henry affirms that "both historical act and its interpretation belong to the totality of revelation."[30] He, too, emphasizes the necessity of propositional statements for revelation. The tenth assertion of Henry's magnum opus, *God, Revelation and Authority*, further highlights his equation of revelation with the Bible and more narrowly propositional statements, "God's revelation is rational communication conveyed in intelligible ideas and meaningful words, that is, in conceptual-verbal form."[31] Packer and Henry not only limit revelation to Scripture, they further narrow it to propositional statements.

In summation, evangelicals do not distinguish the act of revelation with its product, they build a dichotomy whereby some knowledge comes through revelation, but other knowledge comes through reason, and they narrowly describe revelation as a set of propositional statements revealed by God. Though vague and brief, definitions of the term "revelation" do not necessitate the revelation-reason dichotomy, but they do allow for this understanding. Some evangelicals make the revelation-reason dichotomy explicit as they link reason with general revelation and faith with special revelation. Other evangelicals more narrowly describe revelation as select propositional statements. These later evangelicals also separate reason from revelation as ways of receiving and knowing truth. All of the above issues lead to a failure to see the created order as divine revelation.

Elmer Towns, in a popular level theology, provides insight into this reason-revelation divide common among evangelicals. In essence, people discover some things by autonomous human reason, but other matters require the special work of the Spirit of God. Towns asserts that human "[r]eason is the intellectual and moral faculties of man exercised in the pursuit of truth apart from supernatural aid."[32] He continues to affirm autonomous human reason, "Man does not need a special enablement of the Holy Spirit

---

29. Packer, *Fundamentalism and the Word of God*, 92.

30. Henry, *God, Revelation and Authority*, 2:330.

31. Ibid., 12; emphasis removed. Yet, in other places Henry affirms all forms of revelation as necessary. He states, "[N]either the revelation in Jesus nor that in the Bible nor that in conscience nor that in nature can replace one another. Each is an indispensable and individual facet of God's comprehensive disclosure." Ibid., 87–88. Like many evangelicals Henry affirms the reality of the creation as revelation, but then focuses on the Bible and neglects the created order.

32. Towns, *Theology*, 35.

to perceive natural revelation; it is available to all men."³³ However, special revelation requires God's enablement for understanding. Towns affirms that special revelation "must be spiritually discerned. Those who perceive it must not only apply the general methods of literary interpretation, but must also be correctly related to the Holy Spirit to receive and understand His special revelation."³⁴ Towns does point out the limited use of human reason (literary interpretation) to understand special revelation. However, Towns does not mention any notion of God enabling people to understand general revelation. Man discovers general revelation through use of human reason.

The "autonomy of reason is a fiction" for a number of reasons.³⁵ First, mankind can only reason because God created people with the ability to think rationally. As Calvin states, "the admirable light of truth displayed in them [profane authors] should remind us, that the human mind, however much fallen and perverted from its original integrity, is still adorned and invested with admirable gifts from its Creator."³⁶ Humanity's ability to reason, though corrupted because of original sin, remains a good gift from God.

Second, humanity reasons about that which God created. Though humans create something new out of what exists, created people cannot in turn create something out of absolute nothingness.³⁷ Genesis 1 teaches that God created all that exists. Calvin attributes all true knowledge to the work of the Spirit, "For if the skill and knowledge required for the construction of the Tabernacle behoved to be imparted to Bezaleel and Aholiab, by the Spirit of God (Exod. xxxi. 2; xxxv. 30), it is not strange that the knowledge of those things which are of the highest excellence in human life is said to be communicated to us by the Spirit."³⁸ Therefore, reason never occurs autonomously, even for unbelievers.³⁹ Horton similarly states, "[W]e are no less

33. Ibid., 34.
34. Ibid.
35. Holmes, *Truth*, 79.
36. Calvin, *Institutes*, 1:236.

37. Crouch suggests, "For every act of creation involves bringing something into being that was not there before—every creation is *ex nihilo*, from nothing, even when it takes the world as its starting point." Crouch, *Culture Making*, 23.

38. Calvin, *Institutes*, 1:236. Calvin differentiates between the indwelling work of the Spirit (holiness) for believers and the common work done even among unbelievers (physics, dialectics, mathematics, etc.).

39. Human reasoning may not occur outside the realm of divine sovereignty, but the unredeemed do pursue knowledge of creation without seeking insight from the Creator. As Dubay observes, when studying the "history of human thought . . . one is struck by the universal inability of unaided reason to find a satisfying solution to the puzzles of human existence." Without divine intervention people do not rightly understand that which they investigate. Dubay, *Evidential Power of Beauty*, 273.

dependent on God for our knowledge than for our existence."[40] Contrary to Towns' statement above, the Spirit actively works in all true knowing.

Third, true knowledge of all things requires knowing the thing in relation to its Creator and his purposes for the object.[41] Colossians 1:16 teaches that everything exists in relation to Jesus "For by him all things were created; things in heaven and on earth, visible and invisible, whether thrones or powers or rulers or authorities; all things were created by him and for him." Additionally, Paul teaches the reconciliation of all things to God through Christ in Col 1: 20, "through him to reconcile to himself all things, whether things on earth or things in heaven, by making peace through his blood, shed on the cross." Correct understanding of creation requires knowing it in relation to its Creator. Horton echoes this notion, "The same Word who became flesh was the one in whom and through whom all things were made—and are truly known (Jn 1:1–3; Col 1:15–20)."[42]

Fourth, all true knowledge begins with faith. Psalm 14:1 alerts the reader, "The fool says in his heart 'There is no God.'" Proverbs 1:7 teaches, "The fear of the LORD is the beginning of knowledge." The author of Heb 11:3 writes, "By faith we understand that the universe was formed at God's command, so that what is seen was not made out of what was visible." As Augustine states, "Faith seeks; understanding finds."[43]

In addition to the faulty concept of autonomous human reason, the idea that reason and revelation serve as distinct ways of knowing is inaccurate. People use basic reasoning ability to read and understand revelation. People interpret Scripture by way of rational capacity. As Holmes points out, "propositional revelation is by its very nature addressed to men as rational beings, capable of textual study, exegesis, and all the theological sciences."[44] Therefore, seemingly simple propositions like that found in Deut 6:1, "The LORD our God, the LORD is one," requires the use of reason. The reader must understand English, grammar, and concepts such as God, LORD, and one. How a person understands these concepts impacts how the person interprets this simple divinely revealed proposition. Furthermore, knowing Hebrew, Israel, Christianity, and one's own experience of God also come to bear as one reads, understands, and responds to this revelation of God. The revelation does not change, however, the interpretation of it and the response of people to it may vary based on the above factors and more.

40. Horton, *Christian Faith*, 49.
41. Oliphint, *Reasons {for Faith}*, 185–86.
42. Horton, *Christian Faith*, 43.
43. Augustine, "On the Trinity," 200.
44. Holmes, *Truth*, 79.

Problems with Current Definitions and Categorizations 89

In summary, reason and revelation do not represent two independent ways of knowing. Instead, "revelation" refers to the act and the result of God's communication. Holmes points out that "reason is a God-given capacity for *understanding* and organizing and using what is revealed. Revelation and reason are both God-given; both to be valued and used."[45] Similarly, Brewster asserts, "A divine element enters, a coefficient factor, into all the knowledge. Discovery and revelation are respectively the obverse and reverse, the human and divine sides, of the same process . . . To oppose intuitive knowledge to divine revelation is to make a false dilemma."[46] Therefore, revelation "does not extinguish the human reason, but claims it wholly for this process of reception."[47] Furthermore, humans never use reason autonomously of God's sovereignty. True knowledge comes by the work of God. The tension of divine sovereignty and human responsibility must be maintained as the redeemed seek to understand that which they believe.

Some truths regarding God, creation, and the relationship between the two come only through word-based revelation. Scripture exists as a unique and important form of revelation. However, the uniqueness of Scripture does not detract from the fact that God also reveals through the created order. Furthermore, commonalities between forms of revelation do not necessarily diminish the uniqueness of and place of privilege for Scripture. The next chapter explores the similarities and differences between Scripture and creation as forms of revelation. But first, we must examine how evangelicals categorize revelation and the impact of this on understanding revelation.

Categorization

The second problem that leads to neglecting the created order as revelation stems with how evangelicals categorize revelation. Categorizing revelation as general, that which is available to all people at all times, and special as that which is specifically given to certain people at a specific time, causes confusion.[48] Yet, many evangelicals categorize revelation based on

45. Holmes, *Idea of a Christian College*, 26.

46. Brewster, *Revelation*, 40.

47. Brunner, *Revelation and Reason*, 16. Knowing God requires revelation, reason, and faith. Oden teaches the complex relationships between reason, faith, and revelation see Oden, *Systematic Theology*, 203–9.

48. Helm observes that people base their categorization of revelation on one aspect. By way of example, one may categorize based on purpose: redemptive and non-redemptive, another may select form as the basis for categorization: propositional and non-propositional, and yet another may divide revelation based on distribution: general and special. Helm, *Divine Revelation*, 21.

distribution.[49] However, they do not necessarily mean the same thing. Some retain a broader understanding of special revelation, but others narrow it further as they equate it with the Bible. In addition, evangelicals use this categorization as an umbrella under which they subsume all other aspects.[50] In the end, both issues highlight an overly simplified understanding of revelation. They also lead to confusion, and a neglect of the creation as a form of divine revelation.

Evangelicals tend to categorize revelation based on distribution. Garrett states, " 'General' revelation is that disclosure of God which is *available to all human beings* . . . . On the contrary, 'special' revelation is the historical disclosure of God *to the people of Israel and in Jesus Christ*. The distinctly Christian revelation of God is, therefore, special or historical revelation."[51] Though God makes general revelation available to all, he gives special revelation exclusively to Israel in the Old Testament and in Jesus.[52] Garrett narrows the distribution of special revelation more than some.

Saucy agrees with Garrett that God intends general revelation for all. However, the vagueness of his explanation of the distribution of special revelation means it could apply more broadly. Saucy explains, "General revelation is revelation that is addressed to and therefore available to *all people at all times*. Special revelation, on the other hand, is revelation that God has given at *special times to certain people*."[53] Saucy leaves room for non-canonical revelation localized in time and space. As such, one could consider the hymn "A Mighty Fortress" as special revelation given in space and time. As Grudem also explains special revelation more broadly, "Special revelation includes all the words of Scripture but is not limited to the

---

49. Demarest, "Revelation, General," 944; Grenz, et al., "General Revelation," 54–55; Grenz, *Theology for the Community*, 173–74; Plantinga, et al., *Christian Theology*, 52–53; Gulley, *Systematic Theology*, 191; Oden, *Systematic Theology*, 1:19–21; Demarest, *General Revelation*, 14; Lewis and Demarest, *Integrative Theology*, 1:61, 100; Ryrie, *Basic Theology*, 31; Milne, *Know the Truth*, 27, 31; Williams, *Renewal Theology*, 1:32–33, 37; Moore, "Natural Revelation," 114; Kantzer, "Communication of Revelation," 62; Herrick, "Is the Bible the Only Revelation of God"; Allison and Anthony, "Revelation, Scripture, and Christian Education," 73; and Dockery, *Christian Scripture*, 17, 21.

50. Bookman notices this and the problems it causes. He observes the confusion between content and audience, "By mistakenly taking that term [general] to refer to the content of the category (rather than to the audience to which the revelation thus denominated is available) . . . ." Bookman, "Scriptures and Biblical Counseling," 78.

51. Garrett, *Systematic Theology*, 1:45, emphasis added. I am unclear what Garrett means by "the distinctly Christian revelation."

52. Did God reveal only to Israel? Was not God's interaction with the nation of Israel revelation to the surrounding nations? Did God reveal to those outside of Israel, such as Rahab, Ruth, and Nebuchadnezzar?

53. Saucy, "Divine Revelation," 23, emphasis added.

words of Scripture, for it also includes, for example, many words of Jesus that were not recorded in Scripture, and probably there were many words spoken by Old Testament prophets and New Testament apostles that were not recorded in Scripture either."[54] Though still word-based, special revelation according to Grudem exists outside of Scripture.

Erickson agrees with Saucy's description, but further limits special revelation, "General revelation is God's communication of himself to *all persons at all times and in all places*. Special revelation involves God's *particular communications and manifestations of himself to particular persons at particular times*, communications and manifestations that are available now only by consultation of certain sacred writings."[55] Erickson begins with a broader understanding of special revelation, but then adds a caveat that limits special revelation to the Bible.

Dockery also limits special revelation to the Bible. Dockery writes, "God's self-disclosure of Himself in a *general way to all people at all times in all places*," and special revelation as "available to *specific people at specific times in specific places*," but adds "it [special revelation] is available now only by consultation of sacred Scripture."[56] Special revelation therefore does not occur outside of recorded biblical history.

Gamertsfelder, also, equates special revelation with the Bible, "We employ the terms nature and special revelation with the significance commonly attaching to them, meaning by special revelation the Bible, and by nature all the works of God found elsewhere."[57] In addition to Scripture, Enns mentions the Incarnation as a form of special revelation. He writes, "Special revelation involves a narrower focus than general revelation and is restricted to Jesus Christ and the Scriptures."[58] But he, like Erickson and Gamertsfelder, ends by equating special revelation with Scripture. He states: "Of course, all that is known of Christ is through the Scriptures; therefore, it can be said that special revelation is restricted to the Scriptures."[59] Instead of defining special revelation as localized in time and space and given to particular people, such evangelicals simply state that special revelation is the Bible and ultimately propositional statements. Enns observes, "Special revelation as reflected in the Scriptures is given in propositional statements."[60] So, in the

---

54. Grudem, *Systematic Theology*, 123.
55. Erickson, *Christian Theology*, 178, emphasis added.
56. Dockery, "Revelation of God," 1181, 1182, emphasis altered.
57. Gamertsfelder, *Systematic Theology*, 17.
58. Enns, *Handbook of Theology*, 158.
59. Ibid.
60. Ibid.

narrowest sense, evangelicals equate special revelation with propositional statements recorded in Scripture.

Evangelicals, therefore, do not necessarily mean the same thing though they use the same categorization of revelation, general and special. The lack of uniformity raises questions concerning the adequacy of such categorizations. The terminology itself lends to favoring that the "special" over that the "general" without understanding the commonalities and differences between forms of revelation. These problems come into focus as we examine those who offer more detailed explanations of general and special revelation. They often distinguish between general and special revelation based on distribution, but then discuss other aspects of revelation under these headings. Such a practice highlights differences, overlooks commonalities, and leads to neglect of the created order as revelation.

Some evangelicals take the categorization based on distribution and make it absolute. In other words, they force all other aspects of revelation to fit on one side or the other of this dichotomy. Thorsen charts the differences. Under general revelation he states it is "available to all people" whereas under special revelation he states it is "available to a few people."[61] He continues to explain that general revelation is "available at all times and places," whereas special revelation is available at particular times and places."[62] General revelation is "intended for all people; they may discover it for themselves," but special revelation is "intended for all people; they must somehow be told."[63] The chart continues with content, general revelation "declares God's greatness," but special revelation "declares God's grace" therefore general revelation is "sufficient for condemnation," but special revelation is "sufficient for salvation."[64] Thorsen compares revelation's recipients, distribution, characteristics, content, and effect all under a categorization based on distribution.

Phillips and Okholm chart the comparison between general and special revelation. General revelation is "part of the natural order of creation," it is "given through natural means" and it "shows inexcusability."[65] Special revelation is "supernatural or miraculous acts," it is given "through supernatural means," and it "establishes salvation and develops the believer."[66] They use the category of distribution, but compare the characteristics and effect of revelation. Is general revelation natural and special revelation supernatu-

---

61. Thorsen, *Christian Theology,* 18.
62. Ibid., 28.
63. Ibid.
64. Ibid.
65. Phillips and Okholm, *Welcome to the Family,* 45.
66. Ibid.

ral? Or might both forms of revelation be both natural and supernatural in essence? Subsuming the characteristics under a categorization based on distribution does not allow one to explore whether both forms of revelation are natural and supernatural in essence.

In a similar way Diehl differentiates between general and special revelation on the basis of distribution, he labels general revelation "universal" and special revelation "local."[67] But he includes descriptors such as "natural, continuous... indirect and nonpropositional" in his description of general revelation.[68] These extend well beyond the distribution of revelation to its characteristics. Diehl contrasts these descriptors with "usually supernatural, discontinuous (or distinctly historical)... more direct or personal, and often propositional" for special revelation.[69] Diehl also examines the characteristics of revelation, but does so under the umbrella category based on distribution.

Likewise, Plantinga, Thompson, and Lundberg chart an evangelical summarization of revelation. They equate special revelation with revealed knowledge given by means of redemptive acts and words, which people apprehended by faith through the Holy Spirit and which results in sacred theology. Conversely, they equate general revelation with natural knowledge; which comes by means of creation and providence, it is apprehended by reason, intuition, and conscience, and results in natural theology.[70] They use the category of distribution, but then compare forms of revelation in terms of characteristics, form, reception, and content. This comparison does not leave room for faith and reason to come together in order to understand both general and special revelation.

Higgins also affirms that "the two primary categories of divine revelation are general and special revelation."[71] He explains that general revelation "involves God's self-disclosure through some mediate, natural mode," whereas special revelation "is divine self-disclosure through an immediate, supernatural mode."[72] Could both Scripture and the created order be mediated as well as natural and supernatural? Higgins concludes, "Natural theology and revealed theology are the theological understandings arrived at through human reason and reflection as one views general revelation and

67. Diehl, "Evangelicalism and General Revelation," 443–44.
68. Ibid.
69. Ibid., emphasis removed.
70. Plantinga, et al., *Christian Theology*, 52. They do acknowledge that the summary is "simple and straightforward" but this does serve as a basis of their understanding of revelation.
71. Higgins, "God's Inspired Word," 69.
72. Ibid.

special revelation respectively."[73] The two types of revelation provide two distinct theologies; instead, of both forms of revelation correlating to create theology.

Stott lists "six differences between 'general' and 'special' revelation" in chart form.[74] Under general revelation he lists general, natural, continuous, glorious, visible, and judging. However, he characterizes special revelation as special, supernatural, final, gracious, audible, and saving.[75] Using works such as "unlike" and "in contrast," Grenz focuses on the differences between general and special revelation. He explains that God gives general revelation to all people. This revelation is natural, is accessed through use of reason and mediates "general knowledge of God our creator. In contrast, God gives special revelation to specific people by supernatural means which cannot be accessed by use of reason and is meant to bring people into fellowship with God.[76]

Why do problems occur when someone subsumes other aspects of revelation under a categorization based on distribution? Such practices fail to understand the complexity of or acknowledge continuity between forms of revelation. When a person removes the complexity of revelation, then the person can easily neglect one form of revelation. Since I build a theology of revelation based on an analysis of the continuity and discontinuity between forms of revelation in the next chapter, I will provide only one example here.

Some evangelicals equate general revelation with the natural, but special revelation with the supernatural. For example, "unlike special revelation, general revelation is that divine self-disclosure which is 'natural' rather than 'supernatural' or which is disclosed naturally rather than supernaturally."[77] Likewise Saucy writes, "These categories (general and special revelation) are sometimes labeled 'natural' and 'supernatural' revelation, respectively, suggesting that general revelation is communicated through natural phenomena while special revelation is conveyed through supernatural intervention."[78] Similarly, Stott states, "God's general revelation was made through nature (heaven and earth proclaiming his glory), whereas his special revelation was made through miracle (inspiration and incarnation)."[79] Phillips and Okholm agree that special revelation is super-

73. Ibid.
74. Stott, *Evangelical Truth*, 38.
75. Ibid.
76. Grenz, *Theology for the Community*, 173–74.
77. Ibid., 174.
78. Saucy, "Divine Revelation," 23.
79. Stott, *Evangelical Truth*, 38.

natural and general revelation is natural.[80] Kantzer writes, "General revelation (or natural revelation or natural theology) is contrasted with special revelation (or supernatural revelation or revealed theology)."[81]

Though many evangelicals identify general revelation with natural and special revelation with the supernatural not all agree on this differentiation. Furthermore, one can question the accuracy of this description of revelation. Bavinck in one work links general revelation with the natural and special revelation with the supernatural, "God uses usual phenomenon in general revelation and unusual phenomenon in special revelation."[82] Yet in his *Dogmatics* Bavinck points to the teaching of Scripture, "Scripture, though it knows of an established order, in the case of revelation makes no distinction between 'natural' and 'supernatural' revelation."[83] Now Bavinck sees the commonalities between general and special revelation: "Actually, according to Scripture, all revelation, also that in nature, is supernatural."[84] A person who uses distribution as an absolute categorization under which he compares all other aspects of revelation fails to see commonalities between forms of revelation.

Berkof also observes the supernatural nature of all revelation: "In a certain sense it may be said that, according to Scripture, all revelation of God is supernatural, since it comes from God and reveals God, who possesses a life distinct from that of nature."[85] One can label revelation as supernatural since it comes from God. The contextualized and mediated nature of all revelation (see next chapter) means that even special revelation has a natural component. Simple categorizations overlook commonalities between forms of revelation. Oversimplification results in a neglect of the created order discovered by human reason and mediated by nature. Special revelation is supernaturally given by God in propositional form in Scripture.

Rookmaaker notices the Christian preference of grace over nature where the realm of grace is placed "over against the flesh to mean: the spirit is the realm of the soul, the higher things, where faith is. And the flesh is the realm of the lower things, where the body is."[86] So, Rookmaaker concludes, "Maybe we say, very piously, that God created the world but we never study

---

80. Phillips and Okholm, *Welcome to the Family*, 45.
81. Kantzer, "Communication of Revelation," 62.
82. Bavinck, *Our Reasonable Faith*.
83. Bavinck, *Reformed Dogmatics*, 1:307.
84. Ibid.
85. Berkof, *Systematic Theology*, 126.
86. Rookmaaker, *God's Hand in History*, 169.

the world as God's creation; we study it like everyone else does."[87] In the present context, evangelicals prefer the supernatural to the natural. Evangelicals affirm the created order as revelation, but fail to treat it as such.

Anderson provides similar insight. He observes that evangelicals believe "heaven [i]s the goal of life" which he explains as "a direct, intuitive vision of God" which he calls a "beatific vision."[88] He observes, "This view seems to be based on Platonism where the body is a hindrance to the perception of the forms. Christians replaced the forms with God."[89] In our present life, the closest thing believers have to the beatific vision of God is Scripture; therefore some describe special revelation in ways that continue to set apart from the lesser general revelation. They neglect the later as a form of revelation. However, in reality, "The realm of history and matter is not a prison from which we must escape by contemplating unchanging reality, but the theater of God's glory."[90] A theology of revelation must take into consideration the commonalities as well as the differences between forms of revelation.

Conclusion

The nomenclature of general and special revelation can lead to a neglect of that which people label "general." Cosgrove highlights the problem well with a question in *Foundations of Christian Thought: Faith, Learning, and the Christian Worldview*, "You mentioned general revelation in academic subject areas and special revelation in the Bible. Doesn't using the word 'special' mean that the Bible's knowledge is far more important and superior to human learning?"[91] The very categorization of revelation as "general" and "special" leads to problems with the relationship between forms of revelation

Evangelical definitions of revelation imply that some knowledge comes by revelation and other knowledge comes through use of reason. Further explanations of revelation verify the presence of this dichotomy. Many evangelicals believe that God reveals special revelation, but people discover general revelation. This leads to favoring revealed knowledge and neglecting discovered knowledge. A theology of revelation must look at what Scripture teaches concerning revelation with a special focus on the created order as revelation.

87. Ibid.
88. Anderson, *Reason and Worldviews*, 106.
89. Ibid.
90. Horton, *Christian Faith*, 44.
91. Cosgrove, *Foundations of Christian Thought*, 44.

Evangelicals also categorize revelation based on distribution stating in sum that all people, in all times, and all places encounter general *revelation*. Conversely, God gives special revelation to specific people at specific times. Confusion arises where evangelicals begin explaining what they mean by general and special revelation. They subsume discussion of all other aspects of revelation under a categorization based on distribution. Resultantly, they overlook commonalities between forms of revelation. This practice leads to neglect of the created order as a form of revelation. Understanding the commonalities and differences between Scripture and the created order in all major aspects of revelation (source, forms, recipients, characteristics, content, and effects) can overcome simplistic definitions, troublesome categorizations, and lead to the rightful use of the created order as revelation. Taking these issues into consideration, I propose a theology of revelation built around answers to basic questions about the various aspects of revelation.

5

A Theology of Revelation

Introduction

In chapters two and three I argue that evangelicals neglect the created order as a form of revelation. I explain the need for a comprehensive theology of revelation that explores the commonalities and differences between two main forms of revelation (the created order and Scripture). In chapter four I explain the limited usefulness of common definitions as well as problems resulting from current categorizations of revelation. The issues isolated in chapter four shape the current chapter. Here I develop a theology of revelation that highlights the similarities between forms of revelation while acknowledging important distinctions.[1]

Constructing a theology of revelation begins by asking and answering central questions. These include: From whom does revelation come? What form(s) does this revelation take?[2] What does it mean for Scripture to teach

---

1. Why develop a theology of revelation? The reader of the Bible does not find a full-blown propositional theology of revelation in a specific biblical passage or book. The Bible assumes "both the necessity and the reality of revelation" yet says "little about the concept *per se*." Since a theology of revelation "remains undeveloped in scripture, it is the task of Christian theology to elaborate this scriptural assumption into an explicit doctrine of revelation." Plantinga, et al., *Christian Theology*, 52. As the reader will notice below, Scripture instructs its readers regarding revelation throughout.

2. I take into account the complexity of revelation through highlighting similarities and noting differences between forms of revelation. As Latourelle observes, "revelation . . . appears to be extremely complex" and like the Trinity "is a mystery of unity and complexity." Latourelle, *Theology of Revelation*, 443. I, therefore, seek to "accommodate

that God reveals outside of Scripture? What characterizes revelation? Who receives revelation? How do the recipients respond to revelation? What content comes by way of revelation? What effects does revelation produce?[3] How might evangelicals understand the relationship between Scripture and the created order?

Answers to the above questions come from a study of Scripture that extends beyond word studies and the text commonly used (Ps 19, Rom 1). As Latourelle states, in addition to the "*words* of revelation, we must be attentive to the *theme* of revelation" as we construct a theology of revelation.[4] Therefore, the proposed theology of revelation includes observations drawn from passages recording acts of revelation (for example Exod 14, Dan 2, and John 20:30–31) as well as specific statements regarding revelation (Ps 19 and Rom 1).

Although the sixty-six books of the Bible serve as the primary source, I recognize the limitations and dangers of studying Scripture in isolation.[5] Interaction with theologians from different times and cultures "might actually strengthen our present perspectives and convictions."[6] So, I make use of the thoughts of others across space and time. In fact, the contribution of this chapter comes not from novelty of ideas but rather from synthesizing the thoughts of others seeking to understand the teaching of Scripture regarding revelation. Therefore, in addition to Scripture, I use insights from historical figures, contemporary evangelical theologians, and ideas from non-professional theologians.[7]

---

the variety of the forms of revelation and genres of its scriptural mediation that we encounter in the Bible." Horton, *Christian Faith*, 121.

3. Some speak of the purpose of revelation (see below "Effects"). However, as Glenn Kreider pointed out in a casual conversation, God does not tell us why he reveals. Instead, people see the effects of revelation. The language "effects of revelation" comes from Michael Horton. Horton, *Christian Faith*, 122.

4. Latourelle, *Theology of Revelation*, 46. I ask, "What, if anything, does this passage teach about revelation?"

5. The reality of human finitude, the doctrine of original sin, and the concept of the body of Christ, demand that I look to the gifts and abilities of others as I seek articulate an evangelical theology of revelation.

6. Hall, *Learning Theology*, 26. The insights of others might correct faulty understanding or expand limited insight. Central areas of doctrine give shape to the proposed theology of revelation, as well.

7. Historical figures such as Augustine, Calvin, and Edwards contribute to the development of the current chapter. The positive use of evangelicals in this constructive chapter may seem surprising. However, evangelical writings on revelation highlight problems, raise questions, and provide answers. A specific person may provide important insight into *a particular aspect* of revelation. McGrath argues for the importance of learning from experts in other fields of study. McGrath, *Open Secret*, 315.

Examination of the Doctrine of Revelation in Evangelical Theology

The current chapter serves as an invitation for continued dialogue on critical issues pertaining to revelation. I hope the construction that follows leads to careful and deliberate attention among evangelicals on the topic of revelation both in terms of describing it and using the created order as a significant form of revelation.

Source of Revelation

An evangelical theology of revelation opens where Scripture, creeds, and the created order begin, specifically, "[i]n the beginning God" already exists.[8] Father, Son, and Holy Spirit eternally exist as "three persons of one substance."[9] Scripture teaches the eternality of the Son and the Father, "In the beginning was the Word [Son], and the Word was with God, and the Word was God. He was with God in the beginning."[10] Scripture bears witness to the eternality of the Spirit.[11]

The self-existent Godhead freely chose to create things both visible and invisible by speaking them into existence.[12] God, therefore, stands distinct from, but in relationship to, everything that he created.[13] John explains that "Through him [Son] all things were made; without him nothing was made that has been made."[14] Paul, in Colossians teaches, "He [Son] is the image of the invisible God, the firstborn over all creation. For by him all things were created: things in heaven and on earth, visible and invisible, whether thrones or powers or rulers or authorities; all things were created by him

---

8. Gen 1:1. Examples of creeds include: "Irenaeus' Rule of Faith (c. 190)," "The Creed of Nicaea (325)," and "The Augsburg Confession of Faith." Leith, *Creeds of the Churches,* 21, 32, 67.

9. Leith, *Creeds of the Churches,* 197. In other words, the Father, Son, and Spirit are all God, but the Father is not the Son nor the Spirit. Deut 6:4–5 teaches the unity of God. Matt 28:19 and 2 Cor 13:14 teach the diversity of persons in the Godhead.

10. John 1:1–2. The Father loved the Son "before the creation of the world." John 17:24.

11. Heb 9:14. Scripture attests to the deity of the Spirit in Acts 5:3–4 and 2 Cor 3:17.

12. Gen 1:1, 3, 6, 9, 14, 20, and 24. God is worthy of trust and praise because he created all things. Acts 14:15 and Rev 4:9–11.

13. This belief stands in contrast to panentheism which teaches that "God's being includes and permeates the entire universe" though extends beyond it. Panentheists believe that "God's knowledge must change and grow." The belief also opposes pantheism which teaches that "God and the universe are essentially identical." Grenz, et al., *Pocket Dictionary,* 88. Furthermore, God does not create and then leave his creation alone as taught in deism. Christians hold God's transcendence and immanence in tension. Ibid., 32–3. See also Grenz, *Theology for the Community,* 98.

14. John 1:3.

and for him. He is before all things, and in him all things hold together."[15] Creation, therefore, "came into being because of the will of the Father and through the agency of the Son, and it is perfected through the Spirit."[16]

God does not say exactly why he chose to create. Theologians postulate that God created because of a desire to reveal himself.[17] Charnock writes, "The displaying of goodness was the motive and end of all his works of creation and providence."[18] Similarly, Hannah states, "There is, then, a property in God's being that not only delights in himself but longs to show himself."[19] In other words, God is "forever seeking to speak Himself out to His creation."[20] Words such as "display," "show," and "speak" inherently entail revealing. Regardless of specifically why God chose to create, "If we are to know God at all, it is necessary that he reveal himself to us."[21]

God does graciously reveal himself. Divine communication is revelation: "The great and universal end of God's creating the world was to communicate himself. God is a communicative being."[22] Communication, per Packer, "suggests someone approaching us, coming close to us, speaking to us, telling us about himself, opening his mind to us, giving us what he has, telling us what he knows, asking for our attention and seeking our response to what he is saying. This is the true idea of divine revelation, on which we must always keep our minds clear."[23]

---

15. Col 1:15–17.

16. Hall, *Learning Theology*, 113. Grenz similarly states: "The Father creates the world through the Son, by his Spirit." Grenz, *Theology for the Community*, 102.

17. Creation "is not a product of an *internal* necessity within God" nor did God create due to *external* compulsion. Grenz, *Theology for the Community*, 99.

18. Charnock, *Existence and Attributes of God*, 2:228–29. Charnock elsewhere states that "Creation was the first act of goodness without [outside] himself [God]." Ibid., 2:245.

19. Hannah, *How do We Glorify God?* 13–14.

20. Tozer, "Speaking Voice."

21. Grudem, *Systematic Theology*, 149. In addition to knowing God, people only know themselves, the rest of creation, and the relationship between God and his creation because of divine revelation. See "Content" below.

22. Edwards, *"Miscellanies," (Entry Nos. a–z, aa–zz, 1–500)*, 410. Human communication serves as an apt analogy for divine revelation. The format of the chapter reflects the appropriateness of the analogy. The elements of communication (sender-receiver, message, channels, feedback, noise, and setting) compare to the key aspects of revelation (source, recipients, content, forms, effects, and characteristics, respectively). Hybels and Weaver, *Communicating Effectively*, 7–12.

23. Packer, *Knowing Christianity*, 9–10. Tozer observes that God provides answers ahead of time to the *important* questions people ask. These questions include, "What is God like? What kind of God is He? How may we expect Him to act toward us and toward all created things?" The answers, says Tozer, "He [God] has provided in nature,

The careful reader of Genesis observes God communicating with humanity from the very beginning. In Gen 1:28-30, God exhorts the first couple to populate and have dominion over the earth. In the Gen 2:15-17 account, God addresses the first man by giving him freedom and limitation (he may eat from any tree except for one). God then gives man the first recorded lesson. The man must name the animals God created. Through this task man began exercising dominion over the creation which entailed learning about that which God created as well as God himself. The first man learned that he differs from the rest of creation and God. Through this he presumably experienced the feeling of loneliness (Gen 2:19-22). When God created the first women, the man experientially understood God's ability to provide for his needs through that which God created. The first man learned fellowship with someone who corresponded to him.

Tragically, Gen 3 explains the historic and jarring shift in humanity's relationship with God from obedience to rejection. The disobedience of humanity resulted in the fracturing of all relationships (humanity to God, humanity to humanity, and humanity to the rest of creation). God still sought to communicate with people, but man and woman hid from each other and God. The author of Gen 3:8 writes of what appears to be a common occurrence, "the sound of the LORD God as he was walking in the garden in the cool of the day." As the text continues man and woman heard this sound and hid from God. The unexpected event is not that God walks in the garden (personal revelation), but the fact that people now hide from him (turning away from this revelation). Humanity's suppression of divine revelation begins.

Yet even after the fall, God continued to take initiative in revealing to his creation. God covenanted with Noah, his family, and all living creatures (Gen 9:8-17).[24] The covenant "was with all the descendents of Noah, that is, all humanity" and all creature's.[25] God chose a people (Gen 12 and Rom 8). He ratified a covenant in a ceremony like those in Ancient Near Eastern Cultures (Gen 15). He gave the law (Gen 20) and a sacrificial system for

---

in the Scriptures, and in the person of His Son." Tozer, *Knowledge of the Holy*, 13.

24. Notice the juxtaposition of the entire creaturely world fearing man (Gen 9:2) and God's covenant with all living things (Gen 9:9-17). God reveals his love for all he created not just humanity.

25. Oden, *Systematic Theology*, 17. Oden identifies this covenant as "general revelation" because God enters into covenant relationship with all of humanity. In fact, the text of Scripture teaches that God ratifies the covenant with all living creatures. As the text reads, "Then God said to Noah and to his sons with him: 'I now establish my covenant with your descendants after you and with *every living creature* that was with you—the birds, the livestock and all the wild animals, all those that came out of the ark with you—*every living creature on earth*." Gen 9:8-10, emphasis added.

those who break the law (Lev). Ultimately, the Father provided reconciliation through his one and only Son (Col 1:19). All of the above reveal God and come from God.

Revelation, therefore, comes from God. As Oden points out, "There could be no Christian study of God without God's own initiative to become reliably known (Gen. 35:7; Ps. 98:2; Isa. 65:1; Rom. 1:18; 16:25, 26; Rev. 1:1, Origen, *Ag. Celsus* 3.61)."[26] Greer agrees that "the first move in the acquisition of knowledge comes from God, not from us. Not only is God the One revealed; he is also the One who reveals. He speaks through his written Word (verbal communication) and his actions in history (nonverbal communication)."[27] Therefore, "communication—even through creatures—is divine."[28] In other words, "both general and special revelation are (a) from God and (b) about God."[29] Revelation comes from God, but what forms does divine revelation take?

Forms of Revelation

Divine revelation, like human communication, comes in a multitude of forms; both verbal and nonverbal.[30] Chafer reflects on the great variety of modes used by God to reveal, "Divine revelations . . . are discoverable all the way from the grand spectacle of creation down to the lowliest human creature. So stupendous, far-reaching, and complex is this body of truth that any attempt to delineate or classify it will of necessity be incomplete."[31] As shown in the previous chapter, strict classifications can lead to oversimplification. However, it appears that three major forms of revelation exist;

26. Oden, *Classic Christianity*, 176.
27. Greer, *Mapping Postmodernism*, 7.
28. Horton, *Christian Faith*, 129.
29. Ryrie, *Basic Theology*, 31.

30. Ryrie lists four avenues of general revelation and ten avenues of special revelation. Ryrie, *Basic Theology*, 31–36, 71–73. Elwell classifies numerous passages of Scripture into nineteen different modes of revelation. "The Revelation of God," in Elwell and Buckwalter, *Topical Analysis of the Bible*, 223–38. McDermott lists twelve forms through which God spoke. McDermott, *World Religions*, 48–49. Williams lists nine different forms of revelation and states "This is neither an exhaustive nor an ordered account." Stephen N. Williams, "Revelation," in Vanhoozer, *Dictionary for Theological Interpretation of the Bible*, 678. Towns lists roughly a dozen methods used by God to reveal. Towns, *Theology*, 31.

31. Chafer, *Systematic Theology*, 1:52. Chafer lists seven modes of revelation: nature, providence, preservation, miracles, direct communication, the Incarnation, and Scripture. Ibid., 53. Chafer could lump together preservation (God sustaining creation) and nature as one mode of revelation.

namely, Scripture (written Word), the Incarnation (Word who came into the world created through him), and the created order (world). Since I am constructing an *evangelical* theology of revelation, I begin with the Scripture and explore what it teaches concerning other forms of revelation.

God inspired (*theópneustos* or God-breathed) Scripture.[32] In regard to prophecy in particular and all of Scripture in general: "men spoke from God as they were carried along by the Holy Spirit."[33] Jesus modeled for his followers trust in Scripture.[34] He explained the authority and importance of the Law and Prophets in the Old Testament: "Do not think that I come to abolish the Law or the Prophets; I have not come to abolish them but to fulfill them."[35] God revealed through the written Word which the church received and passed down throughout history.[36] The Bible, as God's written revelation, is necessary to help fallen people understand how God relates to his creation.[37]

Scripture instructs that God reveals outside of Scripture. For example, the Incarnation is the supreme revelation of God (Heb 1:1–2).[38] John explains that the Word, whom eternally exists both with God and as God, came to earth and dwelt among his creation.[39] Similarly, the author of Heb 1:1–2a testifies, "In the past, God spoke to our forefathers through the prophets at

---

32. 2 Tim 3:16. When used of Scripture, θεόπνευστος refers to "communication that has been ordained by God's authority and produced by the enabling of his Spirit." Friberg, et al., "*theópneustos, on*," 196.

33. 2 Pet 1:21.

34. For example, Matt 26:23–24; Mark 7:6; Luke 22:37. In these texts, Jesus uses passages from the OT as authoritative and interpretive revelation of his current situation.

35. Matt 5:17.

36. Kelly, *Early Christian Doctrines*, 52, 56, 61. This written revelation takes the form of the sixty-six books of the Old and New Testament.

37. Erickson, *Christian Theology*, 221; Bavinck, *Reformed Dogmatics*, 1:324; Earle, "Revelation and Inspiration," 1:289–95; and Litfin, *Conceiving the Christian College*, 200. The amount of space given to verify each form does not reflect the author's priority or value for each form of revelation. Instead, the amount of attention reflects a greater need to justify the reality of one form (the created order) as a valid revelation of God.

38. Stott believes evangelicals wrongly place more emphasis on Scripture than the Incarnation as revelation. He exhorts evangelicals to return the Incarnation to its rightful place. Stott critiques, "We evangelicals have often made the mistake of isolating and elevating the Bible. But the climax of God's revelation was his incarnate Son, the Word made flesh." He continues, "The climax of God's revelation should be described as the historic, incarnate Christ and the total biblical witness to him." Stott, *Evangelical Truth*, 39.

39. John 1:14.

many times and in various ways, but in these last days he has spoken to us by his Son." Since Jesus is fully God then he uniquely reveals the Father.[40]

As the Son of God walked the earth he taught those around him that he revealed the Father through both words and actions (John 5:19; 7:16; 12:49–50; 14:24, 31). While Scripture preserves some of what Jesus did and said, certainly it does not exhaustively recount every saying or action of the Son of God. In fact, "Jesus did many other miraculous signs in the presence of his disciples, which are not recorded in this book."[41] All that Jesus did and said revealed the Father even if it did not find inclusion in the canon of Scripture.[42]

Additionally, Scripture teaches that God reveals himself through the created order. The sixty-six books of the Bible "bear witness to or teach the reality of general revelation."[43] Though "no one passage expounds a full-blown theology of general revelation," as Russell Moore states, "both the Old and the New Testaments affirm that God has disclosed himself everywhere to all human beings. The special revelation of Scripture brings into focus the varieties and extent of this general revelation."[44] So, the Bible teaches "that there is a knowledge of God available through the created physical order."[45]

Scripture, from Genesis to Revelation, affirms the reality that God reveals himself through the created order. As Lightner points out, "In his Word, God has told us about the revelation of himself in his world."[46] A couple texts more clearly make this point (Ps 19, Rom 1). Psalm 19:1–4 serves as an important Old Testament text that identifies the created order as divine revelation. The Psalmist writes, "The heavens *declare* the glory of God; the skies *proclaim* the work of his hands. Day after day they *pour forth speech*; night after night they *display* knowledge. There is no speech or language where their voice is not heard. Their voice goes out into all the earth,

---

40. Being fully human, without sin, Jesus also revealed *an* (not the only) example of humanness. Therefore Paul could say, "Follow my example, as I follow the example of Christ." 1 Cor 11:1.

41. John 20:30.

42. Grudem labels "words of Jesus that were not recorded in Scripture" as special revelation as well. Grudem, *Systematic Theology*, 123.

43. Garrett, *Systematic Theology*, 1:45. Garrett qualifies this statement using the word "seem." I am uncertain as to why he finds it strange that the Bible teaches the reality of revelation given through the created order. But, after a citing the usual texts in support of general revelation (Ps 19, Rom 1), Garrett again states they "seemingly teach general revelation." He appears reticent to acknowledge the reality that God reveals through the created order.

44. Moore, "Natural Revelation," 72.

45. Erickson, *Christian Theology*, 179.

46. Lightner, *Evangelical Theology*, 45.

their words to the ends of the world."[47] The heavens declare, proclaim, pour forth speech, and display God continuously and everywhere. Calvin, commenting on Ps 19, states the glory of God "not only shines, but also resounds in the heavens."[48]

Both the heavens and the earth reveal God. While the "heavens proclaim his righteousness," so the "*earth is filled* with [his] love."[49] Again, the Psalmist states, "The Lord loves righteousness and justice; the *earth is full* of his unfailing love."[50] In the later text, the psalmist, in the midst of exclaiming his reverence for God's written word, pauses to notice God's love displayed throughout the earth. From these passages we learn that creation reveals God and his works continuously and everywhere.

Paul quotes the text of Ps 19:4 in Rom 10:18. Through this verse Paul argues that the Israelites heard the message proclaimed by the created order. Paul states that not all of the Israelites "accepted the good news" in verse 16. In verse 17 he writes that "faith comes from hearing the message." He asks in verse 18 "Did they not hear?" and answers "Of course they did," then he quotes Ps 19:4 ("Their voice has gone out into all the earth, their words to the ends of the world.") as proof. Paul continues to build his case in verse 19 asking "Did Israel not understand?" He responds by quoting Deut 10:19 and Isaiah 65:1–2 stating that God revealed himself to other nations who did not seek him. Paul uses both the physical creation and God's dealings with other nations to reveal himself. Israel should have known and understood. Witmer comments on the text, "Israel had ample opportunity by both general and special revelation to respond to God. Certainly she heard."[51]

Earlier in the book of Romans, Paul teaches that the created order reveals God. People "suppress the truth by their wickedness."[52] Or as Horner observes, unbelievers not only suppress revelation, they also "suppress their suppression" of revelation.[53] The verb *katechô* (suppress) "does not mean that people do not know the truth," rather they know because *God makes it clear* (I return to the issue of clarity under "Perspicuity" later in this section).[54] Moo summarizes, "the characterization of all those upon whom the wrath of God falls as those who *possessed the truth* of God but turned

---

47. Ps 19:1–4, emphasis added.
48. Calvin, *Book of Psalms*, 1:309.
49. Pss 97:6 and 119:64, emphasis added.
50. Ps 33:5, emphasis added.
51. Witmer, "Romans," 481–2.
52. Rom 1:18.
53. Horner, *Meaning at the Movies*, 44.
54. Hoehner, "Romans," 131.

from it."[55] Paul states that "what may be known about God is plain to them, because God has made it plan to them."[56] The word *phaneros* in the NT primarily refers "to what is visible to sensory perception."[57] When *eimi* follows it (in verse 19 Paul writes, *phaneron estin*) "the reference is still to what can be perceived by the senses but in such a way that the perception involves understanding."[58] God reveals through the created order and makes it plain, but people suppress what they know.

Paul continues, "For since the creation of the world God's invisible qualities—his eternal power and divine nature—have been clearly seen, being understood from what has been made, so that men are without excuse."[59] From creation to the present day God reveals through the created order. As Cranfield states, "There is little doubt that *apo ktiseôs kosmou* should be taken to mean 'since the creation of the world,' *apo* being understood in a temporal sense . . . and κτίσις in its sense of 'act of creating': this is much more natural than to take the phrase to mean 'from the created universe.' "[60] Therefore, "the self-revelation of God here referred to has been continuous ever since the creation."[61]

Furthermore, the verb *kathoratai* in verse 20 means "people can clearly see God's invisible attributes in what he created."[62] The clarity mentioned in verses 19 and 20 stems not from man's ability, but God's work in making it plain to man. God reveals intentionally, as the "clause here emphasizes that God's knowability is not merely a characteristic or 'spin-off' of creation but was willed and effected by God."[63] God's self-revelation through the created order is so clear that those who suppress it stand condemned; without excuse (*anapologêtos*).

Milne observes the reality of Rom 1:18–20 in the Old Testament. The prophets of the Old Testament "frequently speak of God's just judgments on the Gentile nations, although these nations had not been taught the OT law (e.g. Jer. 46–41; Amos 1:6–2:3)."[64] He connects this with the New Testament

---

55. Moo, *Romans*, 98, emphasis added.
56. Rom 1:19.
57. Bultmann and Lührmann, "*phanerós*," 9:2.
58. Ibid.
59. Rom 1:20.
60. Cranfield, *Epistle to the Romans*, 1:114.
61. Ibid., 114. For others who agree to the temporal nature of *apo* see also Osborne, *Romans*, 47; and Moo, *Romans*, 105n64.
62. Hoehner, "Romans," 131.
63. Dunn, *Romans 1–8*, 57.
64. Milne, *Know the Truth*, 28.

"recogni[tion] that the non-Christian conscience is qualified to pass judgment on Christians' behavior (e.g. 1 Tim. 3:7, 1 Pet. 2:12)."[65] He specifies that "the moral appeal of the gospel, its assertion that all have sinned (Rom. 3:9–23), its call to repentance (Acts 17:30), its interpretation of the work of Christ in moral terms (Rom. 3:21–26; 1 Cor. 15:3), all imply a genuine continuity between universal moral experience and that of the believer; this in turn implies some awareness of God's will on the part of non-Christians."[66] The judgment of God on the nations comes because they know and yet suppress the truth.

Jesus also taught that the Father reveals through the created order.[67] Jesus exhorted the crowds to "look at the birds of the air" and the "lilies of the field" to learn of God's character and their appropriate response.[68] Creation teaches people not to worry because God provides essentials for life. Someone might object, "Jesus could rightly interpret creation. However, we cannot infallibly interpret it so we simply need to read Scripture." While such a person makes a fair point, the account in Scripture attests that Jesus told the crowd to look around them at familiar things in the creation. He exhorted them to look at creation as revelation in this passage. He very well could have pointed back to Scripture and the faithfulness of God throughout Israel's history. However, he did not. He intentionally pointed his audience to creation and helped them see that creation reveals the character of the Father. The careful reader also notices that Jesus uses the birds and lilies as examples of trusting God. The created order, therefore, reveals both the character of the Father and appropriate responses to the Father.

The created order is "the visible display of God's glory."[69] Revelation given through creation (creatures, cultures, and consciences) "is *real* revelation" and "not just subjective impressions."[70] As Erickson writes, "God has given us an objective, valid, rational revelation of himself in nature, history, and human personality. Regardless of whether anyone actually observes it, understands it, and believes it, even though it may well have been disturbed

---

65. Ibid.

66. Ibid.

67. He used a number of metaphors to help people understand transcendent truth. The use of metaphors suggests points of commonality between transcendent truth and creation. Some metaphors help people understand Jesus and his relationship to creation (word, vine, lamb, temple, bread, shepherd, son, lion, and lamp). Other metaphors to communicate important truths regarding life (fruit, prodigal son, birth/born, marriage, fishers of men, tongue as rudder or fire).

68. Matt 6:25–34.

69. Butler, "God's Visible Glory," 19.

70. Moore, *Consider the Lilies*, 89.

by the fall, it is nonetheless present."[71] Revelation given through the created order is as real as God's revelation through Scripture. In fact, the early church referred to this revelation as a second book from God.[72] Augustine argues, "The page of divine scripture is open for you to read, and the wide world is open for you to see. Only the literate can read the books, but even the illiterate can read the book of the world."[73] He encourages the illiterate to read the "book of created nature. Look carefully at it top and bottom, observe it, read it. God did not make letters of ink for you to recognize him; he set before your eyes all the things he has made."[74]

What forms, then, does this revelation take? God employs the entirety of creation.[75] The created order as a form of revelation includes: the physical universe including plants and animals, people (both redeemed and unredeemed), divinely ordained institutions, and that which humans create. As noted in the previous section, the reader of Gen 1–3 notices revealing through a number of different forms. He reveals through actions (Gen 1), commands (Gen 1: 28–30; 2:16–17), personal experience and a guided lesson (Gen 2:19–21), provision (Gen 2:22–23; 3:21), personally by walking with people (Gen 3:8), and through judgment (Gen 3:14–19). And lest we miss it, God reveals through these historic events, he reveals through the oral tradition that passed these events on, he reveals when Moses wrote the inspired words, and the book of Genesis is God's written revelation. God

---

71. Erickson, *Christian Theology*, 194. This stands in contrast to Chafer's assertion: "In general, divine revelation is accomplished whenever any manifestation of God is *discerned* or any evidence of His presence, purpose, or power is communicated." Chafer, *Systematic Theology*, 1:52; emphasis added. Chafer here confuses the reality of revelation and the appropriation of revelation. God reveals whether or not people discern his revelation.

72. The early church often used the analogy of the two books of God in reference to Scripture and creation. Tanzella-Nitti lists a number of Church Fathers using the metaphor. These include St. Basil, St. Gregory of Nyssa, and John Cassian. He then states, "If we also include those authors who implicitly refer to the book of nature . . . the list would become much larger and quite uncontrollable." Tanzella-Nitti, "Two Books," 237. Cooey observes that Edwards also views nature as divine communication and uses the book analogy. Cooey, *Jonathan Edwards*, 117.

73. Augustine, "Exposition of Psalm 45," 315. Augustine took the created order seriously as a form of revelation.

74. Augustine, "Sermon 68," 225–26. See also Edwards, *Typological Writings*, 67.

75. As pointed out by Doug Blount, something as basic as knowing one's own name reveals God. He created the mental faculties the person uses to know his own name. Any time people use such faculties we reveal God. Therefore, stating that everything reveals God does not render the concept "revelation" useless. Instead, it most accurately portrays the absolute dependence of people on God. Humans therefore become secondary authors who reveal God, though often poorly, in every sphere of life. Sayers identifies ways the author of literature reveals God. Sayers, *Mind of the Maker*.

reveals the knowledge that led to speaking and reading. The literary knowledge needed to interpret Genesis is divine revelation. The ability of people to understand and portray these events in story, movie, song, or picture reveals God.

God reveals through animals.[76] Divinely inspired Scripture (Prov 6:6) exhorts the sluggard to study the work of the ant to gain wisdom.[77] The lessons derived thereby come from observations of ants (Prov 6:6–11). As Merrill concludes, "We can learn and become wise by observing the habit of an ant."[78] The ant does not stand alone as the only animal open for human investigation. Agur recounts in Prov 30:24–28 his observation of the wisdom of ants, coneys, locusts, and lizards. Whybray comments that "the notion that one can learn lessons from animals appears several times" in the Old Testament.[79] The bullfrog and the whippoorwill call forth at night, while the ant and the bee steadily work during the day, all revealing God. God, therefore, reveals through animals.

God also reveals through human beings. God intentionally created both male and female in his own image to reveal him (Gen 1:27). In Ps 139:14 the human author reflects on his own frame and turns to praise God because "I am fearfully and wonderfully made; your works are wonderful." Likewise, Saucy, in summarizing Isa 29:15–16 and Ps 94:9, states, "In essence, God says, 'Look at yourselves. Your nature and abilities as humans point to Me, your Creator, who is greater than you are.'"[80] Humans, from our physical construction to our character and God-given abilities, reveal our Creator.

Additionally, God reveals through divinely ordained institutions. For example, God uses marriage as a suitable metaphor for the relationship between Christ and the church (Eph. 5:22–33). Furthermore, the physical union of marriage also reveals. As West writes, "God created sexual desire 'in the beginning' to be the very power to love as he loves—in a free, sincere,

---

76. Job 12:7–9.

77. Hollywood unwittingly understands this. Movies like *Ant Bully* and *Antz* teach the viewer lessons *from* ants as well as lessons *through* ants. Additionally, the careful viewer discerns the motif of creation, fall, and redemption in both movies; a motif not only taught in Scripture, but embedded in the created order. Hanks, et al., *Ant Bully*; and Lewis, *Antz*.

78. Merrill, "Wisdom." Merrill reads this passage as a divine rebuke, since God created people to have dominion over the creation.

79. Whybray, *Proverbs*, 96. Examples include Job 12:7–9; Isa 1:3; and Jer 8:7.

80. Saucy, "Scripture," 38.

and total gift of self. *This is how the couple described in Genesis experienced it.*"[81]

Revelation through the created order includes not only physical creation, God-given abilities, and divinely ordained institutions, it extends to those items made by people. When those created in God's image use their creative abilities they reveal the one who created them and gave them such talents. The effort of humanity to fulfill the creation mandate (Gen 2) by creating culture appears as a form of revelation. Culture reveals God. Geisler includes art and music in God's revelation through the created order.[82] Additionally, Grider highlights warrant for the inclusion of buildings and roads in the revelation given through creation. He asserts, "What the individual Christian observes more often than not is fabricated nature—roads, buildings, machines, instruments. . . . The ingenuity of our fellows is imbedded in fabricated nature, as well as God's ingenuity . . . . All of it is the theater for the glorification of God."[83] God reveals through the creations of those he fashioned to bear his image.

Revelation through the created order also includes God's work of redemption in his people. The importance of remembering the work of God rings throughout the Old Testament.[84] Horton observes that theologians often overlook the testimony of the community of God as a form of revelation "in spite of the centrality of testimony in revelation."[85] In particular, Horton writes, "Its [testimony's] truth-conveying status is undervalued" in Dulles' models of revelation.[86] The Psalmist believes God reveals through his chosen people, Israel. He writes, "The LORD has made his salvation known and revealed his righteousness to the nations. He has remembered his love and his faithfulness to the house of Israel; all the ends of the earth have seen the salvation of our God."[87] God revealed himself through his chosen nation.

Similarly, Matt 5:16 teaches that good works done by God's people reveal God to others. Matthew writes, "In the same way, let your light shine

---

81. West, *Theology of the Body*, 27. West, reflecting on Pope John Paul II's work, explains the extent to which proper sexual relations reveal God's relationship to humanity and our proper relationship to one another.

82. Geisler, *Systematic Theology*, 1:65.

83. Grider, *Theology*, 45.

84. See the use of "remember" or "do not forget" in Deut 7:18; 8:2, 11.The importance of remembrance underlies the ordinance of communion (1 Cor 11:17–33).

85. Horton, *Christian Faith*, 133. The idea of testimony as revelation is found in Ross, "General Revelation."

86. Horton, *Christian Faith*, 133.

87. Ps 98:2–3. The psalmist exhorts the entire world to praise the Lord because he saved Israel (1) and will judge the earth (9).

before men, that they may see your good deeds and praise your Father in heaven." As an illustration, Paul lets the Thessalonians know of the revelatory impact of their testimony,

> The Lord's message rang out from you not only in Macedonia and Achaia—your faith in God has become known everywhere. Therefore we do not need to say anything about it, for they themselves report what kind of reception you gave us. They tell how you turned to God from idols to serve the living and true God, and to wait for his Son from heaven, whom he raised from the dead—Jesus, who rescues us from the coming wrath.[88]

Paul also reminds the Corinthians, "We always carry around in our body the death of Jesus, so that the life of Jesus may also be revealed in our body. For we who are alive are always being given over to death for Jesus' sake, so that his life may be revealed in our mortal body."[89] God reveals his character through his people. For instance, the fruit of the Spirit (Gal 5) not only points to God's redeeming work in the life of his people, it also reveals God's attributes through those being sanctified. The changing life of the believer reveals the ongoing work of the Spirit of God as well as the character of God.

God reveals not only through the history of his work in and through his chosen people, but also through history in general.[90] Thiessen observes God's dealings with Egypt, Assyria, Babylon, and Medo-Persia as revelation.[91] Kreider observes, "For Edwards, secular history is another means God uses to reveal himself and his will to his people. History is not simply the account of what happened in the past, but it is a revelation of the sovereign God's actions in the affairs of his world."[92]

The created order as revelation includes: the physical universe including plants and animals, people, institutions created by God, and that which

---

88. 1 Thess 1:8–10.

89. 2 Cor 4:10–11.

90. At the death of Jesus, the Father used creation to reveal to specific people the deity of his Son. The temple curtain tore in two, the earth shook, rocks split, and people were raised to life. All of these were the work of God through the creation. The centurion responded to this revelation exclaiming, "Surely he was the Son of God!" The earth responded violently to this historic revelation of God. The centurion exclaimed a central theological truth upon observing the crucifixion and creation's response to it. Matt 27:50–54.

91. Thiessen, *Systematic Theology*, 33. Thiessen cites the following texts: Egypt: Exod 9:13–17; Rom 9:17; and Jer 46:14–26; Assyria: Isa 10:12–19; Ezek 31:1–14; and Nah 3:1–7; Babylon: Jer 50:1–16 and 51:1–4.

92. Kreider, *Edwards's Interpretation of Revelation*, 207. If God demonstrates his sovereignty over all of history, then can we call any history "secular"?

humans create. In sum, "God determines not only the *if* and *why* of divine disclosure, but also the *when, where, what, how,* and *who*."[93] Scripture, the Incarnation, and the created order are "a comprehensive unity flowing from the one and only God."[94] Therefore, the three forms of revelation "are all given to us by the one triune God with the intent that we receive in faith what he reveals to us."[95] Scripture teaches that God reveals outside of Scripture. As concluded in the previous section, revelation, regardless of form, always comes from God.[96] We turn now to the implications of this fact.

Characteristics of Revelation

Since revelation originates with God it bears his essential character. Jones argues for the inerrancy, infallibility, authority and sufficiency of Scripture on the basis of "the loftiness, grandeur, and glory of the divine author" since "one cannot divorce the words of the author from His character."[97] However, he does not apply the same logic to other forms of divine revelation. I argue below that *all* forms of revelation are true, authoritative, sufficient, and perspicuous.[98] However, what each adjective means for any given form of revelation may differ from what it means for other forms of revelation.

True

God does not lie.[99] He is true "and communicates only the truth."[100] Revelation comes from God. Therefore, the adjective "true" applies to divine revelation. Some equate truth with "statements that correspond to reality."[101]

---

93. Henry, *God, Revelation and Authority*, 2:9.
94. Higgins, "God's Inspired Word," 68.
95. Wilson, "Theater of God," 85.
96. Bavinck, *Our Reasonable Faith*, 34.
97. Jones, "Scriptural View of Science," 236.
98. Van Til, *Christian Apologetics*, 68–69. Though the same adjectives apply to Scripture and creation, they do not necessarily apply in the same way. For instance, Scripture is authoritative for the salvation of man yet creation is not. Creation reveals details of its inner workings where Scripture does not provide such details. Historic verification of this comes from Calvin. Henry states that "Calvin stresses that God's objective revelation in nature no less than in Scripture is clear and adequate." Henry, *Revelation and Authority*, 1:337.
99. Titus 1:2.
100. Mayhue, "Cultivating a Biblical Mind-Set," 46.
101. Clark, *Know and Love God*, 354. Grenz and Franke observe the same. Grenz and Franke, *Beyond Foundationalism*, 14. Grenz, *Theology for the Community*, 7. Some

Carl Henry limits truth to propositions. He writes, "Only propositions have the quality of truth . . . The only significant view of revelation is rational-verbal revelation; indeed the only adequate alternative to skepticism about God is divine revelation in propositional form."[102]

Some who hold to the correspondence theory of truth and perceive propositions to be objective and absolute.[103] For example, Knox limits revelation to propositional statements and thereby rejects event-based revelation.[104] He asserts that "the event, by itself, reveals nothing" and concludes "that revelation is essentially propositional."[105] Knox uses the Incarnation to make his point. The interpretative statements of the Incarnation reveal, but the Incarnation itself does not. Knox states, "There would *have been no revelation in Christ's ministry*, were it not for the interpretive statements of our Lord and His apostles. It is the proposition, then, that is the revelation, not the act itself."[106] Therefore, "all revelation, insofar as it reveals God to us, is propositional."[107] By equating revelation strictly with propositional statements Knox denies the Incarnation, without verbal explanation, as a form of revelation.

Yet, Scripture provides example after example of event-based revelation. Jesus, the God-man, revealed the Father. His very personhood and actions revealed God. The interpretive statements may better enable finite and fallen people to more faithfully interpret this revelation. They may also provide ways to tell others about this revelation. However, even without interpretive statements the Word made flesh revealed God.

Knox does not stand alone in this assertion. Packer maintains that "the biblical position is that the *mighty acts of God are not revelation* to man at all, except in so far as they are accompanied by words of God to explain

---

examples include: Lindsell, *Battle for the Bible*; Knox, "Propositional Revelation," 1–9; Geisler, "Concept of Truth," 327–39; Lewis, "Propositional Revelation." 269–98; Thomas, "General Revelation," 14; Moreland, "Truth, Contemporary Philosophy, and the Postmodern Turn," 77–88; and Mayhue, "Cultivating a Biblical Mind-Set," 46–47.

102. Henry, *God, Revelation and Authority*, 3:430.

103. White, *What is Truth*, 5. Padgett states, "Some theologians have been so enamored of the power and beauty of modern logic and analytic philosophy that they have sought to reduce all truth to true propositions." Padgett, "I Am the Truth," 109.

104. He fears "[d]enial of propositional revelation goes hand in hand with a denial of inerrant revelation." Knox, "Propositional Revelation," 8. However, the affirmation of event-based revelation does not *necessarily* lead to denying propositional revelation.

105. Ibid., 6.

106. Ibid., 7. Purkiser similarly asserts, "Historical act becomes a revelation of God when interpreted through the eye of faith." Purkiser, *Exploring Our Christian Faith*, 55; emphasis added.

107. Knox, "Propositional Revelation," 1.

them."[108] Additionally, Lewis acknowledges that truth includes more than propositions.[109] He lists a number of "non-cognitive, personal and relational ways" in which "Jesus related to his image bearers personally."[110] However, Lewis assumes that "non-informative content does not have the quality of truth" so he simply labels it infallible.[111] Truth, per Lewis, is propositional. The propositional statements correspond to "or are consistent with the way God the Father knows and has spoken them to his Son."[112] Such views limit revelation to Scripture alone.

Limiting truth to propositional statements leads to synthesizing other forms of revelation into propositional statements. For example, Lewis holds that people can translate general revelation into simple propositional statements. He affirms the reality of "divinely originated propositional truths in both general and special revelation."[113] Lewis provides propositional statements derived from general revelation, "God's general revelation and illumination make clear that all in every community are: (1) dependent on one God; (2) morally obligated to the one God; and (3) guilty before the one God."[114] Commentators do the same with non-propositional segments of Scripture. They summarize a story in propositional statements.[115] Kulikovsky observes that "propositional revelation most often takes the form of historical narrative."[116] He then mentions in a footnote that "other biblical genres . . . contain propositional statements" and that "statements from these genres" can be "rephrased or transformed into propositional statements."[117] In similar fashion, Geisler subsumes personal revelation un-

---

108. Packer, *Fundamentalism and the Word of God*, 92; emphasis added.

109. In fact, Lewis states, "Not all the Bible is made up of indicative sentences conveying or implying propositions." Lewis, "Propositional Revelation," 270.

110. Lewis, "Jesus, Truth and The ETS," 4. He states Jesus used expressive (Matt 23:27), evocative (Matt 19:7), exhortative (John 14:1), performative (Matt 8:13), invitational (Matt 11:28), interrogatory (Matt 16:13, 15), petitionary (Matt 6:10–12), metaphorical (John 14:6), and parabolic (Matt 13) language.

111. Ibid., 5.

112. Ibid., 13.

113. Lewis, "Propositional Revelation," 286.

114. Ibid., 285.

115. Commentators do not always agree on the propositional statement taught by the story. Sometimes these statements even contradict. Compare for example the following commentaries on John 4:43–54: Barrett, *Gospel According to John*, 245; Carson, *Gospel According to John*, 238; and Beasley-Murray, *John*, 73. Christian Smith agrees that interpretive pluralism poses problems for biblicism. Smith, *Bible Made Impossible*, 3–54.

116. Kulikovsky, *Creation, Fall, Restoration*, 32.

117. Ibid.

der propositional revelation. He concludes that "only the correspondence view is adequate as a *comprehensive* view of truth."[118]

Each of the above authors make "is it true or false?" the main issue when speaking of revelation in general and Scripture in particular. Wolterstorff observes that this is not always the main issue.[119] For example, asking whether a command, an exhortation, a blessing, or an exclamation is true or false misses the mark. Such speech-forms do not make true or false assertions. He argues that when examining assertions or true propositions in Scripture then asking "Is this assertion true or false?" is appropriate.[120] Simply put, "A proposition is a declarative sentence that affirms or denies something."[121] Such sentences take the form of subject (S), copula (=), predicate (P) or the formula S = P. However, as Lindbeck asserts, propositions are *not* synonymous with sentences.[122] Therefore, a rather small portion of Scripture is in fact assertions that are either true or false. So asking, "Is it true?" must mean something more.

Scripture includes more than propositional statements that correspond to reality. Throughout Scripture, we learn that God uses stories, parables, proverbs, actions and the Incarnation all of which are not propositional in the formal sense of the term. In the Gospel of John alone the reader finds the word "true" used of a commandment (John 2:8), and an action (John 3:21).[123] John also speaks of "true worshipers (4:23), "true vine" (15:1), "true God" (17:3) . . . we find it said that God is true (3:33, 7:28, 8:26) . . . lastly, we get Jesus' well-known saying: 'I am the way, the truth, and the life' (14:6; closely related to 17:17: 'thy word is truth')."[124] Truth, therefore, entails more than true or false assertions. An examination of Scripture alone requires a more expansive understanding of truth.

If we understand truth as "that which measures up," as Wolterstorff does, then we can more clearly understand how "true" applies to all three

---

118. Geisler, "Concept of Truth," 332. Geisler subsumes personal truth under propositional truth in order to achieve a simple system of thought. However, translating personal truth down into propositions steals away from the complexity and results in an inadequate and partial understanding of the rich truth God wants people to understand.

119. Wolterstorff, "True Words," 34. See also Beals, "Truth as a Way of Life," 7–16.

120. Wolterstorff, "True Words," 35.

121. Geisler, *Systematic Theology*, 1:84. See also Lewis, "Propositional Revelation," 270.

122. He explains, "Different sentences can make one and the same affirmation about reality, and, more important for our immediate purposes, the same sentence may be used either propositionally or nonpropositionally." Lindbeck, *Nature of Doctrine*, 67–8.

123. Wolterstorff, "True Words," 38.

124. Ibid.

forms of revelation.[125] He clarifies, "When we speak of 'a true so-and-so,' we are implicitly drawing a contrast between this so-and-so that measures up and other so-and-so's that do not, or would not, measure up. What exactly that contrast is, will differ from case to case."[126] Resultantly, "One has to gather from the context what contrast it is that the speaker had in mind, and hence what sort of failure to measure up he meant to call attention to."[127]

The context, therefore, is essential to understand the comparison being made and "what sort of failure to measure up he meant to call attention to."[128] So, when Jesus states in John 5:31, "If I bear witness to myself, my testimony is not true; there is another who bears witness to me, and I know that the testimony which he bears of me is true"[129] Certainly, the Son of God would not do that which God detests (Prov 12:22). Instead, the context (John 8:17) helps the reader understand in what sense his testimony would be found invalid.[130] Unlike Lewis, Wolterstorff retains "true" as a fit word for the entirety of Scripture (exhortations as well as indicatives). Wolterstorff also validates the full range of theories of truth.

What, then, is the relationship between revelation and truth? All revelation is true because it comes from God. The adjective "true" applies to Scripture, the Incarnation, and the creation. In reference to Scripture, the context must help the reader understand in what way any specific passage is true. Referring to a command as true differs from stating that an assertion is true. What does it mean for Jesus to be the truth? He is truly God and truly man. In other words, he measures up to what it means to be God and he measures up to what it means to be man.[131] The created order truly reveals God. In other words, each aspect of the creation measures up to its proclaimed goodness per Gen 1. More specifically, when the creation "acts in character" or does what God designed it to do, then it is true.[132]

We should therefore "interpret the personal and descriptive uses of the word 'truth' as distinct yet positively related."[133] Both Scripture and the created order communicate "truths for which human beings must give ac-

---

125. Ibid., 42.
126. Ibid.
127. Ibid.
128. Ibid.
129. New American Standard Version.
130. Wolterstorff, "True Words," 38.
131. Chalcedon explains the dual nature of Jesus. Leith, *Creeds of the Churches*, 35–36.
132. The notion that creatures act in character comes from Plantinga. Plantinga, *Engaging God's World*, 31.
133. Clark, *Know and Love God*, 361.

count. Like special revelation, general revelation is intended to unveil the purposes of God for his creation and its human rulers."[134] Truth then can include thoughts, words, and deeds. Beals desires "that we will not rely on actions alone. I hope we will not rely on propositions alone. I hope that the truth as a way of life will include the pursuit of true thoughts, true words, and true deeds."[135]

Revelation is true because of its source, not because of the form it takes. Therefore, the adjective "true" fits Scripture, the Incarnation, and the created order as revelations of God. Although both Scripture and the created order "are utterly true, the potential for error or fragmentary understanding on our part is at hand on every side."[136] The problem lies not with revelation, but with those who interpret it (see "Recipients" below).

Authoritative

Like, true, the authority of revelation stems from its divine origin. Revelation is authoritative because "God speaks with authority wherever and whenever he speaks."[137] Therefore, if God "reveals himself to man, it must be in an authoritative way."[138] Even revelation through creation "reveals God in a *true* and *authoritative* fashion."[139] The question, then, "is how to insure equivalence of authority for truth wherever it shows up and in whatever form . . . Truth has equal warrant as truth, wherever it is found."[140] The answer lies in spheres of authority.

Anything God reveals is true and therefore authoritative because of its source and veracity. Therefore, "All truth is authoritative. And the nature of the authority depends on the nature of the truth."[141] For example, "Math-

---

134. Moore, "Natural Revelation," 106. It not only communicates truths it *is true*.
135. Beals, "Truth," 15.
136. Johnson, "Between Two Wor(l)ds," 82.
137. Van Til, *Christian Apologetics*, 73.
138. Conner, *Revelation and God*, 98.
139. McCune, *Systematic Theology*, 1:174; emphasis added.
140. Ellens, "Biblical Authority," 323. Diehl observes that "general revelation is usually treated only in a brief way in theology books and is quickly set aside in favor of the *exclusive authority of Scripture* once the affects of sin have been specified." Diehl, "Evangelicalism and General Revelation," 445; emphasis added. Moreland notices a tendency among evangelicals to identify the Bible as "the *sole* source of authority for faith and practice." Moreland, "Over-Committed." Thomas is an example of this position. He states that "all truth does not rest on the same authority." He then explains the higher authority of Scripture. Thomas, "Biblical Hermeneutics," 13.
141. Conner, *Revelation and God*, 98.

ematical truth is of such a nature that if one sees it he must accept it; he has little if any option. The truth in this realm is of such a nature that it cannot be denied; to do so is to impeach one's intelligence."[142] The truths of math, therefore, retain authority over all things involving math. However, they are not authoritative over matters in other spheres such as salvation. To be sure, the authority of math stems from its divine origin not something inherent in math or man's ability or inability to rightly understand and use math.

Therefore, the authority of any particular form of revelation extends only as far as its divine purpose. For example, Scripture tells the story of creation, fall, and redemption. In part, redemption involves a renewing of the mind (Rom 12), which requires the active work of the Spirit. Scripture addresses these issues with authority. However, Scripture does not reveal the inner workings of the human brain and how it develops addictive behaviors. Scripture does not speak in terms of dopamine which "is the neurotransmitter involved in the mesolimbic system that coordinates all natural reinforcing behaviors (eating, drinking, and sex). It is the primary neurotransmitter that most addictive drugs are known to release."[143] To the extent that these findings measure up to the reality of the human brain, these findings have authority. In this example, both Scripture and the created order come together as authorities addressing the same issue. However, each speaks authoritatively to differing spheres.

Authority is a corollary of true and both originate with the source not the form of revelation. Divine revelation represents the character of God. He does not speak or act in any way, but with authority. Evangelicals rightly argue for the authority of Scripture because it comes from God.[144] The same argument extends to the created order without fear. The created order, as revelation from God, retains authority. Indeed, caution is warranted, but that belongs under "recipients" below.

---

142. Ibid. The notion that math comes from God and its veracity relies on his character stands in stark contrast to the thought of fallen humankind. Pratchett's character Bent reflects the hubris of humanity when he states: "The human brain *is* capable of infallibility in the world of numbers. Since we invented them, how would it be otherwise?" Pratchett, *Making Money*, 56.

143. Struthers, *Wired for Intimacy*, 188.

144. Allison, *Historical Theology*, 79; Erickson, *Christian Theology*, 267; and Plantinga, et al., *Christian Theology*, 76; Thomas, "General Revelation," 13; and Wolters, *Creation Regained*, 7. David Kelsey uncovers the great complexity of meaning behind the simple statement "Scripture is authoritative." Kelsey, *Proving Doctrine*.

Sufficient

Since revelation comes from God it is sufficient. However, like authority, its sufficiency ties to particular spheres. Sometimes people conclude "general revelation is of minor importance because it is insufficient for salvation."[145] Said another way, general revelation "is limited because it is not sufficient in and of itself to save the sinner," but Scripture "is complete in its revelation of divine revelation."[146] People sometimes label revelation given through the created order as ineffective,[147] insufficient,[148] limited,[149] or inadequate.[150] Use of these descriptors assumes the problem stems from revelation instead of with its recipients. For example, Street holds that humanity's tendency to ignore or misunderstand general revelation serves as a "major limitation [that] hinders general revelation's effect."[151] He concludes, "While special revelation can be distorted or rejected like general revelation, it is different in one major aspect—it is self-authenticated as true and sufficient, while general revelation is not."[152] However, in reality the problem "with the natural revelation of God, and on this we need to be as clear as possible, is *not* from God's side, but from ours."[153] The fact that people suppress and wrongly interpret the created order "does not mean that this revelation is insufficient."[154] In the end, "To claim that general revelation is inadequate [insufficient] because unbelievers [and believers] have distorted it is to reject special revelation for the same reason (Cf. 2 Pet 3:15–16)."[155]

---

145. Thorsen, *Christian Theology*, 19.

146. Evans, *Theology*, 1065. Evans does acknowledge that this does not mean "that God has told us everything." Ibid.

147. Phillips and Okholm state, "*General revelation* refers to God's self-revelation through creation. . . . But these sources seem particularly ineffective in guiding humanity to God." Phillips and Okholm, *Welcome to the Family*, 43.

148. Gamertsfelder, *Systematic Theology*, 21; Boyce, *Systematic Theology*, 34–35; Boice, *Foundations of the Christian Faith*, 21; Lightner, *Evangelical Theology*, 11; Evans, *Theology*, 1065; Milne, *Know the Truth*, 30 (Milne goes a step further stating the insufficiency of general revelation for Adam even before the fall).

149. Wiley, *Christian Theology*, 1:52; Miley, *Systematic Theology*, 1:5; Baker, *Dispensational Theology*, 8; Ryrie, *Basic Theology*, 27; Boice, *Foundations*, 30; Moore, "Natural Revelation," 111; McCune, *Systematic Theology*, 1:176; and Evans, *Theology*, 1065.

150. Grider, *Theology*, 43; Menzies, *Bible Doctrines*, 20; Hart, *Truth Aflame*, 45; and Van Dyke et al., "Integration and the Christian College," 91.

151. Street, "Biblical Counseling," 216.

152. Ibid.

153. Oliphint, "Irrationality of Unbelief," 68.

154. Berkouwer, *General Revelation*, 312.

155. Geisler, *Systematic Theology*, 1:73. For example, Scripture does not provide

A Theology of Revelation

Grudem provides important insight regarding sufficiency. He states, "The sufficiency of Scripture means that Scripture contained all the words of God he intended his people to have at each stage of redemptive history, and that it now contains all the words of God we need for salvation, for trusting him perfectly, and for obeying him perfectly."[156] The sufficiency of Scripture therefore means that God provides what people need for salvation, trust, and obedience. Scripture does not address every question people ask.

Scripture itself teaches that even as God reveals, divine mystery remains. Certainly, revelation "has not told everything there is to know about God."[157] Deut 29:29 most clearly states the partiality of revelation, "The secret things belong to the LORD our God, but the things revealed belong to us and to our children forever, that we may follow all the words of this law." Furthermore, Jesus wanted to reveal more to his disciples, but he knew his disciples could not handle additional revelation. John records, "I [Jesus] have much more to say to you, more than you can now bear."[158] Finally, some things were heard which "man is not permitted to tell."[159]

Scripture is therefore sufficient but not exhaustive. As the Westminster Confession of Faith states, "there are some circumstances concerning the worship of God, and government of the Church, common to human actions and societies, which are to be ordered by the light of nature and Christian prudence, according to the general rules of the Word, which are always to be observed."[160] Often, Scripture provides general guidance not specific answers. People must then look to the created order for guidance as well.

Perspicuous

God makes revelation clear. For Miley, "No truths are so clearly given therein (nature) as in the Scriptures."[161] Milne finds that in special revelation

---

directions on how to set a broken leg. A physician looking to Scripture for such knowledge would find them insufficient, limited, inadequate or ineffective. Such an evaluation is correct in this instance. However, the physician would be foolish to outright reject Scripture because of this. Instead, he should read it and understand for what purposes it is sufficient. Just because the created order is insufficient for salvation does not mean a person should completely reject it as divine revelation.

156. Grudem, *Systematic Theology*, 127. See also Bray, *God is Love*, 88.
157. Towns, *Theology*, 32.
158. John 16:12.
159. 2 Cor 12: 4. Cf. Rev 10:4.
160. Leith, *Creeds of the Church*, 195–96. See also Sawyer, *Survivor's Guide to Theology*, 131.
161. Miley, *Systematic Theology*, 1:2.

"God makes himself known with a clarity and fullness which far surpasses general revelation."[162] Rawley believes general revelation is "rather vague," therefore "general revelation is the servant of specific revelation."[163] Additionally, Warfield labels the written Word superior because of "the fullness, richness, and clearness of its communication."[164] Finally, Beets insists, "Nature's voice is not clear and distinct enough to be heard aright by our sin-corrupted ear."[165] Conversely, he claims "[t]he *clearness* of God's Word is evident as we read Ps. 119:105."[166] Erickson observes, "It is common to point out that general revelation is inferior to special revelation, in both the clarity of the treatment and the range of subjects considered."[167] While, perhaps common, does such belief align with Scripture?

First, Scripture is not equally clear. As the Westminster Confession states, "All things in Scripture are not alike plain in themselves, nor alike clear unto all; yet those things which are necessary to be known, believed, and observed, for salvation, are so clearly propounded and opened in some place of Scripture or other, that not only the learned, but the unlearned, in a due use of the ordinary means, may attain unto a sufficient understanding of them."[168]

Second, as briefly stated under "Forms" Scripture (Rom 1:19–20) teaches that revelation given through the created order is plain, clear, and understood. Myatt and Ferreira state the matter regarding general revelation well, "*A revelação é clara, mas os olhos dos homens são cegos*" (The revelation is clear, but the eyes of men are blind.).[169] Erickson agrees, "God has plainly shown them what can be known about him. This self-manifestation has continued since the creation of the world, being perceived in the things that God has made."[170] As Erickson states, the language of Rom 1:21–25 is "clear and strong."[171] Likewise, Berkouwer affirms that "Paul is profoundly convinced of the clarity and the irrefutability of this [general] revelation."[172]

---

162. Milne, *Know the Truth*, 31.
163. Rawley, "Revelation: General and Specific," 83, 99.
164. Warfield, *Studies in Theology*, 60.
165. Beets, *Reformed Confession Explained*, 31.
166. Ibid., 32.
167. Erickson, *Christian Theology*, 203.
168. Leith, *Creeds of the Church*, 196. Sawyer, *Survivor's Guide to Theology*, 120.
169. Myatt, and Ferreira, *Teologia sistemática*, 23; translation mine.
170. Erickson, *Christian Theology*, 193.
171. Ibid.
172. Berkouwer, *General Revelation*, 148.

Geisler carefully delineates between the clarity of revelation and the problems that stem from the interpretations of fallen people. He writes, "Careful examination of both areas indicates that in spite of the clarity of both revelations, depraved human beings have found a way to deflect, divert, or distort God's commands; therefore, the teachings of God's Word have no more immunity from tortured contortion than does the reality of God's world."[173] The clarity of revelation does not mean infallible interpretation or singularity of interpretation.[174] The clarity of revelation stems from its source more than its form or recipients. In essence, "the revelation of God in nature is genuine and accurate because it is God's."[175]

Recipients of Revelation

The recipients of divine communication include all created beings.[176] However, God created humans in his image and therefore with the ability to uniquely respond to his revelation. He reveals to finite and fallen people. Understanding humanity's finitude God reveals transcendent truth in time and space. Revelation given to finite people is mediated and progressive. The recipients of divine revelation are also fallen. These people, both redeemed and unredeemed, interpret and respond to God's revelation. As Bolt states, "In his works, God is present to all people; the world is the theater of his glory; the human heart responds in faith activated by grace or in rebellious, inexcusable unbelief, but it cannot avoid responding."[177] Because of original sin people depend knowingly or unknowingly on the work of the Spirit for correct interpretation of all revelation.

173. Geisler, *Systematic Theology*, 1:73.
174. Horton, *Christian Faith*, 196–97.
175. Lightner, *Evangelical Theology*, 11.
176. God reveals to all of his creation and creation responds. For example, in Ps 148, "creation itself looks at what Yhwh does with Israel and finds itself drawn with Israel into even more of that inarticulate worship." Goldingay, *Psalms*, 3:735. Might the same occur after the spring rain, when a rainbow appears in the sky and the animals return to their God-given tasks? Another example of creation's response to divine revelation comes from a donkey. Balaam's ass responded more quickly and more obediently than Balaam (Num 22:23–41). God not only reveals through angels he also reveals his character to angels (1 Pet 1:12). Divine revelation "is God making himself known to the objects of that revelation, e.g., angels and people." Herrick, "Is the Bible the Only Revelation of God?" As Paul writes in Eph 3:10–11, "His intent was that now, through the church, the manifold wisdom of God should be made known to the rulers and authorities in the heavenly realms, according to his eternal purpose which he accomplished in Jesus Christ our Lord."
177. Bolt, "Editor's Introduction," 9.

Finite

God reveals to finite people. Finitude limits people's understanding of the created order. For example, "how stands the case, for instance, if we endeavour [sic] to explain the cause of the rising of the Nile? We may say a great deal, plausible or otherwise, on the subject; but what is true, sure, and incontrovertible regarding it, belongs only to God."[178] No matter the depth of knowledge regarding the migration of birds, the ocean tide, and weather events they remain in part mysteries hidden for God and not fully understandable by people. We may know "a great deal while we search into their causes, but God alone who made them can declare the truth regarding them."[179]

Finitude also impacts how people understand Scripture. So, if "with respect to creation," some knowledge belongs to God alone and other knowledge falls "with in [sic] the range of our own knowledge," then how can we complain "if, in regard to those things which we investigate in the Scriptures (which are throughout spiritual), we are able by the grace of God to explain some of them, while we must leave others in the hands of God, and that not only in the present world, but also in that which is to come, so that God should forever teach, and man should for ever learn the things taught him by God?"[180] Finite people, therefore, only know God's revelation, Scripture as well as the created order, in part.

Finitude means no single person "can see everything with equal clarity."[181] Furthermore, different people "do not always notice the same thing even when they are looking at the same object."[182] Therefore, we need to listen to others in the body of Christ. In other words, "we must all have the humility to learn from the perspective of others."[183] Finitude leads to various interpretations of revelation. Diverse interpretations do not *necessarily* signify contradiction. They might mean that two or more people simply see the same thing from a different angle. We study "the same reality, but if we approach it from different angles or with different ends in view, we must not be surprised if we come up with different interpretations of

---

178. Roberts, and Donaldson, *Fathers Down to A.D.* 1:325, 399.
179. Ibid.
180. Ibid.
181. Bray, *God is Love*, 24.
182. Poythress, *Symphonic Theology*, 9.
183. Bray, *God is Love*, 24.

it."[184] God created people as finite beings knowing that we would see things differently. He called this "very good" in Gen 1.

Knowing man's situation, God provides revelation within particular contexts and situations. He communicates transcendent truth in time bound ways. In other words, all revelation comes to humanity mediated.[185] Even the Bible "is a revelation, then, not immediately to us, but mediately through the biblical writers and their situation."[186] God uses that language familiar to people, he "does not break through language and situatedness. Rather, he enters into the linguistic setting and uses language in the act of revelation as a means of accommodation to the situation and situatedness of human beings."[187] Scripture came in particular languages with all the limitations that come with language.[188]

The Incarnation perhaps best exemplifies the mediated nature of revelation. Walls argues: "The Word becoming flesh and pitching tent among us, is itself an act of translation."[189] In other words, Jesus "does not come recurrently into the world . . . He came once, into a particular family at a particular period and place, spoke a particular language, shared a particular culture."[190] The Incarnate Christ, divine revelation, walked this earth in time and space as a man. Therefore, the mediated nature of revelation "is not a problem; it is the solution."[191] The problem, "How does a holy and infinite God communicate with a finite and fallen people?" The answer, "He uses

184. Poythress, *Symphonic Theology*, 9.

185. Bavinck, *Reformed Dogmatics*, 1:301. Some evangelicals teach that Scripture comes immediately from God and is therefore more reliable than the created order which is mediated. For example, Thorsen, *Christian Theology*, 28; and McCune, *Systematic Theology*, 1:172. Both authors link mediated revelation with human discovery and immediate revelation as non-discoverable. As argued in chapter two all revelation comes from God and humans use reason as a means to understand divine revelation. See also Higgins, "God's Inspired Word," 69; and Miley, *Systematic Theology*, 1:8–9. Edwards states that "Jesus Christ is admitted to know God immediately; but the knowledge of all other creatures in heaven and on earth is by means, or by manifestations or signs held forth." Edwards, *"Miscellanies," 501–832*, 428.

186. Conner, *Revelation and God*, 78.

187. Franke, *Character of Theology*, 75.

188. Towns notes, "God has used words to communicate his revelation to mankind and thus the limitations of language will limit our understanding of God. Human words are symbols, only partially able to communicate ideas. While they are useful in most situations, they fall short of perfection." Towns, *Theology*, 22. Tozer states, "But in all this we are thinking creature-thoughts and using creature-words to express them." Tozer, *Knowledge of the Holy*, 15.

189. Walls, *Missionary Movement*, 23.

190. Ibid., 47.

191. Horton, *Christian Faith*, 131.

their language, their world, and their context to communicate transcendent truth." Bavinck explains,

> In a strict sense there is no immediate revelation either in nature or in grace. God always uses a means . . . by which he reveals himself to human beings. By signs and symbols he makes his presence felt by them; by acts he proclaims his attributes; by speech and language he makes known to them his will and mind. Even in cases where he reveals himself internally in the human consciousness by his Spirit, this revelation always occurs organically and hence mediately.[192]

God, therefore, graciously mediates *all revelation* in ways understandable to finite people. In fact, "Christianity has no culturally fixed element," which means the "process of translation is endless."[193]

God also progressively reveals to finite people instead of overwhelming them. God gave Scripture in a progressive fashion instead of all at once.[194] Similarly, the created order "is that communication that God makes continuously to all people by His works."[195] Javier concludes that the created order reveals God and this revelation "unfolds through time." He writes, "La contemplación de un orden y una racionalidad en el mundo, y de un ser humano que no puede dejar de preguntarse de ellos hacen referencia a la permanente posibilidad de percibir la creación como proyecto divino unitario, revelación de Dios, que se despliega a través del tiempo."[196] What exactly does this mean? One example comes in the field of math, "The concept of irrational numbers was not fully resolved until the methods of modern analysis were employed in the nineteenth century. They were there all the time, but God chose to reveal them over time as a part of his continuing revelation to human understanding."[197]

God opens the eyes of man to his revelation in a progressive way. Just as God does not give man all he needs to know in Gen 1, but instead progressively unfolds his plan of salvation. So, progression of the written word

---

192. Bavinck, *Prolegomena*, 309.

193. Walls, *Cross-Cultural Process*, 13.

194. Bavinck, *Reformed Dogmatics*, 1:343; Ryrie, *Basic Theology*, 28; Erickson, *Christian Theology*, 222; Thorsen, *Christian Theology*, 18.

195. Barackman, *Practical Christian Theology*, 43.

196. Cañizares, "Filosofi griega," 201. "Contemplation of the order and rationality of the world as well as man who cannot help but wonder about them point to the possibility of perceiving the divine plan of creation as unitary revelation of God, which unfolds through time." Translation mine.

197. Wooldridge, "Mathematics," 179.

coincides with historical progression whereby history unfolds to its divinely determined end.[198] All divine revelation reflects the fact that he takes the initiative and graciously reveals to finite people.

Fallen

The recipients of revelation are fallen as well as finite.[199] Such people interpret God's revelation. It seems that "If Scriptures be a plain book, and the Spirit performs the functions of a teacher to all the children of God, it follows inevitably that they must agree in all essential matters in their interpretation of the Bible."[200] One might even suggest that the theologian merely repeats God's doctrine as given in Scripture: "das die vom Theologen aus der Schrift geschopste Lehre . . . göttliche Lehre, *doctrina divina*, ist . . . Gottes eigene Lehre, Unschauung und Urteil ist."[201]

However, Scripture and reality teach that this is not the case. The Pharisees "diligently stud[ied] the Scriptures" but then failed to understand Jesus and eternal life.[202] Furthermore, the various denominations demonstrate that believers fail to interpret Scripture rightly. People can "no more step out from behind our pre-understanding to see 'the text itself' or the 'original meaning itself' than we can leave our bodies behind and view the world from a God's eye perspective."[203] What, though, does this mean? Can people even understand revelation?

Finite people know in part, fallen people distort and suppress.[204] The noetic effects of sin do not "render the human intellect incapable of knowing truth."[205] The fall "damaged but did not destroy the image of God in us. Our

---

198. My use of progress here does not follow Enlightenment thinking that assumes modern scientific understanding replaces old naïve and primitive spiritual ideas. Humans do not progress independently of God. History unfolds toward a pre-determined end planned by God. The time in which we live (between fall and redemption) includes a mixture of progress and regress.

199. The enemy (Satan and fallen angels) continue to wage war by attempting to deceive the redeemed. Mayhue, "Cultivating a Biblical Mind-Set," 47-48.

200. Hodge, Systematic Theology, 1:184.

201. Pieper, *Dogmatik*, 1:57. "Doctrine drawn out of Scripture by the theologian . . . is divine, *doctrina divina* . . . God's doctrine, view, and judgment."

202. John 5:39-40.

203. Hart, *Faith Thinking*, 125.

204. Kulikovsky rightly states, "[I]t is impossible to discover the truth about creation by relying on our own knowledge, ideas, and methods, simply because we are finite and fallen human beings." He speaks correctly, but fails to mention that these also hinder people's interpretation of Scripture. Kulikovsky, *Creation, Fall, Restoration*, 25.

205. Moreland, "Philosophy," 56.

reasoning abilities are affected but not eliminated. This can be seen in the fact that the writers of Scripture often appeal to the minds of unbelievers by citing evidence on behalf of their claims, using logical inferences in building their case, and speaking in the language and thought forms of those outside the faith."[206] The redeemed and the unredeemed fail to rightly understand and respond to revelation because of original sin. However, by God's grace and enablement people can rightly understand in part.

In light of the effects of total depravity, God sees fit to reveal to those outside of the community of faith (Exod 7:4–5; Josh 2:9–11; Isa 44:23; 43:7; 46:13; and Deut 28:10, 37).[207] If he did not, then who would ever become his people?[208] Scripture teaches that God reveals to those outside of his chosen community. Saucy writes,

> . . . dreams [were not] limited to God's people. The pharaoh of Egypt and King Nebuchadnezzar of Babylon were given dreams about God's future plans (Gen. 41:1–7; Dan. 2:3, 31–35). In both cases, however, the interpretations were conveyed through those who belonged to God's people. Most of these revelatory dreams included speech from God although some, as with Joseph's dream about himself and his brothers, did not.[209]

Merrill observes the same, "Ironically, enough, the first account of dream revelation features the pagan ruler of Gerar, Abimelech . . . (Gen. 20:3–7) . . . for the LORD God of the Hebrews to reveal himself to the heathen is perhaps unexpected, but it is by no means unique . . . the Lord is sovereign beyond the narrow confines of Israel, acting, and revealing himself as he chooses."[210]

Those outside the community of faith understand revelation given through the created order. Geisler summarizes this point well, "So the problem with unbelievers is not that they do not *see* the truth of natural revelation but that they *shun* the truth it reveals to them (Rom. 1:18)."[211] The unredeemed may "wickedly and unjustly misuse this treasure for the service

---

206. Ibid.

207. For examples see Spina, *Faith of the Outsider*.

208. Moore observes that Edwards saw the Spirit striving with the unredeemed wooing them through both the preached Word as well as the creation. Moore, *Consider the Lilies*, 151.

209. Saucy, "Scripture," 30.

210. Merrill, *Everlasting Dominion*, 78. Bavinck points out, "Scripture repeatedly mentions miracles that God performed before the eyes of pagans (in Egypt, Canaan, Babel, etc.), and supernatural revelations that came to non-Israelites (Gen. 20; 31:24; 40; 41; Judg. 7; Dan. 2:4ff.; etc.)." Bavinck, *Reformed Dogmatics*, 1:311.

211. Geisler, *Systematic Theology*, 1:73.

of demons."²¹² However, the redeemed may benefit from the common grace given by God to the unredeemed. Therefore, "if the Lord has been pleased to assist us by the work and ministry of the ungodly in physics, dialectics, mathematics, and other similar sciences, let us avail ourselves of it, lest, by neglecting the gifts of God spontaneously offered to us, we be justly punished for our sloth."²¹³ As Holmes states, "The most deluded pagan and the most untrustworthy scoundrel possess fragments of truth and might know a great deal more about many things in God's creation (and even about Christian theology) than the finest saint."²¹⁴

Resultantly, not only does God reveal to those outside of the community, he sometimes uses them to teach his people. Scripture reveals that sometimes "God's people in Scripture *learned* things about God from the Gentiles."²¹⁵ If the unredeemed "have said aught that is true and in harmony with our faith, we are not only not to shrink from it, but to claim it for our own use from those who have unlawful possession of it."²¹⁶ As Augustine continues he asserts that along with knowledge, Christians can learn morality and worship from the unredeemed. Heathen learning contains "instruction which is better adapted to the use of the truth, and some most excellent precepts of morality; and some truths in regard to even the worship of the One God."²¹⁷

However, caution is important.²¹⁸ Unbelievers as well as believers reject, suppress, misunderstand or misuse revelation.²¹⁹ In fact, "[t]his applies

212. Ibid.

213. Calvin, *Institutes*, 1:236–37.

214. Holmes, *Truth* , 35. Similarly, Kantzer acknowledges that "[i]n some areas the unbeliever may think as clearly or even more cogently than the believer." Kantzer, "Communication of Revelation," 67.

215. McDermott, *World Religions*, 74. For example, Moses received his education in Egypt and the Chaldeans trained Daniel. God would use people outside of his community to teach those within his chosen people. Spina, *Faith of the Outsider*.

216. Augustine, "St. Augustin's Christian Doctrine," 554.

217. Ibid.

218. Augustine gives this caution as well. Ibid., 545, 554.

219. Moore challenges the traditional reading that Rom 1 applies only to the unredeemed. He asserts, "Paul wants us to believe that anyone and everyone who takes for granted, ignores, or denies the glory and grandeur of God in the things He has made is, at least in some measure, outside the will of God and in danger of coming under His rod of discipline." Therefore, Moore suggests, "the doctrine of general revelation should take on something of a greater urgency for us. For it is apparent from Paul's words that they are foolish and ungrateful who do not take the time to observe what God is revealing of Himself in the creation, to acknowledge with thanks His glory, and to consider what use they ought to make of this revelation in worshiping and serving Him. And they come under His judgment as a result, and can expect something less than the full

to special revelation, to natural revelation, and to incarnational revelation. Not everyone who looks at the stars believes, not everyone who reads Romans believes, and not everyone in Israel who saw Jesus in the course of his earthly ministry believed."[220] Unbelievers as well as believers spurn all three major forms of revelation, but "it does not alter the fact that God has in fact revealed himself."[221] Nor does "our failure to read the revelation" say anything "about whether the revelation was written."[222] The failure of man does not impact the reality of revelation or its veracity.

In our helplessness, God in his mercy and grace provides the Spirit. The Spirit works with the unredeemed as well as the redeemed, but differently. The Spirit of God "may indeed act upon the mind of a natural man; but he acts in the mind of a saint as an indwelling vital principle. He acts upon the mind of an unregenerate person as an extrinsic occasional agent . . . But he unites himself with the mind of the saint, takes him for his temple, actuates and influences him as a new supernatural principle of life and action."[223] Regarding the work of the Spirit with the unregenerate, the Spirit "may excite thoughts in them, may assist their natural reason and understanding, or may assist other natural principles."[224] Only the Spirit of God can unveil the mind of God (1 Cor 2:11).

The Spirit is the necessary agent for right interpretation of any form of revelation. Gulley summarizes this well,

> Without the Holy Spirit there is no right interpretation of nature and God's providence in human life and history, any more than there is a right interpretation of Scripture. Without the Holy Spirit there is no reaching fallen and depraved human beings. It is no innate capacity which contributes to their knowledge any more than to their salvation. Both the knowledge of God and His salvation are a one-hundred-percent gift (as in text).[225]

---

and abundant life promised by our Savior so long as they continue to tread the earth unmindful of the grandeur of God on display all around them." Moore, *Consider the Lilies*, 48–49. See also Milne, *Know the Truth*, 29.

220. Wilson, "Theater of God," 85.

221. Ibid.

222. Ibid.

223. Edwards, *Sermons and Discourses, 1730–1733*, 411.

224. Ibid. Vanhoozer acknowledges the work of the Spirit outside the church as both restraining sin and "even illuminating truth." I share his caution that "it is a mistake to identify an authoritative speaking of the Spirit apart from Christ and Scripture." Vanhoozer, "Everyday Theology," 259n104.

225. Gulley, *Systematic Theology*, 225. See also Van Til, *Common Grace*, 58; and Beets, *Reformed Confession Explained*, 30.

The Spirit, though, "operates in conjunction with normal mental processes so as to make the truth meaningful to the individual. In all His works God employs the natural processes He has ordained."[226] The entire world "about us is a manifestation of the truths of God. It is the Spirit's task to set forth the fullness of this revelation before the eyes of men."[227] Strong writes, "Science and Scripture throw light upon each other. The same divine Spirit who gave both revelations is still present, enabling the believer to interpret the one by the other and thus progressively to come to the knowledge of the truth."[228]

In the final analysis, God reveals (created order, written Word, and the Incarnation) to finite and fallen people. He reveals in a progressive fashion and mediates revelation so that finite people can know, in an analogous way, transcendent truths. Every form of revelation requires interpretation, but fallen people often misinterpret it. God reveals to the unredeemed as well as the redeemed. So, when studying the created order the redeemed may learn from the unredeemed. In either case, the revelation comes from God and correct interpretation of any revelation requires the Spirit of God's enablement. We now look at the content of divine revelation.

Content of Revelation

The content of revelation includes knowledge of God, his relationship to creation, as well as creation itself.[229] Certainly, content between the created order and the written Word overlap, for example both teach the love of God. However, the expression of this content differs between the two forms of revelation. God reveals his attributes through all forms of revelation. Additionally, the content of revelation expands to include what some term "human discovery." The created order reveals details of the inner-workings of creation, which Scripture does not teach.[230]

---

226. Holmes, *Christianity and Philosophy*, 15. Edwards affirms the work of the Spirit with unbelievers as well. Part of the Spirit's common work entails the "illumination of good and evil" as well as "assisting principles of natural reason and judgment against blinding tendency of sin." Edwards, *"Miscellanies,"* 501–832, 732.

227. Van Til, *Common Grace*, 58.

228. Strong, *Systematic Theology*, 27.

229. Wolter's notion of structure and direction provides better questions to ask as we study the created order. What is structural (part of God's good creation) and what is directional (turned either toward self or God)? Wolters, *Creation Regained*, 88.

230. This could be why Calvin, "was extremely reticent . . . to draw detailed, specific scientific inferences from the biblical text." And instead chose to accept "the scientific data and adjusted his interpretation of the text accordingly." Young, *John Calvin and the Natural World*, 159, 160–61.

God reveals in written form the meta-narrative of creation, fall, and redemption.[231] This serves as an interpretive grid through which to understand other areas of Scripture, the created order, and the Incarnation. Scripture teaches that God is one and yet the Father, Son, and Spirit are each God. Scripture also teaches of a current and a future hope.[232] God reveals the same through the created order. His revelation in Scripture adds specificity regarding the current state of the world, God's nature, and the hope of the redeemed.

Divine Attributes

God reveals his attributes through all forms of revelation not just through Scripture.[233] McCune challenges this idea. He acknowledges that Acts 14:17 teaches that "something of God's goodness can be seen" through material and animal creation.[234] However, he states that the aforementioned revelation "reveals nothing about God's love, mercy, and grace, not to mention redemptive information."[235] However, God's decision to reveal and his revelation in both "his world and his Word, are "an evidence and illustration of his love."[236]

In fact, Scripture teaches that the created order reveals God's attributes. In Rom 1 "[t]he word *theiotēs*, translated 'divine nature,' occurs only here in the New Testament and embraces the properties which make God God. Creation, which people see, reveals God's unseen character—the

---

231. Some call this a worldview. Plantinga, *Engaging God's World* and Ostrander, *Why College Matters to God*, 13–23.

232. For example, Rom 8:1 teaches that there is no condemnation for those in Christ. Rev 21 teaches us about the eternal state.

233. A comprehensive examination of God's attributes as displayed through the created order lies beyond the scope of the current work. However, I believe such research is a worthy pursuit.

234. McCune, *Systematic Theology*, 1:176.

235. Ibid. He even states that "Each member of the human race is a revelation of God." Ibid., 177. McCune states this on the basis of man bearing God's image (Gen 1, 1 Cor 11, Ps 139, Eccl 3, Acts 17, and Rom 2). Yet, he misses the fact that people reveal God's love, mercy, and grace. For example, the story of Ruth shows God's love through the faithfulness of a Moabite to an Israelite widow and through a kinsman redeemer who exemplifies the loving kindness of Yhwh. God's provisions through Israelite law for the alien demonstrate his attributes.

236. Lightner, *Evangelical Theology*, 9–10. God reveals his love throughout the pages of Scripture. The ultimate revelation of God's love is revealed through the Incarnation via substitutionary atonement (John 3:16 and 1 John 4:10).

all-powerful Deity. An Old Testament parallel to these verses is Psalm 19:1–6."[237] Calvin, explaining the teaching of Scripture, writes,

> Scripture, indeed, makes known to us the time and manner of the creation; but the heavens themselves, although God should say nothing on the subject, proclaim loudly and distinctly enough that they have been fashioned by his hands: and this of itself abundantly suffices to bear testimony to men of his glory. As soon as we acknowledge God to be the supreme Architect, who has erected the beauteous fabric of the universe, our minds must necessarily be ravished with wonder at his infinite goodness, wisdom, and power.[238]

The Psalms, in poetic fashion, teach that God reveals his attributes through the created order. In Psalm 107 the author recounts works of God exhorting the beneficiaries to praise God (8–9, 15, 21–22, 31–32) on the basis of his works which revealed his character. The Psalm concludes with an exhortation for the wise to look at God's works and consider his character, "Whoever is wise, let him heed these things and consider the great love of the LORD."[239] God displays his attributes through the created order and those with eyes to see should respond with praise. The created order "display[s] his [God's] excellencies."[240] The creation "preaches to us; its creatures declare to us his majesty, his wisdom and power and mercy."[241] Many of God's attributes, "if God had not created the world, never would have had any exercise: the power of God, the wisdom and prudence and contrivance of God, and the goodness and mercy and grace of God, and the justice of God."[242]

God's love shines not only through that which he created, but also through that which vice regents created. Roy Anker observes that cinema understands that "there is a Love that has fashioned a world of shining to make us gape and delight. And films are endlessly inventive in discovering and displaying the curious ways in which the divine shows up in human affairs, of which films themselves may be one instance."[243] He views cinema as a way to "revalidate the significance of sensory experience, to restore to us through the sensorium to a universe shaped and infused by divine love,

237. Witmer, "Romans," 442.
238. Calvin, *Book of Psalms*, 1: 309.
239. See also Pss 33:5, 97:6, 119:64, and 148.
240. Hannah, *Glorify God*, 19, emphasis removed.
241. Edwards, *Sermons and Discourses 1720–1723*, 440.
242. Edwards, *"Miscellanies," 501–832*, 97.
243. Anker, "Like Shining from Shook Foil," 141.

flaming and shining for delight and doxology."[244] Humanity, unredeemed as well as redeemed, sees God's attributes in the created order and mirrors these back to him through representations in the arts.[245]

In short, the creation reveals God's love. The earth is full of God's love (Ps 119:64). When a husband puts his wife's needs before his own, God's love shines forth (Eph 5:28–30). A mother from one species taking in a baby from another species reveals God's love. God's care for the birds reminds those with eyes to see that he takes care of our most basic needs (Matt 6:26). As Grudem explains, "Rains and fruitful seasons, food produced from the earth, and gladness in people's hearts, all bear witness to the fact that their Creator is a God of mercy, of love, and even of joy. These evidences of God are all around us in creation to be seen by those who are willing to see them."[246] God reveals his love not only through the Incarnation and Scripture, but also through the created order.[247]

Charnock models the integration of Scripture and the created order when he speaks of God's goodness. In reference to God's goodness, Charnock writes, "The whole world is a map to represent, and a herald to proclaim this perfection [goodness]. It is as difficult not to see something of it in every creature with the eye of our minds, as it is not to see the beams of the shining sun with those off [sic] our bodies."[248] He continues his observations, "every grain of the creation wears the visible badge" of goodness, so "no creature is silent."[249]

Charnock then explicitly points to both Scripture and the created order as two books that both reveal God's goodness. He states, "In the volume of

---

244. Ibid.

245. For example, Nickelback sings a song that displays a yearning for what Christians identify as the eternal state. They recognize love as caring, truth telling, self-giving and humbling where these exists death no longer exists. Nickelback, "If Everyone Cared."

246. Grudem, *Systematic Theology*, 121.

247. Both Scripture and the created order may reveal the same attributes. However, differences remain. God created us in such a way that experience impacts people differently than words on a page. Reading "God is sovereign" is at once similar and yet different than reading an art form that conveys his sovereignty and this differs yet again from our experience of his sovereign actions in our lives. God created humans as multi-sensory beings. Therefore we learn better when we use multiple senses. Hendricks, *Teaching to Change Lives*, 56. Towns observes the importance of our senses as well. Since God created us as multi-sensory beings he "used all five senses when He gave a revelation to man." Towns, *Theology*, 32. For example, the entire sacrificial system of the Old Testament reveals using creation as part of a grand multi-sensory object lesson for Israel.

248. Charnock, *Attributes of God*, 2:246.

249. Ibid.

the book of the Scriptures it is written of me, and my goodness in redemption: so it may be said of God, In [sic] the volume of the book of the creature it is written of me, and my goodness in creation. Every creature is a page in this book," though not every page reflects the same quality of goodness.[250] For example, "What an admirable piece of goodness is it to communicate life to a fly! How should we stand gazing upon it, till we turn our eye inwards, and view our own frame, which is much more ravishing!"[251] God reveals his attributes, himself, not facts about himself through all three forms of revelation. He also reveals to humans important information needed for ruling over creation.

Inner-workings of Creation

The content of revelation includes the inner-workings of creation. Some state that general revelation refers only to knowledge of God.[252] However, the knowledge of God and the knowledge of self (might I say creation) are interwoven. Calvin begins his *Institutes of the Christian Religion*: "Our wisdom, in so far as it ought to be deemed true and solid wisdom, consists almost entirely of two parts: the knowledge of God and of ourselves. But as these are connected together by many ties, it is not easy to determine which of the two precedes, and gives birth to the other."[253] Since creation is dependent upon God, then right knowledge of creation depends upon knowing creation in relationship to its creator. People depend upon divine instruction for life and to rule over the rest of creation. Scripture provides general, but not specific information in these matters.

Revelation through the created order includes knowledge of the creation. In fact, God reveals the order of the world through creation and exhorts people to learn from it. The knowledge received can rightly be called general revelation. Budziszewski explains,

> To call these first principles part of *revelation* is not a euphemism, for they come from God; they are utterly dependent on his arrangements in creation. We know them for no other reasons than the divinely ordained design of the world, the divinely ordained design of the intellect, and the divinely ordained

---

250. Ibid.
251. Ibid.
252. Stott, "Theology," 5; Bookman, "Biblical Counseling," 63–97; Thomas, "General Revelation," 5–23; Vandenberg, "General Revelation," 16–24; Howard, "General Revelation," 53–75; and Pope, *Christian Theology*, 1:37.
253. Calvin, *Institutes*, 1:37.

> correlation between them. Creation may be fallen, but it has not been destroyed; its structures may be resisted, but they cannot be overthrown; the knowledge of them may be suppressed, but it cannot be abolished.[254]

Divine revelation, thereby, extends beyond knowledge of God and his relationship to the created order and to the function and purpose of the created order.

So, God-fearing and well known scientists understood they were studying God's revelation. As Brewster describes,

> Thus nature is seen in her true relations, vivified by the divine energy, and glorified by the divine presence and the divine purpose. In exploring the secrets of nature, man is discovering the thoughts of God as there manifested. Kepler said: "I think Thy thoughts after Thee, O God." Likewise, when Newton discovers the circulation of the blood, the discoverer is face to face with a revelation of the Almighty; even while they who confined their attention to a single page failed to apprehend the main drift of the whole great argument.[255]

Similarly, theologians think of such knowledge as God's revelation. Shedd writes, "Human knowledge . . . is an unwritten revelation because it is not aboriginal and self-subsistent but derived."[256] Shedd observes precedence for this assertion in the history of the church. He observes, "The wide use of the term *revelation* was more common in the patristic church than it has been since."[257] They would use common understanding to refute polytheists. He states, ". . . the distinction between natural and revealed religion though recognized were not emphasized. All religious knowledge was represented as a revelation from God, partly through the light of nature and partly in a supernatural nature (Justin Martyr's *Apology* 1.8, 18, 57 is an example of this)."[258]

The practice of including general knowledge of creation as revelation stems from Scripture, itself. First, Scripture assumes "that we know certain large truths even prior to its instruction," interpreters find these truths necessary to understand Scripture.[259] Budziszewski lists a few items of knowl-

---

254. Budziszewski, *Evangelicals in the Public Square*, 33.
255. Brewster, *Revelation*, 19.
256. Shedd, *Dogmatic Theology*, 86.
257. Ibid., 87.
258. Ibid.
259. Budziszewski, *Evangelicals in the Public Square*, 31.

edge that Scripture assumes people have such as quantity (1 Kgs 7:15), cause and effect (Jer 40:3), and the principle of noncontradiction and excluded middle (Gen 42:2; Josh 24:15), for instance.[260] Additionally, the knowledge of grammar, genres, and writing were all at one time revealed by God to humanity.

Second, Scripture itself exhorts us to study the creation and includes within its pages information previously known. For example, "the Proverbs counsel humans to look, for instance, to the ant to discern the wisdom of foresight, organization, and labor (Prov. 6:6–9) or to the cause-and-effect principles of agriculture (Prov. 24:30–31) to spur humans to the creative wisdom through which they image their Creator."[261] Likewise, divinely revealed wisdom comes in many forms through the created order. Moore writes,

> . . . wisdom is not identified with the intelligence of philosophers or scholars but with the ways of God has seen in his creation—including the mundane rhythms of creatures such as ants, rock badgers, locusts, and lizards (Prov 30:24–28). Solomon's wisdom was 'wisdom of God' (1 Kings 3:28). He used it to govern people justly (1 Kings 3:9), people marveled (1 Kings 5:3; 1 Kings 4:34), his knowledge extended beyond geopolitics to the natural order, plant and animal life (1 Kings 4:28–33).[262]

Furthermore, the research and record of history finds inclusion in the biblical text. Luke 1:1–4 affirms human research as a form of revelation. Luke "carefully investigated everything from the beginning" and wrote "an orderly account" on this basis.[263] Additionally, it was important to note in 1 Chron 29:29 that the "events of King David's reign . . . are written in the records of Samuel the seer, the records of Nathan the prophet and the records of Gad the seer."

Not only do we find encouragement to study the created order, God specifically taught people how to perform certain tasks. As Turnau deduces in the book of Isaiah, God teaches the farmer the appropriate way to work

---

260. Ibid., 31–32.

261. Moore, "Natural Revelation," 110.

262. Ibid. Moore observes that the very order of nature (changing seasons and the instinct of animals) reveals God. Ibid., 107–8.

263. Luke 1:3. Geisler observes that sometimes the human authors of Scripture use extra-Scriptural resources, "sometimes the biblical authors found God's truth embedded in *human sources*. The Old Testament often used non-canonical writings as sources; the Book of Jashar (Josh. 10:13) and the Book of the Wars of the Lord (Num. 21:14) are examples." Geisler, *Systematic Theology*, 1:157. He references 1 Chr 29:29; Luke 1:1–4; Acts 17:28; 1 Cor 15:33; Titus 1:12; and Jude 9, 14.

the land (Isa 28:23–26).[264] Though this is a metaphor for judgment, Isaiah does state in verse 26 that God "instructs and teaches the farmer the right way" and in verse 29 that "All this also comes from the LORD Almighty, wonderful in counsel and magnificent in wisdom." Rookmaaker also notices more than prophecy in this text,

> In Isaiah 28:23–29, in the midst of very strong and awful prophecies about God's judgment, Isaiah stops and exclaims what a miracle it is that God gave us wheat and the possibility to make bread out of it—a kind of grass that can be turned into bread!—and he reminds the people that it was God who taught the farmers how to handle all the different crops. He stands in wonder that God cares about all these things. Religion is not something high but something that encompasses even the cultivation of our land and the baking of our bread.[265]

Rookmaaker uses this as an example of God's concern for every aspect of life. However, the verses teach more than concern, God acts. God reveals in this passage of Scripture that he reveals outside of Scripture (v. 26), that this revelation concerns more than spiritual truth (vv. 24–28), but even revelation about how to tend to crops teaches people about God's character (v. 29). In essence, God teaches humans about the baking of bread as well as the breaking of bread, both of which are divine revelation.

Likewise, God gives wisdom regarding how to make priestly garments for Aaron to those he selected (Exod 28:3).[266] God even instructs the Israelites about the most base things in life (Deut. 23: 12–13). Revelation through Scripture not only addresses the need of man to turn to God, it also instructs the Israelites "[a]bout having a fence round your roof, otherwise somebody might fall off it."[267] Knowledge regarding the created order which enables humanity to better live finds inclusion among the content of divine revelation.

In summary, God reveals his attributes through all forms of revelation. He encourages humanity to study creation and he reveals to humanity through this created order. We can say that "all knowledge of nature and history as we acquire and apply it in our occupations and business, in commerce and industry, in the arts and sciences, is due to the revelation of

---

264. Turnau, "Popular Culture as Meaningful," 278. See also Bavinck, *Reformed Dogmatics*, 1: 341.

265. Rookmaaker, *God's Hand in History*, 174.

266. Edwards points to this as an example of all knowledge, even of business, coming from God. Edwards, "A Divine and Supernatural Light," 409.

267. Rookmaaker, *God's Hand in History*, 171.

God."[268] As Johnson concludes the various fields of study enable us to hear and respond to God:

> Not only the natural sciences but also the humanities study general revelation, because human cultures constitute responses to the divinely-designed environment. Thus in one way or another not only biology, physics, chemistry and astronomy but also language, literature, philosophy, history, psychology, sociology, politics, economics and the fine arts are means of listening, directly or indirectly, to the voice of God.[269]

Following Calvin, we should not "divide God's revelation of himself in creation from his revelation of himself in his Word."[270] Instead, we might "preach scientifically oriented sermons that focus on natural phenomena" and exhort our "congregation in the pursuit and study of science!"[271] However, to do so, we must diligently study both Scripture and the created order. Before we can examine the relationship between these forms of revelation, we must look at the effects of revelation.

Effects of Revelation

If the goal of life is securing one's salvation and exhorting others to do likewise, then the effects of revelation reflect this goal. Most succinctly, "The purpose of revelation is the salvation of man (2 Ti. 3:15)."[272] And the term revelation "signifies in its last and highest theological meaning the unveiling or disclosing of God's redeeming purpose to mankind."[273] God then reveals

---

268. Bavinck, *Reformed Dogmatics*, 1:341.

269. Johnson, "Between Two Wor(l)ds," 75.

270. Wilson, "Theater of God," 85.

271. Young, *John Calvin*, 192.

272. Towns, *Theology*, 33. The written Word does explain the need for and content of salvation, but by itself it does not save. Instead, salvation is by grace through faith which is a gift from God (Eph 2). Scripture provides the content of faith, but not the means of faith, the Spirit convicts of sin and gives the gift of faith. So, some, like the Pharisees, may study Scripture, but still not find eternal life (John 5). Many people encountered Jesus but still did not believe. Conversely, one may ponder the creation, see the goodness of God, and then the Spirit enables him to believe the message of the Gospel once presented with it. The Westminster Confession of Faith asserts that the necessity of the Spirit "for the saving understanding of such things as are revealed in the Word." Leith, "Westminster," 195.

273. Pope, *Christian Theology*, 1:36. Later he states, "Revelation, in the stricter, deeper, and fuller sense, is the unfolding of the eternal counsel of God in Christ, for the restoration of man to fellowship with Himself" (37).

"himself only inasmuch and insofar as he deems necessary for our invocation of him for *our salvation* and life."[274] Scripture provides information leading to salvation whereas the created order does not.[275] Since the created order does not offer knowledge for salvation, then it serves little purpose. As Anderson and Gangadean summarize, "If the goal [of the Christian life] is justification (salvation), and this is communicated in special revelation, then there is little or no need for natural theology."[276]

The created order, then, merely provides a point of contact between the redeemed and unredeemed as Paul uses it in Acts 17.[277] Though the created order does not provide clear information for the salvation of people it "has for its object the supplying of the natural need of the man and the persuasion of the soul to seek after the true God."[278] The redeemed should therefore "look for 'points of contact' with people in our culture, including 'truth' found in magazines, movies, culture, events, reason, sports, etc. We can then applaud truth where it is found and use it as a means to establish a beachhead with unbelievers."[279] If God reveals only to save people, then revelation given through the created order simply allows for conversation between the redeemed and the unredeemed with the goal of salvation.[280] The created order does provide a point of contact, but this is not its only effect.

The created order also "fulfills its duty by rendering man without excuse."[281] Or as Oden writes, the created order "performs the negative function of leaving humanity without excuse if any should ever claim that they never knew God existed."[282] Said a bit differently, general revelation provides "every human being enough of God's revelation so that no one has an excuse to reject God on the basis of place of residence or status of

---

274. Horton, *Christian Faith*, 123; emphasis added. See also Higgins, "God's Inspired Word," 62.

275. Street, "Biblical Counseling," 217; Thorsen, *Christian Theology*, 28; and Stott, *Evangelical Truth*, 38.

276. Anderson and Gangadean, "Natural Theology," 82. On page 81, Anderson and Gangadean define natural theology as "attempts to show what can be known of God and man and good and evil from general revelation."

277. Dockery, *Renewing Minds*, 81. See also Lightner, *Evangelical Theology*, 11.

278. Thiessen, *Systematic Theology*, 32.

279. Herrick, "Is the Bible the Only Revelation of God?"

280. Ironically evangelicals "have neglected sober analysis of nature, human society and the arts" which they could use as points of contact with the unredeemed. Noll, *Scandal*, 4.

281. Street, "Biblical Counseling," 217. See also Lightner, *Evangelical Theology*, 11.

282. Oden, *Classic Christianity*, 18.

education."[283] The above quotes make it sound as though God is covering his bases. Quite the contrary, humanity faces condemnation because of original sin.[284] God needs no further reason to condemn rebellious people.

Instead, God greatly desires for all to know him. As Peter explains, "The Lord is not slow in keeping his promise, as some understand slowness. He is patient with you, not wanting anyone to perish, but everyone to come to repentance."[285] God graciously reveals himself to all and makes it so plain that people understand. Unfortunately, fallen people suppress his revelation which then results in their inexcusability when they stand before God.[286] The fact that suppressing revelation given through the created order leads to condemnation affirms two things: (1) the clarity and importance of revelation given through creation, and (2) the sinfulness of mankind.[287] The revelation itself does not judge or condemn, but suppression of it does leave people without excuse. What if God reveals for more reasons than the salvation of people? Does revelation produce other effects?

If the "goal of life is knowing and enjoying God," then Charry suggest that this "occurs on two fronts. One is the sphere of God's works in history: creation, the Incarnation, and so forth. The other is the spiritual sphere—a proper understanding of the qualities of God."[288] The Christian life entails more than waiting for the eternal state.[289] Therefore both the created order and Scripture serve important functions.

283. Gulley also states, "The function of universal (general) revelation is to give every human being enough of God's revelation so that no one has an excuse to reject God on the basis of residence or status of education. Even the disadvantaged living in the Third World, without the ability to read, are still humans loved by God, and He can lead them to be open to His revelation and working through nature, history, and human life." Gulley, *Systematic Theology*, 210.

284. Gen 2:17.

285. 2 Pet 3:9.

286. Rom 1 explicitly points out that condemnation results when one suppresses revelation given through the created order. However, rejection of the Incarnation and of Scripture also results in condemnation.

287. Sinners reject all three forms of revelation (Scripture, Incarnation, and the created order). Ultimately, rejecting revelation leads to condemnation. Only those who, by the enablement of the Spirit, respond rightly to revelation and become freed by the "law of the Spirit" avoid condemnation. Rom 8:1–2.

288. Charry, *Renewing of Your Minds*, 128.

289. The Dutch Reformed thinker, Hans Rookmaaker, exhorts Christians to approach life as Christians. He critiques the notion that Christianity is fundamentally about saving souls. Instead, "To save souls is not enough, because a saved soul will go to heaven after the person dies but we need to have people who live and know reality now. We need to turn back to the living God, because God is a God of life." He continues, "Christ died in order that we might be living human beings. He did not die just simply

If justification "is a return to the work of natural theology that was given to humanity in the beginning before the Fall and the need for special revelation" then "[t]his makes natural theology necessary and supremely important. It is not simply a tool of apologetics; it is the source of joy in a believer's life."[290] If justification entails both "setting aside unrighteousness" *and* "seeking and understanding God" then, "Natural theology is therefore necessary not as a means to convert others but as a source of joy in the life of every believer."[291] Joy comes in seeking to know God now as he reveals himself through the Incarnation, Scripture, and the created order.

Revelation (created order, written Word, incarnation) supplies knowledge of God, man, creation and the relationships between each. Scripture provides information about God, man, and the rest of creation. Evangelicals use Scripture to build a worldview by which to live and view life. Scripture shows how God relates to his creation and provides information of God unattainable elsewhere (three in one, Jesus is both God and man). The Incarnate Christ also revealed information regarding God, man and the rest of creation. Similarly, through creation man learns about God, himself and the rest of creation (see above). The created order "teaches God's character and glory; it is a school for the Christian life."[292] Such revelation "can enhance our knowledge of God."[293]

Revelation (in all of its forms) calls forth worship from the created to the Creator.[294] People respond to revelation by praising the God revealed.[295] The Psalmist exhorts all of creation (angels and heavens to praise God [Ps 148:1–5], the earth and its living creatures [Ps 148:7–10], and the nations [Ps 148:11–13]) to praise God because God revealed himself to and through his chosen people (Ps 148:14). Similarly, Matthew expects that the unredeemed will praise God when they see him revealed through the testimony

---

to forgive sins but to achieve much more, to make us new men and women (Romans 6 and Colossians 2). Christ died in order to make normal human life possible, to make freedom and love possible, to make life meaningful." Rookmaaker, *God's Hand in History*, 171.

290. Anderson and Gangadean, "Natural Theology," 82.
291. Ibid.
292. Butler, "God's Visible Glory," 16. See also Baker, *Dispensational Theology*, 33.
293. Moore, *Consider the Lilies*, 89.
294. Dockery, *Christian Scripture*, 19; Allison and Anthony, "Revelation, Scripture, and Christian Education," 77; Moore, *Consider the Lilies*, 89; and Johnston, "Discerning the Spirit in Culture," 60.
295. The Psalmist meditates on God's works (Ps 143:5), tells others about God's works, and praises God because of his works (Ps 145).

of his people.²⁹⁶ The revelation of God throughout creation should lead to worship because "wonder is the normal response to splendor."²⁹⁷

Edwards preaches: "If we look to the heavens or the earth; or birds, beasts, or fishes; or plants and trees: if we do but take notice of it, they all declare to us that we ought to worship, to fear, to love and obey, the God that made all these things. The workmanship of God in our own bodies and souls proclaims the same: all the creatures do declare the same thing."²⁹⁸ Yet, along with praise, honor, obedience, worship, and thanksgiving comprise proper responses to God's revelation. Scripture itself expects such responses from the hearer or reader and they are appropriate responses to the Incarnate Son of God. As Moore affirms, "Pastors and church leaders, then, would do well to point to general revelation—as informed by special revelation—to prompt Christians to worship their covenant God."²⁹⁹

Revelation can lead people to maturity. One purpose of knowledge of God (revelation) is "to foster Christian growth (2 Pet. 3:18)."³⁰⁰ Spiritual growth can come from appropriate responses to God's revelation. Paul tells Timothy that God inspired Scripture for correction, reproof, teaching and training in godliness. The inspired and written Word teaches, corrects, and trains in righteousness so that the believer is "equipped for every good work" (2 Tim 3:16). The God-man challenged those who walked with him toward spiritual growth. Knowledge of God through creation should lead to greater love for and joy in God as well as greater conformity to God.³⁰¹

God creates and reveals for his own personal delight. People do not see much of God's revelation given through the created order. Scripture (Isa 43:7; 48:11; 61:3) teaches that the Creator designed people to "mirror God's holiness and righteousness back to God, not so *we* may benefit (though there are immeasurable benefits to personal godliness), but so God will be glorified in beholding himself in his creatures."³⁰² God takes delight when he looks in the "mirror of creation" and sees himself. As Butler summarizes, "God is an Artist who needs no audience; he delights in his own creation."³⁰³

---

296. Matt 5:16.

297. Dubay, *Evidential Power of Beauty*, 18.

298. Edwards, "The Duty of Hearkening to God's Voice," 440. He also cautions, "It don't make God the happier to be praised." Edwards, *"Miscellanies" (Entry Nos. a–z, aa–zz, 1–500)*, 410.

299. Moore, "Natural Revelation," 114.

300. Ryrie, *Basic Theology*, 29. Though Ryrie might likely narrow this to special revelation, no such differentiation appears as he speaks of knowledge of God.

301. Kreider, *Jonathan Edwards*, 127. See also Moore, *Consider the Lilies*, 89.

302. Hannah, *Glorify God*, 19.

303. Butler, "God's Visible Glory," 18.

God reveals for his own pleasure. For example, Gen 9:16 teaches that the rainbow reminds God of his promise to never flood the earth. Furthermore, much of the creation remains undiscovered or at best rarely seen by people. God reserves this for his enjoyment. Mouw, reflecting on Ps 104:31, posits: "There is good reason to believe that the Lord is gratified by glowing sunsets and ocean waves breaking on a rocky coastline and a cherry tree in bloom and the speed of a leopard on the chase—and all of this without any necessary reference to elect and non-elect human beings."[304] We receive a glimpse of this when we read that the whale frolics for the pleasure of God.[305]

Broadening our understanding of the effects of revelation can result in greater use of the created order as revelation. Salvation may be one effect of revelation, but not the only one. Scripture tells the story of salvation in propositional form. So, evangelicals reserve a special place of prominence for it. Certainly pitfalls exist when overstating the significance of the created order as revelation, but dangers of a "truncated doctrine of God's wider revelation," can include an ineffective witness and "stunting one's own spiritual growth."[306] The question of where sinners find reliable information regarding salvation is important. However, the effects of revelation extend beyond the salvation of mankind. Understanding the numerous functions of revelation increases the value of the created order without diminishing the unique worth of Scripture. Now we turn to the relationship between the created order and Scripture.

Relationship between Forms of Revelation

Descriptions of the relationship between Scripture and the created order as forms of revelation tend to fall into four categories. Scripture (written Word) *corrects* our understanding of the created order (world), Scripture *supplements* the created order, the created order *demonstrates* the teaching of Scripture, or Scripture and the created order relate in a *complementary* way.

First, Scripture *corrects* our understanding of the created order. Williams writes, "The word of God in special revelation comes to people not to supplement what they already know, but to *correct* what is distorted and darkened and to bring forth new truth."[307] Kantzer identifies this as a re-

---

304. Mouw, *He Shines in All That's Fair*, 35
305. Ps 104:26.
306. Johnston, "Discerning the Spirit in Culture," 67.
307. Williams, *Renewal Theology*, 1:38; emphasis added.

storative relationship. Special revelation "restores natural revelation to its pristine glory" and "enables one to read the book of nature with glasses on so that he may see what is really there and was always available, but which he has incorrectly understood because of his own spiritual astigmatism."[308]

One's interpretations of Scripture might correct faulty interpretations of the created order. However, since revelation comes from God and retains his character, one form of revelation does not correct another form of revelation. More specifically, "The purpose of special revelation is not to correct, much less to set aside general revelation. General revelation needs no correction—God has not revealed himself falsely or misleadingly in it."[309] Rather, each form of revelation contributes to greater understanding of the other form of revelation.

Second, Scripture *supplements* the created order. As Wiley concludes, "The revelation in the Holy Scripture is not meant to supersede His revelation in nature but to *supplement* it."[310] Wiley identifies the "Incarnate Word and the Holy Scriptures" as "higher disclosures" than revelation given through the created order.[311] He writes, "General revelation is basic and fundamental, but from the very nature of things implies a revelation on a *higher* and personal plane."[312] Enns explains that general revelation "is essential and preliminary to God's special revelation."[313] Similarly, Gulley identifies the created order as "a means to lead to particular revelation."[314] He also explains the limitation of general revelation as "its inability to say anything about Jesus Christ. Thus the very center of particular revelation is absent in general revelation."[315] Strong points out that Scriptures supplement natural revelation because it does not provide knowledge for salvation.[316] Since the "central message of the Bible is God's redemption of mankind" then "special revelation [is] an absolute necessity as a *supplement* to general revelation."[317] Therefore, "General revelation serves as a *foundation* upon which the special

---

308. Kantzer, "The Communication of Revelation," 69.
309. Warfield, *Revelation and Inspiration*, 27.
310. Wiley, *Christian Theology*, 1:139, emphasis added.
311. Ibid., 1:126.
312. Ibid., 1:135, emphasis added.
313. Enns, *Handbook of Theology*, 156.
314. Gulley, *Systematic Theology*, 213.
315. Ibid.
316. Strong, *Systematic Theology*, 26, 28.
317. Earle, "Revelation and Inspiration," 290, emphasis added.

revelation of the Scriptures is built."[318] Hoffmeier writes, "God provides special revelation to complement and complete creational revelation."[319]

Demarest also illustrates the created order as a foundation upon which Scripture builds. He illustrates "the indivisible relationship between the two kinds of revelation" in a triangle with general revelation as the base and special revelation as the top. But he quotes Kuyper stating the singularity of the knowledge of God " 'the content of which has flowed to use from *both* sources, whose waters have mingled themselves.' "[320] The diagram fails to illustrate the explanatory quote which he borrows from Kuyper. The triangle may represent a singular knowledge, but Demarest clearly divides the triangle into two distinct parts with a hard line separating special revelation from general revelation. Furthermore, the triangle depicts a hierarchy of special revelation over general revelation. The picture may represent general revelation as a foundation for special revelation. However, the image does not show that "general revelation and special revelation constitute a two-volume work that is incomplete and quite useless if either volume is missing" much less the intermingling of the two forms of revelation.[321]

Since Scripture provides unique content (see "Content"), which leads to salvation (see "Effects"), then Scripture does in this sense supplement the created order. However, this is not the only potential relationship between Scripture and the created order. Scripture does not always serve in a hierarchical relationship to the created order.

Third, the created order either *demonstrates* (or *amplifies*) the teaching of Scripture.[322] Horner holds that the created order demonstrates the teaching of Scripture. He writes, "For the believer, these extrascriptural truths do not compete with Scripture, nor do they supplement it in the strictest sense; their value lies in their demonstration that what Scripture says about man is true and valid."[323] As Edwards observes,

> The manifestations God makes of himself in his works are the principal manifestations of his perfections, and the declarations and teaching of his Word are to lead to those; by God's declaring and teaching that he is infinitely powerful or wise, the creature believes that he is powerful and wise as he teaches, but in seeing

---

318. Moore, "Natural Revelation," 114, emphasis added.

319. Hoffmeier, "Limits of General Revelation," 21.

320. Demarest, *General Revelation*, 251. He quotes Kuyper, *Sacred Theology*, 158.

321. Demarest, *General Revelation*, 251.

322. Bouma states that the practice of evangelicals suggests that creation at best confirms the teaching of Scripture. Bouma, "Creation's Persistent Voice," 2.

323. Horner, *Meaning at the Movies*, 29.

his mighty and wise works, the effects of his power and wisdom, the creature not only hears and believes, but sees his power and wisdom.[324]

Moore agrees, "General revelation speaks the same thing as the Word, but illuminates, amplifies and makes them more powerful to alter our lives."[325] For example, reading the proposition "God is sovereign" differs from reading of his sovereignty as the Israelites cross the Red Sea. The narrative story differs from the experience of that particular group of Israelites, but all teach of God's sovereignty. Or as Edwards states, "It is not he that has heard a long description of the sweetness of honey that can be said to have the greatest understanding of it, but he that has tasted."[326] Certainly, at times the created order does demonstrate or amplify the teaching of Scripture, but this is not the only relationship between the two.

Fourth, Scripture and the created order exist in *complementary* relationship. Ostrander sees revelation given through the created order as unique. He writes, ". . . the doctrine of Creation implies that the universe is God's journal which reveals things about him that we *would not learn in any other way*."[327] Since the created order and Scripture originate in God "science (general revelation) and theology (particular revelation) should agree."[328] Revelation comes from God and retains his character therefore one form of revelation does not contradict other forms of revelation.

Chronologically, God revealed through the created order first.[329] The created order "is the first revelation of God, the beginning and foundation of all subsequent revelation."[330] And yet God provides an interpretative framework (creation, fall, and redemption) in Scripture which better enables people to understand the created order. The written Word provides humanity with crucial information regarding redemption. However, even with regard to redemption one can look to the created order for increased understanding. For example, Edwards "typically turns to nature in order to gain a deeper understanding of God's will and his work in accomplishing his grand purpose of redemption. He also finds nature to be a perfect il-

---

324. Edwards, *"Miscellanies,"* 501–832, 430.

325. Moore, *Consider the Lilies*, 128. Revelation given through the creation does amplify that which God gave in Scripture. See the section above on "content" for an explanation of the uniqueness of revelation given through the created order.

326. Edwards, *Sermons and Discourses, 1723–1729*, 80.

327. Ostrander, *Why College Matters to God*, 97–98, emphasis added.

328. Gulley, *Systematic Theology*, 192.

329. Conner, *Revelation and God*, 79.

330. Bavinck, *Reformed Dogmatics*, 1:307.

lustrator. And he uses nature's illustrations to guide others in understanding God's ways."[331] So, the created order precedes Scripture, but "[t]he book of Scripture is the interpreter of the book of nature."[332] These two forms of revelation complement and mutually interpret one another.

In fact, "One does not simply come to the Scriptures with a blank mind and then rationalistically interpret the Bible. For the Bible is always interpreted through experience, tradition and reason."[333] Interpreting the written Word assumes knowledge of the world, linguistics, grammar, history, geography, and psychology, for example. Augustine teaches that God's revelation through creation aids in interpreting Scripture.[334] Augustine affirms that history aids us "in understanding the Scriptures even if it be learnt without the pale of the Church."[335] The knowledge of language, our own as well as Greek, Hebrew, and Aramaic, enables readers to understand Scripture. He also affirms the use of knowledge "about the situation of places and the nature of animals, trees, plants, herbs, stones, and other bodies" because "this kind of knowledge is serviceable [sic] in solving the difficulties of Scripture."[336] Finally, we should employ literature even though "Mercury is reputed to be its presiding deity."[337]

Erickson highlights the complementary relationship of the created order and Scripture, "general revelation therefore required the special revelation. The special revelation, however, requires the general revelation as well. Without the general revelation, humans would not possess the concepts regarding God that enable them to know and understand the God of the special revelation."[338] Erickson affirms that, "The two mutually require each other and are harmonious. Only if the two are developed in isolation from one another does there seem to be any conflict between them. They

---

331. Nichols, *Jonathan Edwards*, 122.

332. Crampton, *Meet Jonathan Edwards*, 43.

333. Wood, "The Wesleyan View," 95.

334. Augustine's "Christian Doctrine" addresses "The entire treatment of the Scriptures is based upon two factors: the method of discovering what we are to understand and the method of teaching what has been understood." Augustine, "Christian Doctrine," 515.

335. Ibid., 549.

336. Ibid.

337. Nor should we shun music "because of the superstitions of the heathen, if we can derive anything from it that is of use for our understanding of Holy Scripture." Ibid., 544–45.

338. Erickson, *Christian Theology*, 203.

have a common subject matter and perspective, yielding a harmonious and complementary understanding."[339]

Bavinck also sees a mutual reinforcement between general and special revelation. He states,

> But as a disclosure of the greatness of God's heart, special revelation far surpasses general revelation, which makes known to us the power of his mind. General revelation leads to special, special revelation points back to general. The one calls for the other, and without it remains imperfect and unintelligible. Together they proclaim the manifold wisdom which God has displayed in creation and redemption.[340]

In his *Reformed Dogmatics*, Bavinck highlights the relationship between the created order and Scripture. He relates Scripture and creation back to the Incarnation when he asserts that all revelation "finds its fulfillment and meaning in Christ."[341] He affirms the creation when he states,

> In no way should the Christian faith be represented as otherworldly or anti-creation. Rather, grace and nature are united in the Christian faith, and general revelation links the kingdom of heaven and the kingdom of earth—it joins creation and redemption together in one great eschatological cantata of praise. Grace restores nature, a religious life is woven into the very fabric of ordinary human experience. Finally, God is one and the same loving God in creation and redemption; grace restores nature.[342]

Both the created order and Scripture come together in Christ as complementary forms of revelation.

What if our *interpretations* of Scripture and creation contradict? Then we should hold the ideas in tension, check presuppositions on both sides, and diligently research all areas. As Packer states,

> The truth is that the facts of nature yield positive help in many ways for interpreting Scripture statements correctly, and the discipline of wrestling with the problem of relating the two sets of facts, natural and biblical, leads to a greatly enriched understanding of both. Not only does the book of Scripture throw light on the meaning of the book of nature; the book of nature reflects some of that light back on to Scripture, so that we

---

339. Ibid.
340. Bavinck, *Philosophy of Revelation*, 28.
341. Bavinck, *Reformed Dogmatics*, 1:302.
342. Ibid.

may read its message more clearly. It is through the ferment of thought created by such interaction that theological insight is deepened and the relevance of the gospel more fully grasped.[343]

As with Calvin and many through church history, we affirm the centrality of Scripture. Wilson observes that, "John Calvin wrote, taught, and preached as though the Bible were the sun around which everything else revolved."[344] Scripture maintains authority as a central point. Wilson notices the "authoritative *centrality* of God's Word" in Calvin.[345] But this centrality included room for the created order as revelation from God. In other words, "Regarding knowledge of God, the claim is not that we must hold the Bible as a *first* premise, but that Scripture is of *prime* importance."[346]

Yet, technically, Scripture does not interpret the created order nor does the created order interpret Scripture. They both exist as two forms of divine revelation. People read and interpret the text of the created order and Scripture. People do not read one form *through* the other. Instead, we read both as people within time and space. Correct understanding of either and both comes as people understand them in relation to Christ (Col 3). However, finite and fallen people depend upon the work of the Spirit for accurate interpretation. The Spirit gives the gift of faith, but also opens the eyes of people (and communities) to more accurately understand that which they believe. Bavinck explains how revelation through creation remains the same, but the perspectives of people change. In reference to the founding of natural science by Francis Bacon, Bavinck writes,

> . . . they found God again in their own lives and hearts, and they also again discovered him all around in nature. This nature remained the same, but the human person had changed. They viewed nature differently, looking at it in a new light, in the light that had arisen in their own soul through God's revelation. And when such people looked at nature from that perspective, they stood amazed at its beauty and glory . . . Nature, seen in God's light, was not a seducing, satanic power but a revelation of God's glory and a marvelous creation of unity and harmony.[347]

They studied nature "because they wanted to know God from his works."[348]

---

343. Packer, *Fundamentalism*, 134–35.
344. Wilson, "Theater of God," 92.
345. Ibid., 93; emphasis added.
346. Clark, *Know and Love God*, 87.
347. Bavinck, "Christianity and Natural Science," 98–99.
348. Ibid., 99.

Furthermore, the Spirit works to transform the church and the individual. The active involvement of the Spirit comes as people encounter God's revelation. He uses both forms of revelation to transform the life and thinking of the church. Such transformation in turn enables people to more faithfully interpret his revelation in its various forms. Marsden writes, "Edwards believed that he could develop a unified account of all knowledge but it could not be discovered by experience and reason alone."[349] He believed that "God might speak in all of nature and in all of life, but the only place where one could find the key to unlock the whole system was in Scripture.... The starting point for unraveling the mysteries of the universe must be the shattering revelation of one's total inadequacy and a recognition of God's love in Jesus Christ."[350] Personal transformation is vital to begin grasping the relationship between forms of revelation, "One who was so changed could then experience how all creation was one harmonious hymn of praise to the glories of the Creator and the mercies of Christ. Without the grace that gave sinful and rebellious people ears to hear, they would never hear the sublime Christ-like choruses or see how the particular notes of reality all fit together."[351] Edwards exemplifies this approach.

Jonathan Edwards: An Example

Jonathan Edwards serves as an example of one for which "nature . . . is as much God's self-revelation as the Scripture."[352] We see this reflected in subsections of some of his works. For example, his *Dissertation Concerning the End for which God Created the World* contains the following chapter titles "Wherein is Considered What Reason Teaches Concerning this Affair," and "Wherein it is Inquired, What is to be Learned from Holy Scripture Concerning God's Last End in the Creation of the World."[353] The reader finds this approach throughout his works. Another example comes when Edwards argues for original sin "from the empirical evidence of human evil (most of Part One), from Scripture (Parts Two and Three), and from reason (most of part Four and some of Part One)."[354]

Similarly Edwards begins some of his sermons by explaining Scripture, but then follow up by demonstrating the reasonableness of the belief.

349. Marsden, *Jonathan Edwards*, 81.
350. Ibid.
351. Ibid.
352. Lee, "Edwards on God and Nature," 35.
353. Edwards, *History of the Work of Redemption*.
354. Helm, "Great Christian Doctrine (Original Sin)," 177.

For example, in "A Divine and Supernatural Light," Edwards explains Matt 16:17, then he summarizes the doctrine taught by this passage and expounds upon each point of the doctrine, finally, he sets to "show the truth of the doctrine; that is, to show that there is such a thing as that spiritual light that has been described thus immediately let into the mind by God. And here I would show briefly, that this doctrine is both scriptural, and rational."[355]

Edwards maintains a special place for Scripture. In his notebook on types Edwards states "The book of Scriptures is the interpreter of the book of nature . . . ."[356] However, "if Edwards had been asked to rank Scripture, reason, and experience in order of importance for theology, he would undoubtedly have ranked Scripture first. But he would have thought that the choice we were offering him was rather unnecessary, and indeed superficial. For it is evident from his patterns of thought . . . that he saw each of the three as complementing each other."[357] Edwards even held that knowledge from creation can enlarge our understanding of Scripture. As Kreider observes, "Jonathan Edwards was convinced that what he could learn about the rainbow through studying nature and science would aid in his interpretation of this symbol."[358] However, in his miscellanies, Edwards consistently noted the importance of Scripture in contrast to the position of the deists.

Applying typology to Scripture is not unique with Edwards. The extent to which he applied it and the idea that typology applies to nature is unique for Edwards.[359] "Although Edwards interpreted nature as providing signs or images of divine things, Scripture takes priority."[360] Through this methodology Edwards affirms the relationship between Scripture and the created order as forms of divine revelation. He is not alone in his affirmation.

Herman Bavinck: An Example

Dutch Reformed theologian Herman Bavinck "is an excellent example of how Christian theology integrates with other disciplines."[361] His work *Essays on Religion, Science, and Society* covers topics such as religious studies,

---

355. Edwards, "A Divine and Supernatural Light," 408–17, 417.

356. Edwards, *Typological Writings*, 106.

357. Helm, "Great Christian Doctrine (Original Sin)," 177.

358. Kreider, *Jonathan Edwards*, 98.

359. Ibid., 99.

360. Ibid., 100.

361. Kreider, Review of *Essays on Religion*, 107. Hans Rookmaaker, another Dutch Reformed thinker, also serves as a fine example. Rookmaaker, *God's Hand in History*.

psychology, aesthetics and education.[362] As Bolt observes, one must grasp Bavinck's "insistence on taking creation seriously as God's revelation without in any way diminishing the necessity of biblical revelation" in order to understand these essays.[363]

Each essay provides a fine example of how both Scripture and the created order come together to form a Christian understanding of some particular area. Bavinck brings to bear both forms of revelation (Scripture and the created order) on each topic. For example, his chapter on aesthetics demonstrates a keen awareness of art theory and prominent philosophies of aesthetics.[364] His reflection on these along with the created order and the Bible spill onto the page as he puts forth his own theology of aesthetics: "We cannot express in words what a valuable gift the Creator of all things has granted to his children. He is the Lord of glory and spreads his beauty lavishly before our eyes in all his works. His name is precious in the whole earth, and while he did not leave us without a witness, he also fills our hearts with happiness when we observe that glory."[365] Bavinck continues, "Beauty is the harmony that still shines through the chaos in the world; by God's grace, beauty is observed, felt, translated by artists; it is prophecy and guarantee that this world is not destined for ruin but for glory—a glory for which there is a longing deep in every human heart."[366] Bavinck's work illustrates how reading and responding to both forms of revelation over time impacts how one understands each form of revelation in turn. The product of a lifetime of diligently studying the created order and Scripture yield an integrated product.

Conclusion

Revelation is divine disclosure. God freely chooses to reveal to those whom he created. This revelation comes in three primary forms; namely, the created order, Scripture, and the Incarnation. The three forms have many similarities, such as; they come from God and therefore are true, authoritative, and sufficient. Though what each of the above adjectives means for each form may vary. For instance, the created order does not have authority over matters of salvation, but it does over mathematical principles. God

---

362. Bavinck, *Essays on Religion*.

363. Bolt, "Editor's Introduction," 8.

364. Bavinck, *Essays on Religion*, 245–60. He covers in brief Plato, Shelling, Kant, and Fechner.

365. Ibid., 259.

366. Ibid.

accommodates revelation by disclosing transcendent truth progressively and in mediated ways. Finite and fallen people interpret each form. Inevitably, finite people only know in part and many times in error. The Spirit of God enables people to rightly interpret or respond to all divine revelation. Therefore, the redeemed may learn from the unredeemed as each responds to the created order.

Scripture and the created order overlap as God reveals himself; his attributes through each form. And yet, each form provides information in ways not provided by the other form. As one author observed, "One can picture both kinds of revelation in a relationship of ongoing continuity."[367] In the end, Scripture and the created order are two forms of divine revelation read by people. As people read both forms of revelation the transforming work of the Spirit then changes how the person or community then reads the other form of revelation. In this sense, both forms of revelation come from God to many and form a unity of truth to which people must respond. The effects of revelation include the salvation of man, but they extend beyond that to maturity and divine pleasure. When examining the commonalities between forms of revelation a greater case is made for reading revelation given through the created order and using it in theological development and efforts at integration.

---

367. Felker Jones, *Christian Doctrine*, 37.

6

Conclusion

In the above, I provided a critical examination of the doctrine of revelation in evangelical theology. I attempted to show the confusion that exists regarding revelation and in particular the created order as revelation (commonly referred to as general revelation). Evangelicals teach that God reveals through created order and use Ps 19 and Rom 1 as text supporting this teaching. Most refer to this form of revelation as "general revelation" stating that all people, at all times, and in all places have access to it. Furthermore, evangelicals routinely tie revelation to truth and affirm that all truth comes from God, regardless of form. However, when explaining the relationship between Scripture and the created order, as two primary forms of revelation, many evangelicals emphasize Scripture to the neglect of the created order. The neglect of the created order is seen in both evangelical systematic theologies as well as works on the topic of integration.

I evaluated roughly eighty systematic theologies, dividing them into three categories based on stated method. Those explaining systematic theology as systematizing verses taught the reality of the created order as revelation. They also used sources outside of Scripture and made some use of the created order.[1] The theologians defining systematic theology as systematizing doctrine often mentioned that the doctrines come from Scrip-

---

1. Use of the created order often meant that the author included the philosophical proofs for God's existence, cited or quoted positions in opposition to their own from the field of science, provided illustrations to clarify their teaching, or made suggestions for application of the doctrine. Some used the created order as additional evidence for some teaching found in Scripture. On a rare occasion, some theologians integrated the created order and Scripture.

ture alone. Though, like those systematizing verses, these theologians often used sources from outside of Scripture and made minimal use of the created order. Finally, those who view systematic theology as systematizing all truth (Scripture and the created order) differed little from the other two groups in actual methodology. They largely systematized Scripture with some use of tradition and little use of the created order.

In light of the above findings, I argued in favor of an understanding of systematic theology that emphasizes bringing together truth from all sources (both Scripture and creation). Such a methodology assumes a role for the created order in forming systematic theology. One example comes from Chafer who writes, "Systematic Theology may be defined as the collecting, scientifically arranging, comparing, exhibiting, and defending of all facts from any and every source concerning God and His works."[2] I pointed to other contemporary theologians exhorting evangelicals to examine the created order or at least dialogue with specialists in other fields of study. Systematic theology that takes the created order into serious consideration understands that theology is man's response to divine revelation. Systematic theologies attempt to communicate transcendent truth in time and space. These theologies understand that addressing contemporary issues requires studying both Scripture and the world around us (culture and physical creation). Understanding that the Bible does not contain all truth, the works reflect inter-disciplinary dialogue.

I also examined how evangelicals in various fields of study explain and practice faith-learning integration. At its core, integration represents evangelicals trying to understand the relationship between the created order and Scripture as two forms of revelation. The central beliefs that lead to faith-learning integration suggest the process should result in a two-way dialogue between interpretations of Scripture and the created order. Presuppositions underlying integration include an understanding that reality is unified, belief that all truth comes from and points to God, God reveals truth, and Scripture retains a prime role in integration. I assert that these beliefs suggest that the created order and Scripture mutually inform one another.

However, the tendency of evangelicals toward neglecting the created order as a form of revelation also manifests in efforts at the integration of faith and learning. In practice, evangelicals take one of four stances regarding the relationship between Scripture and the created order. Some take a "Bible only" approach stating that the created order, at best, reiterates what Scripture clearly teaches. Others speak of integration in uni-directional terms where Scripture (or one's worldview derived from Scripture) informs

---

2. Chafer, *Systematic Theology*, 1:6.

one's study of the created order, but the created order does not in turn inform our reading of Scripture. Yet others begin with mutual integration, but then if one's interpretation of these two forms conflicts then he prefers the reading. In other words, thorough study of both forms of revelation occurs, all else is completely equal, the person relies on his interpretation of Scripture instead of holding the findings in tension. Some evangelicals do seek to look at both Scripture and the created order on a particular topic of study.

I argued for the position of mutual integration. Divine revelation comes to us in both Scripture and the created order. Since both of these revelations come from God, then evangelicals must study them. Investigation of both forms of revelation requires dialogue. Only through discussions with others can a fuller picture of God, his creation, and the relationship between the two unfold. The goal of integration is not necessarily seeing the same thing the same way. Instead, the goal often is appreciating a diversity of perspectives and approaches. However, whether we explore our own questions or study the pressing issues determined by the unbelieving world, we always do so as Christians.

So, evangelicals teach that God reveals through the created order. They neglect the created order's usefulness in areas one would expect to see it; namely in systematic theology and integration. I asserted that a theology of revelation might provide a way to fruitfully and appropriately use the created order. However, before proposing such a theology I studied evangelical definitions and categorizations of revelation. I found that a misunderstanding of the relationship between reason and revelation leads to problematic definitions. I also noticed that some contemporary evangelicals categorize revelation based on one aspect (distribution), but then subsume all other aspects under this categorization. They, then, focus on the differences between forms of revelation and fail to see the similarities.

Finally, I proposed a theology of revelation intended to overcome current problems. I synthesized the teachings of Scripture, church history, and contemporary thinkers. I began by asking and answering central questions. These questions include: From whom does revelation come? What form(s) does this revelation take? What are the characteristics of revelation? What is the content of revelation? Who receives revelation? How do the recipients respond to revelation? What effects does revelation have? What does it mean for Scripture to teach that God reveals outside of Scripture? What is the relationship between the Bible as revelation and creation as revelation? Answers to these formed my theology of revelation.

Instead of being the last word on the issue of evangelicals and revelation this work serves as a springboard for discussion and further thinking. A number of directions for future study come to mind. Foremost, build a theology of revelation.³ The proposed theology of revelation above needs expansion. Each facet of revelation could itself turn into a significant article. Covering each area well would require a book devoted solely to the topic.

An improved categorization of revelation can stem from a satisfactory understanding of revelation. The categorizations of general and special revelation prove better than many other terms, yet they lend themselves to a simplistic and "Bible only" preference.⁴ The new category must reflect the commonality and the diversity between forms of revelation. The terms might also tie more closely to ideas from Scripture such as created world, Incarnate word, and written Word. The use of "word" for the three major forms of revelation (created word, Incarnate word, and written Word) may have biblical precedence.⁵ God speaks "in diverse ways: his deeds are words, as in the creation account we read, 'He spoke and so it came to be.' He speaks in the splendors of the universe and through all within it. He teaches in human language, and especially in the words of his incarnate Word."⁶ These reflect two potential ways to speak of the forms of revelation.

Logical next steps include creating a systematic theology that includes learning from the created order in a way that makes positive and substantial contributions. Carter's theology takes steps in this direction with chapters on psychology and social involvement.⁷ Topics such as creation or anthropology provide natural starting points whereby theologians can enter into fruitful dialogue with specialists in other fields of study on issues of mutual

---

3. The evangelical community needs to read the Bible cover to cover asking, "What does this passage teach about revelation?" And conversely read the created order asking "What does this teach us about God, ourselves, and the creation?"

4. It might prove helpful to identify when and why the language of "general" and "special revelation" began.

5. Scripture affirms the use of "word" for both the Incarnation and Scripture itself. Though I use "world" in reference to the created order, one might consider using "word" here as well. Genesis 1 repeatedly refers to creation as a result of God's spoken word. Colossians 1:17 (and Heb 1:3) teach that the Son of God holds together all things. Precedent in the early church for using "book" as a metaphor for nature may suggest the appropriateness of using "word" in reference to creation. Tanzella-Nitti explains, "God creates by his Increated Word and the world conveys a divine logos, i.e., contains and expresses the words of God." Tanzella-Nitti, "Two Books," 236–37. Similarly, Latourelle writes that "[s]ince creation is something said by God it is also revelation." Latourelle, *Theology of Revelation*, 31. Jonathan Edwards states that nature is a divine word: "And as the system of nature and the system of revelation are both divine works, so both are in different senses a divine word, both are the voice of God to intelligent creatures, a manifestation and declaration of Himself to mankind." Edwards, *"Miscellanies," 1153–1360*, 374. See also Ps 33:6 and Tozer, "Speaking Voice."

6. Dubay, *Evidential Power of Beauty*, 335.

7. Ridgway, "Psychology," 875–950; and Thompson, "Social Involvement," 689–732.

interest. Dialogue between theologians and those in other fields of study is necessary. Polkinghorne states:

> If we believe in the unity of knowledge and experience, then advances in understanding in one realm of knowledge modify the tone and limit the range of acceptable insight in all others. There is an inescapable interaction between science and theology, as the whole of intellectual history from Copernicus through Darwin to the present day makes abundantly clear. That history is by no means one of continual warfare. Einstein once said that religion without science is blind and science without religion is lame. The two disciplines need each other.[8]

The same applies to other fields of study. There is much evangelicals can learn from Jonathan Edwards and Dutch Reformed thinkers such as Herman Bavinck and Hans Rookmaaker.

Similarly, examining mutual integration done within a community of evangelicals from various disciplines on specific issues is the next step in integration literature. Discussions of integration must begin with a firm understanding that people *seek to understand the unity that already exists*. Though finite people must analyze the parts "the form of the whole must be seen as a unity ad a totality. Dissecting done aside from this wholeness can distort and mislead, especially when the entire living reality is downplayed or neglected."[9] The term "integration" and the way some write about the topic still suggest a divided reality. Ultimately, mutual integration finds expression in books and articles co-authored by theologians and specialists in other fields on topics of mutual interest.

God reveals through his written Word as well as creation. All evangelicals agree that the written Word provides information that enable people to interpret the created order. Many affirm beliefs that suggest mutual integration can happen, but then either practice or explain uni-directional integration. In reality, people come to Scripture with prior beliefs, experiences, and priorities. These already inform our reading of Scripture. Evangelicals use the written Word to interpret the world, which we use to interpret the written Word. This simply must be done more intentionally. Evangelicals need to embrace the reality of finitude and the interconnectedness of God's creation.

Then, we must intentionally seek out how both the written Word and the created world teach us about God, fellow man, and the rest of creation. The process is less pedantic than the mutual interpretation outlined above.

8. Polkinghorne, "Structure of the Physical World," 40.
9. Dubay, *Evidential Power of Beauty*, 330.

The Spirit and the brain work continuously as people observe the created order and read Scripture. In ways neither theologian nor neuroscientist understand both the created order and the written Word come together to inform the believer of who God is, who we are, and how we relate to him and the rest of the created order. I am merely exhorting evangelicals to read; intentionally and actively, *both* the created order and the Bible and teach others to do likewise. The very "intelligibility of visible reality is a staggering fact that calls for serious pondering."[10]

Finally, we must carry out the Great Commandment (Matt 22:39) which requires knowing my own neighbor by understanding his culture.[11] We must also fulfill the Great Commission. Matthew 28: 18–20 teaches that the redeemed must make disciples and teach them to obey his commandments which occurs in particular cultural contexts. While the redeemed carry out the Great Commandment and the Great Commission we must not forget the Cultural Mandate given in Gen 1: 28. As Plantinga argues "human beings are charged not only with care for earth and animals ('subduing' what's already there) but also with developing certain cultural possibilities ('filling' out what is only potentially there). To unfold such possibilities—for example, to speak languages, build tools and dies, enter contracts, organize dance troupes—is to act in character for human beings designed by God."[12] All of these commands require seeking to understand revelation given by God through the created order.

God did not create every person with an ability to study his creation professionally, but he does charge all of us to explore his creation. Hoezee states that "a major part of our Christian vocation should be the nurturing of delight in this universe of wonders—a delight similar to God's own playful joy in creation, which we see traced for us in Scripture. This world teems with opportunities for such delight—the question is whether we take the time to notice."[13]

---

10. Dubay, *Evidential Power of Beauty*, 12.

11. Vanhoozer argues that "cultural literacy" or the "ability to understand patterns and products of everyday life" is essential to fulfilling the Great Commandment. Vanhoozer, "Everyday Theology," 19.

12. Plantinga, *Engaging God's World*, 33.

13. Hoezee, *Remember Creation*, 8.

Bibliography

Abraham, William J. *Crossing the Threshold of Divine Revelation*. Grand Rapids, MI: Eerdmans, 2006.

Adams, Edward. "Calvin's View of Natural Knowledge of God." *International Journal of Systematic Theology* 3 (2001) 280–92.

Adams, Jay E. *How to Help People Change: The Four-Step Biblical Process*. Grand Rapids, MI: Zondervan, 1986.

Agee Bob R., and Douglas V. Henry. "Introduction." In *Faithful Learning and the Christian Scholarly Vocation*, edited by Douglas V. Henry and Bob R. Agee. Grand Rapids, MI: Eerdmans, 2003.

Akin, Daniel L. "Preface." In *A Theology for the Church*, edited by Daniel L. Akin, vii–x. Nashville: B & H Academic, 2007.

Allert, Craig D. *Revelation, Truth, Canon and Interpretation: Studies in Justin Martyr's Dialogue with Trypho*. Supplements to Vigiliae Christianae 64. Edited by J. Den Boeft, et al. Boston: Brill, 2002.

———. "What are We Trying to Conserve? Evangelicalism and Sola Scriptura." *Evangelical Quarterly* 76 (2004) 327–48.

Allison, Gregg R. *Historical Theology: An Introduction to Christian Doctrine: A Companion to Wayne Grudem's Systematic Theology*. Grand Rapids, MI: Zondervan, 2011.

Allison, Gregg R., and Michael J. Anthony. "Revelation, Scripture, and Christian Education." In *A Theology for Christian Education*, edited by James Estep, et al., 73–101. Nashville: B & H Academic, 2008.

Anderson, Owen. *Reason and Worldviews: Warfield, Kuyper, Van Til and Plantinga on the Clarity of General Revelation and Function of Apologetics*. New York: University Press of America, 2008.

Anderson, Owen, and Benjamin B. Warfield. *Right Reason: The Clarity of General Revelation and Function of Apologetics*. New York: University Press of America, 2005.

Anderson, Owen, and Surrenda Gangadean. "On the Necessity for Natural Theology." In *Reason and Worldviews: Warfield, Kuyper, Van Til and Plantinga on the Clarity of General Revelation and Function of Apologetics*. New York: University Press of America, 2008.

Bibliography

Anker, Roy. "Like Shining from Shook Foil: Art, Film, and the Sacred." In *The Beauty of God: Theology and the Arts*, edited by Daniel J. Treier, et al., 121–42. Downers Grove, IL: InterVarsity, 2007.

Augustine, Aurelius. "Christian Instruction." Translated by John J. Gavigan. In *Writings of Saint Augustine*. The Fathers of the Church: A New Translation 4. Edited by Ludwig Schopp, 2–235. New York: CIMA, 1947.

———. *Expositions of the Psalms 33–50*. The Works of Saint Augustine: A Translation for the 21st Century 16. Translated by Maria Boulding. Edited by John E. Rotelle. Hyde Park, NY: New City, 2000.

———. *On Christian Doctrine*. Translated by D. W. Robertson, Jr. New York: Macmillan, 1986.

———. *On Order*. Translated by Silvano Borruso. South Bend, IN: St. Augustine's Press, 2007.

———. "On the Trinity." Translated by Arthur West Haddan. In *A Select Library of the Nicene and Post-Nicene Fathers* 3, edited by Philip Schaff, Series 1, 17–228. 1887. Reprint. New York: Charles Scribner's Sons, 1917.

———. "Revelation and Natural Theology." In *Alister E. McGrath and Evangelical Theology: A Dynamic Engagement*, edited by Sung Wook Chung, 264–79. Grand Rapids, MI: Baker, 2003.

———. *Saint Augustine on the Trinity*. Translated by Stephen McKenna. The Fathers of the Church: A New Translation 45. Edited by Roy Joseph Deferrari. Washington, DC: The Catholic University of America Press, 1963.

———. *Sermons III 51–94 on the New Testament*. The Works of Saint Augustine: A Translation for the 21st Century 3.3. Translated by Edmund Hill. Edited by John E. Rotelle. Brooklyn, NY: New City, 1991.

———. "St. Augustin's Christian Doctrine." Translated by J. F. Shaw. In *A Select Library of the Nicene and Post-Nicene Fathers* 2, edited by Philip Schaff, Series 1, 515–97. New York: Charles Scribner's Sons, 1887.

Bacon, Francis. *Advancement of Learning: Novum Organum, New Atlantis*. Great Books of the Western World 3. Edited by Robert Maynard Hutchins. Chicago: Encyclopaedia Britannica, 1952.

Bacote, Vincent E., and Stephen R. Spencer. "What are the Theological Implications for Natural Science?" In *Not Just Science: Questions where Christian Faith and Natural Science Intersect*, edited by Dorothy F. Chappell and E. David Cook, 61–78. Grand Rapids, MI: Zondervan, 2005.

Badley, Kenneth R. "The Community of Faith as the Locus of Faith-Learning Integration." In *Alive to God: Studies in Spirituality Presented to James Houston*, edited by J. I. Packer and Loren Wilkenson, 286–95. Downers Grove, IL: InterVarsity, 1992.

———. "'Integration' and 'The Integration of Faith and Learning.'" PhD diss., University of British Columbia, 1986.

———. "Two 'Cop-Outs' in Faith-Learning Integration: Incarnational Integration and Worldviewish Integration." *Spectrum* 28 (1996) 105–18.

Baillie, John. *The Idea of Revelation in Recent Thought*. New York: Columbia University Press, 1964.

Baker, Charles F. *A Dispensational Theology*. Grand Rapids, MI: Grace Bible College Publications, 1971.

Bancroft, Emery H. *Christian Theology: Systematic and Biblical*. Bible School Park, NY: Echoes, 1925.

Bandow, Doug. *Beyond Good Intentions: A Biblical View of Politics*. Turning Point Christian Worldview Series. Edited by Marvin Olasky. Westchester, IL: Crossway, 1988.

Barackman, Floyd H. *Practical Christian Theology: Examining the Great Doctrines of the Faith*. 3rd ed. Grand Rapids, MI: Kregel, 1998.

Barr, James. *Biblical Faith and Natural Theology: The Gifford Lectures for 1991*. Oxford: Clarendon, 1993.

Barrett, C. K. *The Gospel According to John: An Introduction with Commentary and Notes on the Greek Text*. Philadelphia: Westminster, 1978.

Battles, Ford L. "God Was Accommodating Himself to Human Capacity." *Interpretation* 31 (1977) 19–38.

Bavinck, Herman. "Christianity and Natural Science." In *Essays on Religion, Science and Society*, edited by John Bolt, translated by Harry Boonstra and Gerrit Sheeres, 81–104. Grand Rapids, MI: Baker, 2008.

———. "Common Grace." Translated by R.C. Van Leeuwen. *Calvin Theological Journal* 24 (1989) 38–65.

———. *The Doctrine of God*. Edited and translated by William Hendricksen. Grand Rapids, MI: Eerdmans, 1977.

———. *Essays on Religion, Science and Society*. Edited by John Bolt. Translated by Harry Boonstra and Gerrit Sheeres. Grand Rapids, MI: Baker, 2008.

———. *Our Reasonable Faith*. Translated by Henry Zylstra. Grand Rapids, MI: Eerdmans, 1956.

———. *The Philosophy of Revelation*. The Stone Lectures for 1908–1909, Princeton Theological Seminary. 1953. Reprint. Grand Rapids, MI: Baker, 1979.

———. *Reformed Dogmatics*. 4 vols. Edited by John Bolt. Translated by John Vriend. Grand Rapids, MI: Baker, 2006–2008.

Beals, Corey. "Truth as a Way of Life." *Quaker Religious Thought* 102 (2004) 7–16.

Beasley-Murray, George R. *John*. Word Biblical Commentary 36. Waco, TX: Word, 1987.

Bebbington, D. W. *Evangelicalism in Modern Britain: A History from the 1730s to the 1980s*. Boston: Unwin Hyman, 1989.

Beck, James R. "The Integration of Psychology and Theology: An Enterprise Out of Balance." *Journal of Psychology and Christianity* 22 (2003) 20–29.

———. "Sola Scriptura: Then and Now." *Journal of Psychology and Christianity* 16 (1997) 293–302.

Beck, W. David, ed. *Opening the American Mind: The Integration of Biblical Truth in the Curriculum of the University*. Grand Rapids, MI: Baker, 1991.

Beets, Henry. *The Reformed Confession Explained: A Popular Commentary and Textbook on the Netherland or Belgic Confession of Faith*. Grand Rapids, MI: Eerdmans, 1929.

Begbie, Jeremy. "Creation, Christ and Culture in Dutch Neo-Calvinism." In *Christ in Our Place: The Humanity of God in Christ for the Reconciliation of the World. Essays Presented to Professsor James Torrance*, edited by Trevor A. Hart and Daniel P. Thimell, 113–32. Allison Park, PA: Pickwick, 1989.

———. *Resounding Truth: Christian Wisdom in the World of Music*. Engaging Culture. Grand Rapids, MI: Baker, 2007.

Begbie, Jeremy, ed. *Beholding the Glory: Incarnation through the Arts*. Grand Rapids, MI: Baker, 2001.

Berkhof, Hendrikus. *Christian Faith: An Introduction to the Study of the Faith*. Translated by Sierd Woudstra. Rev. ed. Grand Rapids, MI: Eerdmans, 1986.
Berkof, Louis. *Manual of Reformed Doctrine*. Grand Rapids, MI: Eerdmans, 1933.
———. *Systematic Theology*. 1939. Reprint. Grand Rapids, MI: Eerdmans, 1965.
———. *Systematic Theology: New Edition Containing the Full Text of Systematic Theology and the Original Introductory Volume to Systematic Theology*. Grand Rapids, MI: Eerdmans, 1996.
Berkouwer, B. C. *General Revelation*. Studies in Dogmatics. 1955. Reprint. Grand Rapids, MI: Eerdmans, 1968.
Berry, C. Markham. "Approaching the Integration of the Social Sciences and Biblical Theology." *Journal of Psychology and Theology* 81 (1980) 33–44.
Bingham, D. Jeffrey. *Pocket History of the Church*. Downers Grove, IL: InterVarsity, 2002.
Bird, Michael F. *Evangelical Theology: A Biblical and Systematic Introduction*. Grand Rapids, MI: Zondervan, 2013.
Bloch, Richard. " 'What you do speaks so loudly I cannot hear what you are saying': What Ralph Waldo Emerson Really Said." No pages. Online: https://medium.com/@rbloch/what-you-do-speaks-so-loudly-i-cannot-hear-what-you-are-saying-92fbfdf52472.
Blocher, Henri. "The Biblical Concept of Truth." *Themelios* 6 (1969) 47–61.
Bloesch, Donald G. *God, Authority and Salvation*. Essentials of Evangelical Theology 1. New York: Harper & Row, 1978.
———. *Holy Scripture: Revelation, Inspiration and Interpretation*. Christian Foundations. Downers Grove, IL: InterVarsity, 1994.
———. *A Theology of Word and Spirit: Authority and Method in Theology*. Christian Foundations. Downers Grove, IL: InterVarsity, 1992.
Boice, James Montgomery. *Foundations of the Christian Faith: A Comprehensive and Readable Overview of Christian Beliefs*. Rev. ed. Downers Grove, IL: InterVarsity, 1986.
———. *Psalms 1–41*. Psalms 1. Grand Rapids, MI: Baker, 1994.
Bolt, John. "Editor's Introduction." In *Essays on Religion, Science and Society*, edited by John Bolt, translated by Harry Boonstra and Gerrit Sheeres, 7–11. Grand Rapids, MI: Baker, 2008.
Bonaventure. *The Soul's Journey into God; The Tree of Life; The Life of St. Francis*. Translated by Ewert Cousins. The Classics of Western Spirituality. New York: Paulist, 1978.
Bookman, Douglas. "The Scriptures and Biblical Counseling." In *Introduction to Biblical Counseling: A Basic Guide to the Principles and Practice of Counseling*, edited by John F. MacArthur Jr. and Wayne A. Mack, 63–97. Dallas: Word, 1994.
Bouma, Rolf. "Creation's Persistent Voice: Critiquing the Secondary Status of Creation as Revelation." *Journal of Faith and Science Exchange* 1 (1997) 1–6.
Boyce, James Pettigru. *Abstract of Systematic Theology*. 1887. Reprint. n.p.: Christian Gospel Foundation, 1970.
Boyd, Gregory A., and Paul R. Eddy. *Across the Spectrum: Understanding Issues in Evangelical Theology*. Grand Rapids, MI: Baker Academic, 2002.
Bray, Gerald. *God is Love: A Biblical and Systematic Theology*. Wheaton: Crossway, 2012.
———. "Sola Scriptura." *Churchman* 118 (2004) 99–104.

Brewster, Chauncey B. *Aspects of Revelation. Being the Baldwin Lectures for 1900.* New York: Longmans, Green, 1901.
Bromiley, G. W. "Natural Revelation." *Evangelical Quarterly* 13 (1941) 161–76.
Bruce, F. F. *The Letter of Paul to the Romans: An Introduction and Commentary.* Grand Rapids, MI: Eerdmans, 1988.
Brunner, Emil. *Revelation and Reason: The Christian Doctrine of Faith and Knowledge.* Translated by Olive Wyon. Philadelphia: Westminster, [1946].
Budziszewski, J., ed. *Evangelicals in the Public Square: Four Formative Voices on Political Thought and Action.* Grand Rapids, MI: Baker, 2006.
Bultmann, Rudolph, and Dieter Lührmann. "Φανερός." *Theological Dictionary of the New Testament 9.* Edited by Gerhard Kittel and Gerhard Friedrich. Grand Rapids, MI: Eerdmans, 1964. Logos Bible Software.
Buswell, James Oliver, Jr. *God and His Revelation and Man the Sinner and His Life in this World.* A Systematic Theology of the Christian Religion 1. Grand Rapids, MI: Zondervan, 1962.
Butler, Diana. "God's Visible Glory: The Beauty of Nature in the Thought of John Calvin and Jonathan Edwards." *Westminster Theological Journal* 52 (1990) 13–26.
Byl, John. "General Revelation and Evangelicalism." *Mid-American Journal of Theology* 5 (1989) 1–13.
Cairns, Alan. *Dictionary of Theological Terms.* Rev. ed. Greenville, SC: Ambassador Emerald International, 2002.
Calvin, John. *Commentaries on The First Book of Moses Called Genesis.* Translated and revised by John King. Calvin's Commentaries 1. Grand Rapids, MI: Baker, 1999.
———. *Commentary on the Book of Psalms.* Vol. 1. Translated by Rev. James Anderson. Grand Rapids, MI: Eerdmans, 1949.
———. *Commentary on the Book of the Psalms.* Translated by Henry Beveridge. Grand Rapids, MI: Baker, 1999.
———. *Commentary on Romans.* Vol. 2. Translated by Henry Beveridge. Grand Rapids, MI: Baker, 1999.
———. *The First Epistle of Paul the Apostle to the Corinthians.* Translated by John W. Fraser. Calvin's New Testament Commentaries 9. Edited by David W. Torrance and Thomas F. Torrance. Grand Rapids, MI: Eerdmans, 1960.
———. *Institutes of the Christian Religion.* Translated by Henry Beveridge. 2 vols. in 1. Grand Rapids, MI: Eerdmans, 1989.
Cameron, Nigel M. de S. "The Idea of Revelation." In *Evangelical Dictionary of Biblical Theology,* edited by Walter A. Elwell, 679–82. Grand Rapids, MI: Baker, 1996.
Cañizares, Javier Sánchez. "Filosofi griega y revelación cristiana. La recepción patrística del Discurso del Areópago." *Scripta theological* 39 (2007) 185–201.
Caragounis, Chrys. "Divine Revelation." *Evangelical Review of Theology* 12 (1988) 226–39.
Carmer, Gregory W. "All Things Reconciled: A Dialogue with the Sciences from a Reformed Perspective." *Journal of Faith and Science Exchange* 1 (1997) 7–15.
Carson, D. A. "Can There Be a Christian University?" *Southern Baptist Journal of Theology* 1 (1997) 20–38.
———. *Christ and Culture Revisited.* Grand Rapids, MI: Eerdmans, 2008.
———. *The Gospel According to John.* Grand Rapids, MI: Eerdmans, 1991.
Carter, Craig A. *Rethinking Christ and Culture: A Post-Christendom Perspective.* Grand Rapids, MI: Brazos, 2006.

Carter, John D., and Bruce Narramore. *The Integration of Psychology and Theology: An Introduction*. Rosemead Psychology Series. Grand Rapids, MI: Academie, 1979.

Chafer, Lewis Sperry. "Bibliology: Revelation." *Bibliotheca sacra* 94 (1937) 264–80.

———. *Major Bible Themes: Presenting Forty-Nine Vital Doctrines of the Scriptures, Abbreviated and Simplified for Popular Use, Including Suggestive Questions on each Chapter; with Topical and Textual Indices*. Chicago: Moody, 1945.

———. *Major Bible Themes: 52 Vital Doctrines of the Scriptures Simplified and Explained*. Revised by John F. Walvoord. Grand Rapids, MI: Zondervan, 1974.

———. *Systematic Theology: An Unabridged, Original Study of Systematic Theology from a Biblical Viewpoint—Evangelical, Premillennial and Dispensational*. 6 vols. 1947–1948. Reprint. Dallas: Dallas Seminary Press, 1957–1974.

Charnock, Stephen. *The Existence and Attributes of God*. 2 vols. in 1. Grand Rapids, MI: Baker, 2000.

Charry, Ellen T. *By the Renewing of Your Minds: The Pastoral Function of Christian Doctrine*. New York: Oxford University Press, 1997.

Chewing, Richard C., et al. *Business Through the Eyes of Faith*. San Francisco: Harper & Row, 1990.

Chiareli, Antonio A. "Christian Worldview and the Social Sciences." In *Shaping a Christian Worldview: The Foundations of Christian Higher Education*, edited by David S. Dockery and Gregory A. Thornbury, 240–63. Nashville: Broadman & Holman, 2002.

Chow, Wilson W. "Biblical Foundations for Evangelical Theology in the Third World." In *Biblical Theology in Asia*, edited by Ken Gnanakan, 112–3. Bangalore: Theological Book Trust, 1995.

Claerbaut, David. *Faith and Learning on the Edge: A Bold New Look at Religion in Higher Education*. Grand Rapids, MI: Zondervan, 2004.

Clark, David K. *To Know and Love God: Method for Theology*. Wheaton: Crossway, 2003.

Clarke, William N. *An Outline of Christian Theology*. 1899. Reprint. New York: Scribner's & Sons, 1901.

Clinton, Stephen M. "A Critique of Integration Models." *Journal of Psychology and Theology* 18 (1990) 13–19.

Cochrane, Arthur C., ed. *Reformed Confessions of the 16th Century*. Philadelphia, PA: Westminster, 1966.

Coe, John H. "An Interdependent Model of Integration and the Christian University." *Faculty Dialogue* 21 (1994) 111–37.

Coe, John H., and Todd W. Hall, "A Transformational Psychology View." In *Psychology and Christianity: Five Views*, edited by Eric L. Johnson, 199–226. 2nd ed. Downers Grove, IL: InterVarsity, 2010.

Coffey, David M. "Natural Knowledge of God: Reflections on Romans 1:18–32." *Theological Studies* 31 (1970) 674–91.

Collins, Kenneth J. *The Evangelical Moment: The Promise of an American Religion*. Grand Rapids, MI: Baker, 2005.

Conner, Walter T. *Revelation and God: An Introduction to Christian Doctrine*. 1936. Reprint. Nashville: Broadman, 1946.

Conyers, A. J. "Can Postmodernism Be Used as a Template for Christian Theology?" *Christian Scholar's Review* 33 (2004) 293–309.

Cooey, Paula. *Jonathan Edwards on Nature and Destiny: A Systematic Analysis.* Lewiston, NY: E. Mellen, 1985.

Cosgrove, Mark P. *Foundations of Christian Thought: Faith, Learning, and the Christian Worldview.* Grand Rapids, MI: Kregel Academic & Professional, 2006.

Crabb, Lawrence J. "Biblical Authority and Christian Psychology." *Journal of Psychology and Theology* 9 (1981) 305–11.

Craigie, Peter C. *Psalms 1–50.* Word Biblical Commentary 19. Waco, TX: Word, 1983.

Crampton, W. Gary. *Meet Jonathan Edwards: An Introduction to America's Greatest Theologian/Philosopher.* Morgan, PA: Soli Deo Gloria, 2004.

Crane, Richard. "Postliberal, Truth, Ad Hoc Apologetics, and (Something Like) General Revelation." *Perspectives in Religious Studies* 30 (2003) 29–53.

Cranfield, C. E. B. *A Critical and Exegetical Commentary on the Epistle to the Romans.* International Critical Commentary 1. 6th ed. Edinburgh: T. & T. Clark, 1975.

Crouch, Andy. *Culture Making: Recovering Our Creative Calling.* Downers Grove, IL: InterVarsity, 2008.

Culver, Robert D. *Systematic Theology: Biblical and Historical.* Fearn, Ross-shire: Mentor, 2005.

Curtis, Edward M. "Some Biblical Contributions to a Philosophy of Education." *Faculty Dialogue* 21 (1994) 91–110.

Curtius, Ernst Robert. *European Literature and the Late Middle Ages.* Translated by Willard R. Trask. New York: Pantheon, 1953.

Daane, James. *A Theology of Grace: An Inquiry into and Evaluation of Dr. C. Van Til's Doctrine of Common Grace.* Grand Rapids, MI: Eerdmans, 1954.

Dabney, Robert L. *Lectures in Systematic Theology.* Grand Rapids, MI: Zondervan, [1972].

Dahood, Mitchell. *Psalms 1–50.* Psalms 1. Garden City, NY: Doubleday, 1965.

Davis, Edward B. "The Word and the Works: Concordism in American Evangelical Thought." In *The Book of Nature in Early Modern History*, edited by Klaas van Berkel and Arjo Vanderjagt, 195–209. Groningen Studies in Cultural Change 17. Edited by M. Gosman. Dudley, MA: Peeters, 2006.

Davis, John J. *Foundations of Evangelical Theology.* Grand Rapids, MI: Baker, 1984.

Dayton, Donald W. "Some Doubts about the Usefulness of the Category 'Evangelical.'" In *The Variety of American Evangelicalism*, edited by Donald W. Dayton and Robert K. Johnston, 245–51. Downers Grove, IL: InterVarsity, 1991.

Deffinbaugh, Bob. "Nature's Part in God's Perfect Plan (Psalm 19; Romans 8:18–25; Isaiah 65:17–25)." No pages. Online: http://bible.org/seriespage/natures-part-gods-perfect-plan-psalm-19-romans-818-25-isaiah-6517-25/.

Deinhardt, C. I. "General Revelation as an Important Theological Consideration for Christian Counselling and Therapy." *Didaskalia* 7 (1995) 40–60.

Deinhardt, Carol I., and Heather J. Rochon. "Is Our Truth God's Truth?" *Didaskalia* 12 (2000) 1–24.

Demarest, Bruce. *General Revelation: Historical Views and Contemporary Issues.* Grand Rapids, MI: Zondervan, 1982.

Demarest, Bruce, and Keith J. Matthews, eds., *Dictionary of Everyday Theology and Culture.* The Navigators Reference Library. Colorado Springs, CO: NavPress, 2010.

Demarest, Bruce A., and Richard J. Harpel. "Don Richardson's 'Redemptive Analogies' and the Biblical Idea of Revelation." *Bibliotheca sacra* 146 (1989) 330–40.

Dennison, William D. "Natural and Special Revelation: A Reassessment." *Kerux* 21 (2006) 13–34.

DeVries, Michael J. "The Conduct of Integration: A Response to Farnsworth." *Journal of Psychology and Theology* 10 (1982) 320–25.

Dick, John. *Lectures on Theology*. 2 vols. in 1. New York: Robert Carter & Brothers, 1864.

Diehl, David W. "Evangelicalism and General Revelation: An Unfinished Agenda." *Journal of the Evangelical Theological Society* 30 (1987) 441–55.

Dillenberger, John. "The Diversity of Disciplines as a Theological Question: The Visual Arts as Paradigm." *Journal of the American Academy of Religion* 48 (1980) 233–43.

Dockery, David S. *Christian Scripture: An Evangelical Perspective on Inspiration, Authority and Interpretation*. Eugene, OR: Wipf & Stock, 2004.

———. *Faith and Learning: A Handbook for Christian Higher Education*. Nashville: Broadman & Holman, 2012.

———. *Renewing Minds: Serving Church and Society through Christian Higher Education*. Nashville: Broadman & Holman, 2008.

———. "Revelation of God." In *Holman Bible Dictionary*, edited by Trent C. Butler, 1180–83. Nashville: Holman Bible Publishers, 1991.

Dockery, David S., and Gregory A. Thornbury. *Shaping a Christian Worldview: The Foundations of Christian Higher Education*. Nashville: Broadman & Holman, 2002.

Dooyeweerd, H. *Roots of Western Culture: Pagan, Secular, and Christian Options*. Toronto: Wedge Publishers, 1979.

Dowey, Edward A., Jr. *The Knowledge of God in Calvin's Theology*. 3rd ed. Grand Rapids, MI: Eerdmans, 1994.

Dubay, Thomas. *The Evidential Power of Beauty: Science and Theology Meet*. San Francisco: Ignatius, 1999.

Dulles, Avery. "Donald Bloesch on Revelation." In *Evangelical Theology in Transition: Theologians in Dialogue with Donald Bloesch*, edited by Elmer M. Coyler, 61–76. Downers Grove, IL: InterVarsity, 1999.

———. *Models of Revelation*. 1992. Reprint. Maryknoll, NY: Orbis, 2005.

———. "The Symbolic Structure of Revelation." *Theological Studies* 41 (1980) 51–73.

Dunn, James D. G. *Romans 1–8*. Word Biblical Commentary 38A. Dallas: Word, 1988.

Dyrness, William A. "Evangelical Theology and Culture." In *The Cambridge Companion to Evangelical Theology*, edited by Timothy Larsen and Daniel J. Treier, 145–59. New York: Cambridge University Press, 2007.

Earle, Ralph "Revelation and Inspiration." In *A Contemporary Wesleyan Theology: Biblical, Systematic, and Practical 1*, edited by Charles W. Carter, 287–330. Grand Rapids, MI: Francis Asbury, 1983.

Eckel, Mark. *The Whole Truth: Classroom Strategies for Biblical Integration*. N.p.: Xulon, 2003.

Edgar, Thomas R. "Through the Written Word, Spiritual Truth Can Be Known." In *The Fundamentals for the Twenty-First Century: Examining the Crucial Issues of the Christian Faith*, edited by Mal Couch, 57–71. Grand Rapids, MI: Kregel, 2000.

Edwards, Jonathan. *Ethical Writings*. Edited by Paul Ramsey. The Works of Jonathan Edwards 8. New Haven, CT: Yale University Press, 1989.

———. *A History of the Work of Redemption*. Edited by John F. Wilson. The Works of Jonathan Edwards 9. New Haven, CT: Yale University Press, 1989.

———. *The "Miscellanies," (Entry Nos. a-z, aa-zz, 1-500)*. Edited by Thomas A. Schafer. The Works of Jonathan Edwards 13, edited by Harry S. Stout. New Haven, CT: Yale University Press, 1994.

———. *The "Miscellanies," 501-832*. Edited by Ava Chamberlain. The Works of Jonathan Edwards 18. New Haven, CT: Yale University Press, 2000.

———. *The "Miscellanies," 833-1152*. Edited by Amy Plantinga Pauw. The Works of Jonathan Edwards 20. New Haven, CT: Yale University Press, 2002.

———. *The "Miscellanies," 1153-1360*. Edited by Douglas A. Sweeney. The Works of Jonathan Edwards 23. New Haven, CT: Yale University Press, 2004.

———. *Notes on Scripture*. Edited by Stephen J. Stein. The Works of Jonathan Edwards 15. New Haven, CT: Yale University Press, 1998.

———. *Sermons and Discourses, 1720-1723*. Edited by Wilson H. Kimnach. The Works of Jonathan Edwards 10. New Haven, CT: Yale University Press, 1992.

———. *Sermons and Discourses, 1723-1729*. Edited by Kenneth P. Minkema. The Works of Jonathan Edwards 14. New Haven, CT: Yale University Press, 1997.

———. *Sermons and Discourses, 1730-1733*. Edited by Mark Valeri. The Works of Jonathan Edwards 17. New Haven, CT: Yale University Press, 1999.

———. *Sermons and Discourses, 1734-1738*. Edited by M. X. Lesser. The Works of Jonathan Edwards 19. New Haven, CT: Yale University Press, 2001.

———. *Sermons and Discourses, 1739-1942*. Edited by Harry S. Stout, Nathan O. Hatch and Kyle P. Farley. The Works of Jonathan Edwards 22. New Haven, CT: Yale University Press, 2003.

———. *Typological Writings*. Edited by Wallace E. Anderson, Mason I. Lowance and David H. Watters. The Works of Jonathan Edwards 11. New Haven, CT: Yale University Press, 1993.

———. *Writings on Trinity, Grace and Faiths*. Edited by Sang Hyun Lee. The Works of Jonathan Edwards 21. New Haven, CT: Yale University Press, 2003.

Eells, Robert. "Creation, Redemption, and Doing Your Best: Gaebelein's Approach to Learning." In *Christian Approaches to Learning Theory: A Symposium: Major Papers Delivered at the First Annual Conference: Trinity Christian College*, edited by Norman DeJong, 13-29. New York: University Press of America, 1984.

Efferin, Henry. "A Study on General Revelation: Romans 1:18-32; 2:12-16." *Stulos Theological Journal* 4 (1996) 147-55.

Ellens, J. Harold. "Biblical Authority and Christian Psychology." *Journal of Psychology and Theology* 9 (1981) 318-25.

Elwell, Walter A. "Preface." In *Handbook of Evangelical Theologians*, edited by Walter A. Elwell, vii. Grand Rapids, MI: Baker, 1993.

Elwell, Walter A., and Douglas Buckwalter, eds. *Topical Analysis of the Bible with the New International Version*. Grand Rapids, MI: Baker, 1991.

Engelsma, David J. *Common Grace Revisited: A Response to Richard J. Mouw's He Shines in All That's Fair*. Grandville, MI: Reformed Free, 2003.

———. *Reformed Education: The Christian School as Demand of the Covenant*. Rev. ed. Grandville, MI: Reformed Free, 2000.

Enns, Paul. *The Moody Handbook of Theology*. Chicago: Moody, 1989.

Enns, Phil. "Reason and Revelation: Kant and the Problem of Authority." *International Journal for Philosophy of Religion* 62 (2007) 103-14.

Entwistle, David N., and Aaron Preston. "Epistemic Rights vs. Epistemic Duties: A Reply to Porter." *Journal of Psychology and Christianity* 29 (2010) 27-32.

Erickson, Millard J. *Christian Theology*. 2nd ed. Grand Rapids, MI: Baker, 2001.

———. *Introducing Christian Doctrine*. Edited by L. Arnold Hustad. 1992. Reprint. Grand Rapids, MI: Baker, 2000.

———. *The Living God*. Readings in Christian Theology 1. Grand Rapids, MI: Baker, 1973.

———.*The New Evangelical Theology*. Westwood, NJ: Fleming H. Revell Company, 1968.

———. *Truth or Consequences: The Promise & Perils of Postmodernism*. Downers Grove, IL: InterVarsity, 2001.

Estep, James R., et al. *A Theology for Christian Education*. Nashville: B & H Academic, 2008.

Evangelical Theological Society. "ETS Constitution, Article III: Doctrinal Basis." No pages. Online: http://www.etsjets.org/about/constituion#A3.

Evans, Tony. *Theology You Can Count On*. Chicago: Moody, 2008.

Fackre, Gabriel. *A Narrative Interpretation of Basic Christian Doctrine*. The Christian Story 1. 3rd ed. Grand Rapids, MI: Eerdmans, 1996.

———. *The Doctrine of Revelation: A Narrative Interpretation*. Edinburgh Studies in Constructive Theology. Grand Rapids, MI: Eerdmans, 1997.

Felker Jones, Beth. *Practicing Christian Doctrine: An Introduction to Thinking and Living Theologically*. Grand Rapids, MI: Baker Academic, 2014.

Finney, Charles G. *Finney's Lectures on Systematic Theology*. 1878. Reprint. Grand Rapids, MI: Eerdmans, 1951.

Fischer, John. *Finding God Where You Least Expect Him*. Eugene, OR: Harvest House, 2003.

Fitzmyer, Joseph A. *Romans: A New Translation with Introduction and Commentary*. The Anchor Bible 33. New York: Doubleday, 1992.

Fitzwater, P. B. *Christian Theology: A Systematic Presentation*. 2nd ed. Grand Rapids, MI: Eerdmans, 1948.

Fooz, Harold D., and L. Paige Patterson. "The Revelation, Inspiration, and Inerrancy of the Bible." In *The Fundamentals for the Twenty-First Century: Examining the Crucial Issues of the Christian Faith*, edited by Mal Couch, 85–109. Grand Rapids, MI: Kregel Publications, 2000.

Fortner, Robert S. *Communication, Media, and Identity: A Christian Theory of Communication*. New York: Rowman and Littlefield Publishers, 2007.

Foster, Robert V. *Systematic Theology*. Nashville: Cumberland Presbyterian Publishing House, 1898.

Frame, John M. *Cornelius Van Til: An Analysis of His Thought*. Phillipsburg, NJ: P & R, 1995.

———. "In Defense of Something Close to Biblicism: Reflections on Sola Scriptura and History in Theological Method." *Westminster Theological Journal* 59 (1997) 269–91.

———. *The Doctrine of the Word of God*. A Theology of Lordship 4. Phillipsburg, NJ: P & R, 2010.

Franke, John. *The Character of Theology: An Introduction to its Nature, Task, and Purpose: A Postconservative Evangelical Approach*. Grand Rapids, MI: Baker, 2005.

Fraser, David A., and Tony Campolo. *Sociology Through the Eyes of Faith*. San Francisco: Harper & Row, 1992.

Fretheim, Terence E. *God and World in the Old Testament: A Relational Theology of Creation*. Nashville: Abingdon, 2005.
Friberg, Timothy, et al."Θεόπνευστος, ov." In *Analytical Lexicon of the Greek New Testament*, 196. Grand Rapids, MI: Baker, 2000.
Frye, Roland Mushat. "The Two Books of God." *Theology Today* 39 (1982) 260–6.
Gaebelein, Frank E. *A Varied Harvest: Out of a Teacher's Life and Thought*. Grand Rapids, MI: Eerdmans, 1967.
———. "Corollaries of Biblical Scholarship." *Christianity Today* 6 (1962) 7–8.
———. *The Christian, The Arts, and Truth: Regaining the Vision of Greatness*. Edited by D. Bruce Lockerbie. Portland, OR: Multnomah, 1985.
———. *The Pattern of God's Truth: The Integration of Faith and Learning*. 1954. Reprint. Chicago: Moody, 1968.
———. "Towards a Christian Philosophy of Education: I. The Need and Nature of a Christian Philosophy of Education." *Grace Journal* 3 (1962) 3–11.
———. "Towards a Christian Philosophy of Education: II. The Major Premise of Christian Education." *Grace Journal* 3 (1962) 12–18.
Gallagher, Susan V., and Roger Lundin. *Literature Through the Eyes of Faith*. San Francisco: Harper & Row, 1989.
Gamertsfelder, Samuel J. *Systematic Theology*. 1921. Reprint. Harrisburg, PA: Evangelical, 1938.
Gangel, Kenneth O. "Biblical Integration: The Process of Thinking Like a Christian." *Evangelical Review of Theology* 20 (1996) 209–19.
———. "Christian Higher Education and Contemporary Culture: Isolation or Penetration?" *Bibliotheca sacra* 135 (1978) 291–302.
———. "Integrating Faith and Learning: Principles and Process." *Bibliotheca sacra* 135 (1978) 99–108.
———. "Preface." In *Toward a Harmony of Faith and Learning: Essays on Bible College Curriculum*, edited by Kenneth O. Gangel, vii–xv. Farmington Hills, MI: William Tyndale College Press, 1983.
———. "Thinking Like a Christian: An Evangelical Analysis of Rationality." *Christian Education* 8 (1987) 61–72.
———. *Toward a Harmony of Faith and Learning: Essays on Bible College Curriculum*. Farmington Hills, MI: William Tyndale College Press, 1983.
Garrett, James L. *Systematic Theology: Biblical, Historical, Evangelical*. 2 vols. Grand Rapids, MI: Eerdmans, 1990–1995.
Gärtner, Bertil. *The Areopagus Speech and Natural Revelation*. Acta Seminarii Neotestamentici Upsaliensis 21. Translated by Carolyn H. King. Uppsala: Almquist & Wiksells, 1955.
Geehan, E. R. *Jerusalem and Athens: Critical Discussions on the Theology and Apologetics of Cornelius Van Til*. [Phillipsburg, NJ]: P & R, 1971.
Geisler, Norman L. "Biblical Studies." In *Opening the American Mind: The Integration of Biblical Truth in the Curriculum of the University*, edited by W. David Beck, 25–46. Grand Rapids, MI: Baker, 1991.
———. *Systematic Theology*. 4 vols. Minneapolis: Bethany House, 2002–2005.
———. "The Concept of Truth in the Inerrancy Debate." *Bibliotheca sacra* 137 (1980) 327–39.
Genderen, J. van, and W. H. Velema. *Concise Reformed Dogmatics*. Translated by Gerrit Bilkes & Ed M. van der Maas. Phillipsburg, NJ: P & R, 2008.

George, Timothy. "The Nature of God: Being, Attributes and Acts." In *A Theology for the Church*, edited by Daniel L. Akin, 176–241. Nashville, TN: B & H Academic, 2007.

George, Timothy, and David S. Dockery, eds. *Theologians of the Baptist Tradition*. Nashville: Broadman & Holman, 2001.

Gerstner, John H. *Jonathan Edwards: A Mini-Theology*. Wheaton: Tyndale House, 1987.

Geyer-Kordesch, Johanna. "Nature Writing and the Book of Nature: From Taxonomy to Narrative Truth." In *The Book of Nature in Early Modern History*, edited by Klaas van Berkel and Arjo Vanderjagt, 121–40. Groningen Studies in Cultural Change 17. Edited by M. Gosman, Dudley, MA: Peeters, 2006.

Goldingay, John. *Psalms 1–41*. Psalms. Baker Commentary on the Old Testament Wisdom and Psalms 1. Edited by Tremper Longman III. Grand Rapids, MI: Baker, 2006.

Goodman, Marvin L. "Non-Literal Interpretations of Genesis Creation." *Grace Journal* 14 (1973) 25–38.

Gootjes, N. H. "General Revelation in Its Relation to Special Revelation." *Westminster Theological Journal* 51(1989) 359–68.

Gray, Albert F. *Christian Theology*. 2 vols. Anderson, IN: Warner, 1944.

Green, Brad. "Theological and Philosophical Foundations." In *Shaping a Christian Worldview: The Foundations of Christian Higher Education*, edited by David S. Dockery and Gregory A. Thornbury, 62–91. Nashville: Broadman & Holman, 2002.

Greer, Robert C. *Mapping Postmodernism: A Survey of Christian Options*. Downers Grove, IL: InterVarsity, 2003.

Greidanus, Sidney. "The Use of the Bible in Christian Scholarship." *Christian Scholar's Review* 11 (1982) 138–47.

Grenz, Stanley J. "Articulating the Christian Belief-Mosaic: Theological Method after the Demise of Foundationalism." In *Evangelical Futures: A Conversation on Theological Method*, edited by John G. Stackhouse Jr., 107–38. Grand Rapids, MI: Baker, 2000.

———. "Evangelical, Evangelicalism, Neo-evangelicalism." In *Pocket Dictionary of Theological Terms*, 47–48. Downers Grove, IL: InterVarsity, 1999.

———. "Fideistic Revelationalism: Donald Bloesch's Antirationalist Theological Method." In *Evangelical Theology in Transition: Theologians in Dialogue with Donald Bloesch*, edited by Elmer M. Coyler, 35–60, 216–9. Downers Grove, IL: InterVarsity, 1999.

———. *Pocket Dictionary of Theological Terms*. Downers Grove, IL: InterVarsity, 1999.

———. *Renewing the Center: Evangelical Theology in a Post-Theological Era*. Grand Rapids, MI: Baker Academic, 2000.

———. *Theology for the Community of God*. Nashville: Broadman and Holman, 1994.

———. "What Does Hollywood Have to Do With Wheaton? The Place of (Pop) Culture in Theological Reflection." *Journal of the Evangelical Theological Society* 43 (2000) 303–14.

Grenz, Stanley J., and John R. Franke. *Beyond Foundationalism: Shaping Theology in a Postmodern Context*. Louisville, KY: Westminster John Knox, 2001.

Grenz, Stanley J., and Roger E. Olson. *Who Needs Theology? An Invitation to the Study of God*. Downers Grove, IL: InterVarsity, 1996.

Grider, J. Kenneth. *A Wesleyan-Holiness Theology*. Kansas City, MO: Beacon Hill, 1994.

Groothuis, Douglas. "Why Truth Matters Most: An Apologetic for Truth-Seeking in Postmodern Times." *Journal of the Evangelical Theological Society* 47 (2004) 441–54.

Grudem, Wayne. "Do We Act as if We Really Believe that 'The Bible Alone, and the Bible in its Entirety, is the Word of God Written'?" *Journal of the Evangelical Theological Society* 43 (2000) 5–26.

———. *Systematic Theology: An Introduction to Biblical Doctrine*. 1994. Reprint. Grand Rapids, MI: Zondervan, 2000.

Guarino, Thomas G. "Why Avery Dulles Matters." *First Things* 193 (2009) 40–46.

Gulley, Norman R. *Systematic Theology: Prolegomena*. Berrien Springs, MI: Andrews University Press, 2003.

Gunton, Colin. *A Brief Theology of Revelation: The 1993 Warfield Lectures*. Edinburgh: T. & T. Clark, 1995.

———. *Christ and Creation*. The Didsbury Lectures. Grand Rapids, MI: Eerdmans, 1992.

———. *Revelation and Reason: Prolegomena to Systematic Theology*. Edited and transcribed by P. H. Brazier. New York: T. & T. Clark, 2008.

Gushee, David P. "Integrating Faith and Learning in an Ecumenical Context." In *The Future of Baptist Higher Education*, edited by Donald D. Schmeltekopf and Dianna M. Vitanza, 25–51, 236–9. Waco, TX: Baylor University, 2006.

Guthrie, George H. "The Authority of Scripture." In *Shaping a Christian Worldview: The Foundations of Christian Higher Education*, edited by David S. Dockery and Gregory A. Thornbury, 19–39. Nashville: Broadman & Holman, 2002.

Guy, James D. "The Search for Truth in the Task of Integration." *Journal of Psychology and Theology* 8 (1980) 27–32.

Hall, Christopher A. *Learning Theology with the Church Fathers*. Downers Grove, IL: InterVarsity, 2002.

Hall, David W., and Marvin Padgett, eds. *Calvin and Culture: Exploring a Worldview*. The Calvin 500 Series. Phillipsburg, NJ: P & R, 2010.

Hall, David W., and Peter A. Lillback. *A Theological Guide to Calvin's Institutes: Essays and Analysis*. Phillipsburg, NJ: P & R, 2008.

Hanks, Tom, et al. *The Ant Bully*. DVD. Directed by John A. Davis. Burbank, CA: Warner Brothers, 2006.

Hannah, John D. *How do We Glorify God? Basics of the Reformed Faith*. Phillipsburg, NJ: P & R, 2008.

Harbin, Michael A. "The God Who Acts: A Preliminary Study of General Revelation in History." Evangelical Theological Society Annual Meeting, Santa Clara, CA, Nov. 20–22, 1997.

Harris, Robert A. *The Integration of Faith and Learning: A Worldview Approach*. Eugene, OR: Cascade, 2004.

Harrison, Everett F. *Romans–Galatians*. The Expositor's Bible Commentary 11. Edited by Tremper Longman and David E. Garland. Rev. ed. Grand Rapids, MI: Zondervan, 2008.

Harrison, Everett F., et al. *Wycliffe Dictionary of Theology*. 1960. Reprint. Peabody, MA: Hendrickson, 1999.

Hart, D. G. *Deconstructing Evangelicalism: Conservative Protestantism in an Age of Billy Graham*. Grand Rapids, MI: Baker, 2004.

———. "The Princeton Mind in the Modern World and the Common Sense of J. Gresham Machen." *Westminster Theological Journal* 46 (1984) 1–25.

———. "Systematic Theology at Old Princeton Seminary: Unoriginal Calvinism." In *The Pattern of Sound Doctrine: Systematic Theology at the Westminster Seminary: Essays in Honor of Robert B. Strimple*, edited by David Van Drunen, 3–26. Phillipsburg, NJ: P & R, 2004.

Hart, Larry D. *Truth Aflame: Theology for the Church in Renewal*. Rev. ed. Grand Rapids, MI: Zondervan, 2005.

Hart, Trevor. *Faith Thinking: The Dynamics of Christian Theology*. Downers Grove, IL: InterVarsity, 1995.

Hasel, Gerald F. "The Relationship between Biblical Theology and Systematic Theology." *Trinity Journal* 5 (1984) 113–27.

Hasker, William. "Faith-Learning Integration: An Overview." *Christian Scholar's Review* 21 (1992) 234–48.

Hatch, Nathan O. *The Democratization of American Christianity*. New Haven, CT: Yale University Press, 1989.

Hatch, Nathan O., and Mark A. Noll, eds. *The Bible in America: Essays in Cultural History*. New York: Oxford Press, 1982.

Hawkin, David J. "The Johannine Concept of Truth and its Implications for a Theological Society." *Evangelical Quarterly* 59 (1987) 3–13.

Healy, Nicholas M. "What is Systematic Theology?" *International Journal of Systematic Theology* 11 (2009) 24–39.

Helm, Paul. *Divine Revelation: The Basic Issues*. Foundations for Faith. Edited by Peter Toon. Westchester, IL: Crossway, 1982.

———. "The Great Christian Doctrine (Original Sin)." In *A God Entranced Vision of All Things*, edited by John Piper and Justin Taylor, 175–200. Wheaton: Crossway, 2004.

Helseth, Paul Kjoss. "B. B. Warfield on the Apologetic Nature of Christian Scholarship: An Analysis of His Solution to the Problem of the Relationship Between Christianity and Culture." *Westminster Theological Journal* 62 (2000) 89–111.

Hendricks, Howard. *Teaching to Change Lives: Seven Proven Ways to Make Your Teaching Come Alive*. Rev. ed. Sisters, OR: Multnomah, 1987.

Henry, Carl F. H. *God, Revelation and Authority*. 6 vols. Carlisle, Cumbria, UK: Paternoster, 1976–83.

———. *Revelation and the Bible: Contemporary Evangelical Thought*. Grand Rapids, MI: Baker, 1958.

———. "Revelation, Special," In *Evangelical Dictionary of Theology*, edited by Walter A. Elwell, 946. 1984. Reprint. Grand Rapids, MI: Baker Books, 1997.

———. *The Uneasy Conscience of Modern Fundamentalism*. Grand Rapids, MI: Eerdmans, 1947.

Henry, Douglas V., and Bob R. Agee, eds. *Faithful Learning and the Christian Scholarly Vocation*. Grand Rapids, MI: Eerdmans, 2003.

Herrick, Greg. "Is the Bible the Only Revelation of God?" No pages. Online: http://bible.org/article/bible-only-revelation-god/.

Heslam, Peter S. "Faith and Reason: Kuyper, Warfield and the Shaping of the Evangelical Mind." *Anvil* 15 (1998) 299–313.

Heywood, David. *Divine Revelation and Human Learning: A Christian Theory of Knowledge*. Burlington, VT: Ashgate, 2004.

Higgins, John R. "God's Inspired Word." In *Systematic Theology*, edited by Stanley M. Horton, 61–116. Rev. ed. Springfield, MO: Logion, 1998.

Hindson, Edward E. "The Historical Significance of The Fundamentals." In *The Fundamentals for the Twenty-First Century: Examining the Crucial Issues of the Christian Faith*, edited by Mal Couch, 15–27. Grand Rapids, MI: Kregel, 2000.

Hodge, Archibald A. *Outlines of Theology: For Students and Laymen*. 1879. Reprint. Grand Rapids, MI: Zondervan, 1972.

Hodge, Charles. *Systematic Theology*. 3 vols. 1999. Reprint. Peabody, MA: Hendrickson, 2003.

Hodges, Bert H. "Faith-Learning Integration: Appreciating the Integrity of a Shop-Worn Phrase." *Faculty Dialogue* 22 (1994) 95–106.

Hoehner, Harold W. "Romans." In *The Bible Knowledge Word Study: Acts-Ephesians*, edited by Darrell L. Bock, 125–204. Colorado Springs, CO: Cooks Communications Ministries, 2006.

Hoezee, Scott. *Remember Creation: God's World of Wonder and Delight*. Grand Rapids, MI: Eerdmans, 1998.

Hoffmeier, James K. " 'The Heavens Declare the Glory of God': The Limits of General Revelation." *Trinity Journal* 21 (2000) 17–24.

Holmes, Arthur F. *All Truth is God's Truth*. Grand Rapids, MI: Eerdmans, 1977.

———. *Building the Christian Academy*. Grand Rapids, MI: Eerdmans, 2001.

———. *Contours of a World View*. Grand Rapids, MI: Eerdmans, 1983.

———. *Faith Seeks Understanding*. Grand Rapids, MI: Eerdmans, 1971.

———. *The Idea of a Christian College*. Grand Rapids, MI: Eerdmans, 1975.

Holth, Sverre. "The Christian Doctrine of Revelation." *South East Asia Journal of Theology* 2 (1961) 20–30.

Horner, Grant. *Meaning at the Movies: Becoming a Discerning Viewer*. Wheaton: Crossway, 2010.

Horton, Michael. *The Christian Faith: A Systematic Theology for Pilgrims on the Way*. Grand Rapids, MI: Zondervan, 2011.

Horton, Stanley M., ed. *Systematic Theology*. Rev. ed. Springfield, MO: Logion, 1998.

Howard, Daniel. "A Critical Analysis of General Revelation." *Criswell Theological Review* 8 (2010) 53–75.

Howell, Russell W., and W. James Bradley, eds. *Mathematics in a Postmodern Age: A Christian Perspective*. Grand Rapids, MI: Eerdmans, 2001.

Hybels, Sandra, and Richard L. Weaver, II. *Communicating Effectively*. 5th ed. Boston: McGraw Hill, 1998.

James, Theodore E. "Reason, Revelation, and Romans 1:18–21." In *Unity in Diversity: Essays in Religion by Members of the Faculty of the Unification Theological Seminary*, edited by Henry O. Thomson, 325–58. Barrytown, NY: The Unification Theological Seminary, 1984.

Jensen, Peter. *The Revelation of God*. Contours of Christian Theology. Edited by Gerald Bray. Downers Grove, IL: InterVarsity, 2002.

Jerome. "Letter to Nepotian." Translated by W. H. Fremantle. *The Nicene and Post-Nicene Fathers* 6. Series 2. Edited by Philip Schaff and Henry Wace. Reprint. Grand Rapids, MI: Eerdmans 1989.

Johnson, Alan F., and Robert E. Webber. *What Christians Believe: A Biblical and Historical Summary*. Grand Rapids, MI: Zondervan, 1993.

Johnson, Dennis. "Between Two Wor(l)ds: Worldview and Observation in the Use of General Revelation to Interpret Scripture, and Vice Versa." *Journal of the Evangelical Theological Society* 41 (1998) 69–84.

Johnson, Eric L., ed. *Psychology and Christianity: Five Views*. 2nd ed. Downers Grove, IL: InterVarsity, 2010.

Johnson, Gary L. W., ed. *B. B. Warfield: Essays on His Life and Thought*. Phillipsburg, NJ: P & R, 2007.

Johnston, Robert K. "Discerning the Spirit in Culture: Observations arising from Reflections on General Revelation." *Ex Auditu* 23 (2007) 52–69.

———. *God's Wider Presence: Reconsidering General Revelation*. Grand Rapids, MI: Baker Academic, 2014.

Jones, Taylor B. "Why a Scriptural View of Science?" In *Think Biblically! Recovering A Christian Worldview*, edited by John MacArthur, 221–38. Wheaton: Crossway, 2003.

Jorink, Eric. "Reading the Book of Nature in the Seventeenth-Century Dutch Republic." In *The Book of Nature in Early Modern History*, edited by Klaas van Berkel and Arjo Vanderjagt, 45–68. Groningen Studies in Cultural Change 17; general ed. M. Gosman. Dudley, MA: Peeters, 2006.

Kaiser, Walter C., Jr. "Evangelical Hermeneutics: Restatement, Advance or Retreat from the Reformation?" *Concordia Theological Quarterly* 46 (1982) 167–80.

Kantzer, Kenneth S. "Contemporary Thinking about Revelation," *Bibliotheca sacra* 115 (1958) 302–12.

———. "The Communication of Revelation." In *The Bible: The Living Word of Revelation*, edited by Merrill C. Tenney, 53–80. Grand Rapids, MI: Zondervan, 1968.

———. "The Method of Revelation: How Does God Reveal Himself?" *Bibliotheca sacra* 115 (1958) 218–28.

———. "What is Revelation?" *Bibliotheca sacra* 115 (1958) 120–7.

Keck, Leander E. *The Book of the Psalms*. The New Interpreter's Bible 4. Nashville: Abingdon, 1996.

Kelly, Douglas F. *Systematic Theology: Grounded in Holy Scripture and Understood in the Light of the Church*. Fearn, Ross-shire: Mentor, 2008.

Kelly, J. N. D. *Early Christian Doctrines*. Rev. ed. Peabody, MA: Hendrickson, 2004.

Kelsey, David H. *Proving Doctrine: The Uses of Scripture in Modern Theology*. Harrisburg, PA: Trinity, 1999.

Kempe, Michael. "Sermons in Stone: Johann Jacob Scheuchzer's Concept of the Book of Nature and the Physics of the Bible." In *The Book of Nature in Early Modern History*, edited by Klaas van Berkel and Arjo Vanderjagt, 111–19. Groningen Studies in Cultural Change 17; general ed. M. Gosman. Dudley, MA: Peeters, 2006.

Kendall, R. T. *Developing a Healthy Church in the 21st Century*. Understanding Theology 1. Ross-Shire, Great Britian: Christian Focus, 1996.

Kidner, Derek. *Psalms 1–72: An Introduction and Commentary on Books I and II of the Psalms*. Downers Grove, IL: InterVarsity, 1973.

Kistler, Don, ed. *Standing in Grace: A Treatise on Grace by Jonathan Edwards*. Morgan, PA: Soli Deo Gloria, 2002.

Klinger, Jerzy. "The Second Epistle of Peter: An Essay in Understanding." *St. Vladimir's Theological Quarterly* 17 (1973) 152–69.

Knierim, Rolf P. *The Task of Old Testament Theology: Substance, Method, and Cases.* Grand Rapids, MI: Eerdmans, 1995.

Knight, Christopher C. *Wrestling with the Divine: Religion, Science, and Revelation.* Minneapolis, MN: Fortress, 2001.

Knox, D. B. "Propositional Revelation the only Revelation." *Reformed Theological Review* 19 (1960) 1–9.

Kraemer, Hendrik. *Religion and the Christian Faith.* Philadelphia: Westminster, 1956.

Kraft, Charles H. "Can Anthropological Insight Assist Evangelical Theology?" *Christian Scholar's Review* 7 (1977) 165–202.

———. "Cultural Anthropology: Its Meaning for Christian Theology." *Theology Today* 41 (1985) 390–400.

Kraus, Hans-Joachim. *Psalms 1–59: A Commentary.* Translated by Hilton C. Oswald. Minneapolis: Augsburg, 1988.

Kreider, Glenn R. *Jonathan Edwards's Interpretation of Revelation 4:1–8:1.* Lanham, MD: University Press of America, 2004.

———. Review of *Essays on Religion, Science, and Theology*, by Herman Bavinck. *Bibliotheca sacra* 168 (2011) 105–7.

Kulikovsky, Andrew S. *Creation, Fall, Restoration: A Biblical Theology of Creation.* Fearn, Ross-shire: Mentor, 2009.

———. "Scripture and General Revelation." No pages. Online: http://www.creationtheweb.org/content/view/4763.

Kurian, George Thomas, ed. *Nelson's New Christian Dictionary: The Authoritative Resource on the Christian World.* Nashville: Thomas Nelson, 2001.

Kuyper, Abraham. *Wisdom and Wonder: Common Grace in Science and Art.* Translated by Nelson D. Kloosterman. Grand Rapids, MI: Christian's Library, 2011.

Ladd, George E. "The Knowledge of God: The Saving Acts of God." In *Basic Christian Doctrines*, edited by Carl F. H. Henry, 7–13. Contemporary Evangelical Thought. New York: Holt, Rineheart and Winston, 1962.

Latourelle, René. *Theology of Revelation: Including a Commentary on the Constitution "Dei Verbum" of Vatican II.* Staten Island, NY: Alba House, 1966.

Lawson, Kevin E. "Theological Reflection, Theological Method, and the Practice of Education Ministry: Exploring the Wesleyan Quadrilateral and Stackhouse's Tetralectic." *Christian Education Journal* 1 (1997) 49–64.

Leavenworth, Lynn, ed. *Great Themes in Theology: Study Papers Prepared for American Baptist Theological Conferences.* Chicago: The Judson, 1958.

Lecerf, Auguste. *An Introduction to Reformed Dogmatics.* 2 vols. London: Lutterworth, [1949].

Lee, Sang Hyun. "Edwards on God and Nature: Resources for Contemporary Theology." In *Edwards in Our Time: Jonathan Edwards and the Shaping of American Religion*, edited by Sang Hyun Lee and Allen C. Guelzo, 15–44. Grand Rapids, MI: Eerdmans, 1999.

Lee, Sang Hyun, and Allen C. Guelzo, eds. *Edwards in Our Time: Jonathan Edwards and the Shaping of American Religion.* Grand Rapids, MI: Eerdmans, 1999.

Leitch, Addison H. "The Knowledge of God: General and Special Revelation." In *Basic Christian Doctrines*, edited by Carl F. H. Henry, 1–6. Contemporary Evangelical Thought. New York: Holt, Rineheart and Winston, 1962.

Leith, John H. *Basic Christian Doctrine.* Louisville, KY: Westminster John Knox, 1993.

———. *Creeds of the Churches: A Reader in Christian Doctrine from the Bible to the Present*. 3rd ed. Louisville, KY: Westminster John Knox, 1982.

Letham, Robert. "Amandus Polanus: A Neglected Theologian?" *Sixteenth Century Journal* 21 (1990) 463–76.

Leupold, H. C. *Exposition of the Psalms*. Grand Rapids, MI: Baker, 1959.

Lewis, Brad, et al. *Antz*. DVD. Directed by Eric Darnell and Tim Johnson. Glendale, CA: DreamWorks Animation, 2009.

Lewis, Donald, and Alister McGrath, eds. *Doing Theology for the People of God: Studies in Honor of J. I. Packer*. Downers Grove, IL: InterVarsity, 1996.

Lewis, Gordon R. "Is Propositional Revelation Essential to Evangelical Spiritual Formation?" *Journal of the Evangelical Theological Society* 46 (2003) 269–98.

———. "Jesus, Truth, and the ETS." Evangelical Theological Society: National Meeting, San Antonio, TX, November 2004: 1–17.

Lewis, Gordon R., and Bruce A. Demarest. *Integrative Theology: Historical, Biblical, Systematic, Apologetical, Practical*. 3 vols. in 1. Grand Rapids, MI: Zondervan, 1996.

Lewis, John M. *Layman's Library of Christian Doctrine: Revelation, Inspiration, Scripture*. Nashville: Broadman, 1985.

Lightner, Robert P. *Evangelical Theology: A Survey and Review*. Grand Rapids, MI: Baker, 1986.

Lindsay, Dennis G. *Harmony of Science and Scripture*. Creation Science Series 2. Rev. ed. Dallas: Christ for the Nations, 1998.

Lindsay, Dennis R. "What is Truth?: Ale[macron over e]theia in the Gospel of John." *Restoration Quarterly* 35 (1993) 129–45.

Lindsell, Harold. *The Battle for the Bible*. Grand Rapids, MI: Zondervan, 1976.

Lints, Richard. "Two Theologies or One? Warfield and Vos on the Nature of Theology." *Westminster Theological Journal* 54 (1992) 235–53.

Litfin, Duane. *Conceiving the Christian College: A College President Shares His Vision of Christian Higher Education*. Grand Rapids, MI: Eerdmans, 2004.

Litton, Edward Arthur. *Introduction to Dogmatic Theology*. New ed. Edited by Philip E. Hughes. London: J. Clarke, [1960].

Lockerbie, D. Bruce. *A Passion for Learning: The History of Christian Thought on Education*. Chicago: Moody, 1994.

Lundin, Roger. "Offspring of an Odd Union: Evangelical Attitudes Toward the Arts." In *Evangelicalism and Modern America*, edited by George Marsden, 135–49, 203–5. Grand Rapids, MI: Eerdmans, 1984.

Luther, Martin. *Sermons on the Gospel of St. John Chapters 1–4*. Luther's Works 22. Edited by Jaroslav Pelikan. [Saint Louis, MO]: Concordia Publishing House, 1957.

MacArthur, John. *Colossians & Philemon*. The MacArthur New Testament Commentary. Chicago: Moody, 1992.

———. *Romans 1–8*. The MacArthur New Testament Commentary 1. Chicago: Moody, 1991.

———. *Think Biblically! Recovering a Christian Worldview*. Wheaton: Crossway, 2003.

Machen, J. Gresham. *Christianity and Liberalism*. New ed. Grand Rapids, MI: Eerdmans, 2009.

MacLeod, Donald. "Bavinck's Prolegomena: Fresh Light on Amsterdam, Old Princeton, and Cornelius Van Til." *Westminster Theological Journal* 68 (2006) 261–82.

Marsden, George M. "Fundamentalism and American Evangelicalism." In *The Variety of American Evangelicalism*, edited by Donald W. Dayton and Robert K. Johnston, 22–35. Downers Grove, IL: InterVarsity, 1991.

———. *Jonathan Edwards: A Life*. New Haven, CT: Yale University Press, 2003.

Masselink, William. *General Revelation and Common Grace*. Grand Rapids, MI: Eerdmans, 1953.

Mathison, Keith A. *The Shape of Sola Scriptura*. Moscow, ID: Canon, 2001.

Mayhew, Eugene J. "God's Use of General Revelation in His Response to Job: A Critique of 2000 Years of Interpretation in Judaism and Christianity." *Evangelical Theological Society Annual Meeting*, Nov. 20–22, 1998.

Mayhue, Richard L. "Cultivating a Biblical Mind-Set." In *Think Biblically! Recovering A Christian Worldview*, edited by John MacArthur, 37–54. Wheaton: Crossway, 2003.

McAvoy, Steven L. "Can Truth Be Known?" In *The Fundamentals for the Twenty-First Century: Examining the Crucial Issues of the Christian Faith*, edited by Mal Couch, 29–55. Grand Rapids, MI: Kregel, 2000.

McCune, Rolland. *A Systematic Theology of Biblical Christianity*. 2 vols. Allen Park, MI: Detroit Baptist Theological Seminary, 2009.

McDermott, Gerald R. *Can Evangelicals Learn from World Religions? Jesus, Revelation and Religious Traditions*. Downers Grove, IL: InterVarsity, 2000.

McDonald, H. D. *Theories of Revelation: An Historical Study 1700–1960*. Grand Rapids, MI: Baker, 1979.

McGavran, Donald. *The Clash Between Christianity and Cultures*. Washington, DC: Canon, 1974.

McGrath, Alister E. *Christian Theology: An Introduction*. 3rd ed. Malden, MA: Blackwell, 2001.

———. *Creation. Truth and the Christian Imagination*. Minneapolis: Fortress, 2005.

———. *Evangelicalism and the Future of Christianity*. Downers Grove, IL: InterVarsity, 1995.

———. "Loving God with Heart and Mind: The Theological Foundations of Spirituality." In *For All the Saints: Evangelical Theology and Christian Spirituality*, edited by Timothy George and Alister McGrath, 11–26. Louisville, KY: Wesminster John Knox, 2003.

———. *The Open Secret: A New Vision for Natural Theology*. Malden, MA: Blackwell, 2008.

———, ed. *The Blackwell Encyclopedia of Modern Thought*. Cambridge, MA: Blackwell Reference, 1993.

McLean, John A. "The Importance of Hermeneutics." In *The Fundamentals for the Twenty-First Century: Examining the Crucial Issues of the Christian Faith*, edited by Mal Couch, 73–84. Grand Rapids, MI: Kregel, 2000.

McMinn, Mark R., and Jeannine M. Graham. "Theology as Science: A Response to 'Theology as Queen and Psychology as Handmaid.'" *Journal of Psychology and Christianity* 29 (2010) 15–19.

Meaders Gary T., ed. *Four Views on Moving Beyond the Bible to Theology*. Counterpoints. Edited by Stanley N. Gundry. Grand Rapids, MI: Zondervan, 2009.

Medley, Mark S. "An Evangelical Theology for a Postmodern Age: Stanley J. Grenz's Current Theological Project." *Perspectives in Religious Studies* 30 (2003) 71–94.

Meeter, John E., ed. *Selected Shorter Writings of Benjamin B. Warfield –I*. Nutley, NJ: Presbyterian and Reformed, 1970.

———. *Selected Shorter Writings of Benjamin B. Warfield –II*. Nutley, NJ: Presbyterian and Reformed, 1973.

Meneses, Eloise Hiebert. "No Other Foundation: Establishing a Christian Anthropology." *Christian Scholar's Review* 29 (2000) 531–49

Menzies, William W. *Bible Doctrines: A Pentecostal Perspective*. Edited by Stanley M. Horton. 1993. Reprint. Springfield, MO: Logion, 1998.

Merrill, Eugene H. *Everlasting Dominion: A Theology of the Old Testament*. Broadman & Holman, 2006.

———. "The Wisdom That is From Above." http://wwww.dts.edu/media/play/the-wisdom-that-is-from-above-eugene-h-merrill/.

Migliore, Daniel L. *Faith Seeking Understanding: An Introduction to Christian Theology*. 2nd ed. Grand Rapids, MI: Eerdmans, 2004.

Miley, John. *Systematic Theology*. 2 vols. New York: Methodist Book Concern, 1892–1894.

Miller, Ed L., ed. *Classical Statements on Faith and Reason*. New York: Random House, 1970.

Milne, Bruce. *Know the Truth: A Handbook of Christian Belief*. 3rd ed. Downers Grove, IL: InterVarsity, 2009.

Miner, Raymond. *Systematic Theology*. 3 vols. 1879. Reprint. Cincinnati, OH: Walden and Stowe, 1880.

Mohler, R. Albert. "What is Truth? Truth and Contemporary Culture." *Journal of the Evangelical Theological Society* 48 (2005) 63–75.

Moo, Douglas J. *The Epistle to the Romans*. Grand Rapids, MI: Eerdmans, 1996.

Moore, Andrew. "Should Christians do Natural Theology?" *Scottish Journal of Theology* 63 (2010) 127–45.

Moore, Russell D. "Natural Revelation." In *A Theology for the Church*, edited by Daniel L. Akin, 109–16. Nashville: B & H Academic, 2007.

———. "Personal and Cosmic Eschatology." In *A Theology for the Church*, edited by Daniel L. Akin, 858–926. Nashville, TN: B & H Academic, 2007.

Moore, T. M. *Consider the Lilies: A Plea for Creational Theology*. Phillipsburg, NJ: P & R, 2005.

———. *Culture Matters: A Call for Consensus on Christian Cultural Engagement*. Grand Rapids, MI: Brazos, 2007.

Moreland, J. P. "How Evangelicals Became Over-Committed to the Bible and What can be Done about It." No pages. Online: http://www.kingdomtriangle.com/discussion/moreland_EvangOverCommBible.pdf.

———. "A Philosophical Examination of Hugh Ross' Natural Theology." *Philosophia Christi* 21 (1998) 33–39.

———. "Philosophy." In *Opening the American Mind: The Integration of Biblical Truth in the Curriculum of the University*, edited by W. David Beck, 47–66. Grand Rapids, MI: Baker Book, 1991.

———. "Truth, Contemporary Philosophy, and the Postmodern Turn." *Journal of the Evangelical Theological Society* 48 (2005) 77–88.

Morris, Henry M. "The Bible is a Textbook of Science." *Bibliotheca sacra* 121 (1964): 341–50.

Morris, L. *I Believe in Revelation*. Grand Rapids, MI: Eerdmans, 1976.

Mouw, Richard. *He Shines in All That's Fair: Culture and Common Grace.* The Strobe Lectures. Grand Rapids, MI: Eerdmans, 2001.

———. *The Smell of Sawdust: What Evangelicals Can Learn from Their Fundamentalist Heritage.* Grand Rapids, MI: Zondervan, 2000.

Mueller, John Theodore. *Christian Dogmatics: A Handbook of Doctrinal Theology for Pastors, Teachers and Laymen.* St Louis, MO: Concordia, 1934.

Muller, Richard A. *The Divine Essence and Attributes.* Post-Reformation Reformed Dogmatics 3. Grand Rapids, MI: Baker, 1987.

———. *Prolegomena to Theology.* Post-Reformation Reformed Dogmatics 1. Grand Rapids, MI: Baker, 1987.

———. "Scholasticism Protestant and Catholic: Francis Turretin on the Object and Principles of Theology." *Church History* 55 (1986) 193–205.

———. *The Study of Theology: From Biblical Interpretation to Contemporary Formulation.* Foundations of Contemporary Interpretation 7. Edited by Moisés Silva. Grand Rapids, MI: Zondervan, 1991.

Mullins, Edgar Young. *The Christian Religion in its Doctrinal Expression.* Philadelphia: Roger Williams, 1917.

Murphy, Nancey. *Beyond Liberalism & Fundamentalism: How Modern and Postmodern Philosophy Set the Theological Agenda.* Rockwell Lecture Series. Edited by Werner H. Kelber. Valley Forge, PA: Trinity, 1996.

Murray, John. *Select Lectures in Systematic Theology.* Collected Writings of John Murray 2. Carlisle, PA: Banner of Truth Trust, 1976.

Myatt, Alan, and Franklin Ferreira. *Teologia sistemática.* Rio de Janeiro: Seminário Teológico Batista do Sul do Brasil, 2002.

Myers, David G., and Malcolm A. Jeeves. *Psychology Through the Eyes of Faith.* Rev. ed. San Francisco: Harper & Row, 2003.

Nash, Ronald. "Southern Baptists and the Notion of Revealed Truth." *Criswell Theological Review* 2 (1988) 371–84.

———. *The Word of God and the Mind of Man.* Grand Rapids, MI: Zondervan, 1982.

Newell, William L. *Truth is Our Mask: An Essay on Theological Method.* Lanham, MD: University Press of America, 1990.

Newell, William R. *Romans Verse-by-Verse.* A Classic Evangelical Commentary. Grand Rapids, MI: Kregel, 1973.

Nickelback. "If Everyone Cared." In *All the Right Reasons.* New York: Roadrunner Records, 2005.

Niebuhr, H. Richard. *Christ and Culture.* 1951. Reprint. San Francisco, CA: Harper Collins Publishers, 2001.

———. *The Meaning of Revelation.* 1941. Reprint. Louisville, KY: Westminster John Knox, 2006.

Nickel, James. *Mathematics: Is God Silent?* Rev. ed. Vallecito, CA: Ross House, 2001.

Noll, Mark A. *American Evangelical Christianity: An Introduction.* Malden, MA: Blackwell, 2001.

———. "Common Sense Traditions and American Evangelical Thought." *American Quarterly* 37 (1985) 216–38.

———. *A History of Christianity in the United States and Canada.* 1992. Reprint. Grand Rapids, MI: Eerdmans, 2000.

———. *Jesus Christ and the Life of the Mind.* Grand Rapids, MI: Eerdmans, 2011.

———. *The Princeton Theology 1812–1921: Scripture and Theological Method from Archibald Alexander to Benjamin Warfield*. 1983. Reprint. Grand Rapids, MI: Baker, 2001.

———. *The Rise of Evangelicalism: The Age of Edwards, Whitefield, and the Wesleys*. A History of Evangelicalism: People, Movements and Ideas in the English-Speaking World. Edited by David W. Bebbington and Mark A. Noll. Downers Grove, IL: InterVarsity, 2003.

———. *The Scandal of the Evangelical Mind*. Grand Rapids, MI: Eerdmans, 1994.

Norman, R. Stanton. "Human Sinfulness." In *A Theology for the Church*, edited by Daniel L. Akin, 409–79. Nashville, TN: B & H Academic, 2007.

Numbers, Ronald L. "The Dilemma of Evangelical Scientists." In *Evangelicalism and Modern America*, edited by George Marsden, 150–60, 205–6. Grand Rapids, MI: Eerdmans, 1984.

Nygren, Anders. *Commentary on Romans*. Philadelphia: Fortress, 1949.

Oden, Thomas C. "Response to Hugh Ross on 'General Revelation: Nature's Testament.'" *Philosophia Christi* 21 (1998) 41–48.

———. *Systematic Theology*. 3 vols. Peabody, MA: Hendrickson, 2006.

———. *A Systematic Theology: Classic Christianity*. New York: Harper One, 2009.

———. "Without Excuse: Classic Christian Exegesis of General Revelation." *Journal of the Evangelical Theological Society* 41 (1998) 55–68.

Oehler, Gustav Friedrich. *Theology of the Old Testament*. Revised trans. George E. Day. Original T. & T. Clark, 1873. Reprint Minneapolis, MN: Klock and Klock, 1978.

Ohlmann, Eric H. "Baptists and Evangelicals." In *The Variety of American Evangelicalism*, edited by Donald W. Dayton and Robert K. Johnston, 148–60. Downers Grove, IL: InterVarsity, 1991.

Oliphint, K Scott. "Jerusalem and Athens revisited." *Westminster Theological Journal* 49 (1987) 65–90.

———. *Reasons {for Faith}: Philosophy in the Service of Theology*. Phillipsburg, NJ: P & R, 2006.

———. "The Irrationality of Unbelief." In *Revelation and Reason: New Essays in Reformed Apologetics*, edited by K. Scott Oliphint and Lane G. Tipton, 59–73. Phillipsburg, NJ: P & R, 2007.

Olson, Roger E. *The Mosaic of Christian Belief: Twenty Centuries of Unity and Diversity*. Downers Grove, IL: InterVarsity, 2002.

———. *Pocket History of Evangelical Theology*. Downers Grove, IL: InterVarsity, 2007.

O'Rourke, John J. "Romans 1, 20 and Natural Revelation." *Catholic Biblical Quarterly* 23 (1961) 301–6.

Orr, J. *Revelation and Inspiration*. New York: Scribner's, 1910.

Osborne, Grant R. *Romans*. The IVP New Testament Commentary Series. Edited by Grant R. Osborne. Downers Grove, IL: InterVarsity, 2004.

Ostrander, Rick. *Why College Matters to God: Faithful Learning and Christian Higher Education*. Abilene, TX: Abilene Christian University Press, 2009.

Ottati, Douglas F. "Christian Theology and Other Disciplines." *Journal of Religion* 64 (1984) 173–87.

Outler, Albert C. "Augustine and the Transvaluation of the Classical Tradition." *The Classical Journal* 54 (1959) 213–20.

Owen, H. P. "The Scope of Natural Revelation in Rom. 1 and Acts 17." *New Testament Studies 1958-1959*, edited by Matthew Black, vol. 5, 133–43. Cambridge: University Press, 1959.
Packer, J. I. *Concise Theology: A Guide to Historic Christian Belief.* Wheaton: Tyndale House, 1993.
———. *Fundamentalism and the Word of God: Some Evangelical Principles.* 1958. Reprint. London: InterVarsity Fellowship, 1963.
———. *Knowing Christianity*. Wheaton: Harold Shaw, 1995.
Padgett, Alan G. "'I Am the Truth': An Understanding of Truth from Christology for Scripture." In *But is it All True? The Bible and the Question of Truth*, edited by Alan G. Padgett and Patrick R. Keifert, 104–14. Grand Rapids, MI: Eerdmans, 2006
Pailin, David A. "Revelation." In *The Westminster Dictionary of Christian Theology*, edited by Alan Richardson and John Bowden, 503–6. Philadelphia: Westminster, 1983.
Panel Discussion. "Evangelical Theological Method." Evangelical Theological Society: Southwest Regional Meeting, Dallas Theological Seminary, Dallas, TX, March 19, 2011.
Pate, P. Elizabeth, et al. *Making Integrated Curriculum Work: Teachers, Students, and the Quest for Coherent Curriculum.* New York: Teachers College Press, 1997.
Patterson, Bob E. "James Leo Garrett Jr. and the Doctrine of Revelation." *Perspectives in Religious Studies* 33 (2006) 25–40.
Patterson, Bob E., and Carl F. H. Henry. *The Makers of the Modern Mind.* Edited by Bob E. Patterson. Waco, TX: Word, 1983.
Pearcey, Nancy R. *Total Truth: Liberating Christianity from Its Cultural Captivity.* Wheaton: Crossway, 2004.
Pelikan, Jaroslav, and Valerie Hotchkiss, eds. *Creeds and Confessions of the Reformation Era.* Creeds & Confessions of Faith in the Christian Tradition 2. New Haven, CT: Yale University Press, 2003.
———. *Early, Eastern & Medieval.* Creeds & Confessions of Faith in the Christian Tradition 1. New Haven, CT: Yale University Press, 2003.
Peter, J. F. "Revelation and Propositions." *Evangelical Quarterly* 33 (1961) 67–80.
Phillips, Timothy R., and Dennis L. Okholm. *Welcome to the Family: An Introduction to Evangelical Christianity.* Grand Rapids, MI: Baker, 1996.
Pieper, D. Franz. *Christliche dogmatik.* Band 1. Saint Louis, MO: Concordia, 1924.
Pieper, Francis. *Christian Dogmatics.* 4 vols. Saint Louis, MO: Concordia, 1950–1957.
Pierard, Richard V. "Evangelicalism." In *Evangelical Dictionary of Theology*, edited by Walter A. Elwell, 379–80. 1984. Reprint. Grand Rapids, MI: Baker Books, 1997.
Pinnock, Clark H. *Biblical Revelation: The Foundations of Christian Theology.* Chicago: Moody, 1971.
Piper, John. *The Pleasures of God: Meditations on God's Delight in Being God.* Sisters, OR: Multnomah, 1991.
Piper, John, and Justin Taylor, eds. *A God Entranced Vision of All Things.* Wheaton: Crossway, 2004.
Plantinga, Alvin. "Advice to Christian Philosophers." *Faith and Philosophy* 1 (1984) 253–71.
Plantinga, Cornelius, Jr. *Engaging God's World: A Reformed Vision of Faith, Learning, and Living.* Grand Rapids, MI: Eerdmans, 2002.

Plantinga, Richard J., Thomas R. Thompson, and Matthew D. Lundberg. *An Introduction to Christian Theology*. New York: Cambridge University Press, 2010.

Polkinghorne, John R. "Creation and the Structure of the Physical World." In *Readings in Modern Theology*, edited by Robin Gill, 25–42. London: SPCK, 1995.

———. *Science and the Trinity: The Christian Encounter with Reality*. New Haven, CT: Yale University Press, 2004.

———. *Traffic in Truth: Exchanges between Science and Theology*. Facets. 2000. Reprint. Minneapolis: Fortress, 2002.

Pope, William Burt. *A Compendium of Christian Theology: Analytical Outlines of a Course of Theological Study: Biblical, Dogmatic, Historical*. 3 vols. 2nd ed. New York: Phillips & Hunt, 1882.

Porter, Steve L. "A Reply to the Respondents of 'Theology as Queen and Psychology as Handmaid.'" *Journal of Psychology and Christianity* 29 (2010) 33–40.

———. "Theology as Queen and Psychology as Handmaid: The Authority of Theology in Integrative Endeavors." *Journal of Psychology and Christianity* 29 (2010) 3–14.

Poythress, Vern S. *Symphonic Theology: The Validity of Multiple Perspectives in Theology*. 1987. Reprint. Phillipsburg, NJ: P & R, 2001.

Pratchett, Terry. *Making Money*. New York: Harper Collins, 2007.

Purkiser, W. T., ed. *Exploring Our Christian Faith*. Rev. ed. Kansas City, MO: Beacon Hill, 1978.

Rabey, Steve, and Monte Unger. *Milestones: 50 Events of the 20th Century that Shaped Evangelicals in America*. Nashville: Broadman & Holman, 2002.

Ramm, Bernard. *Special Revelation and the Word of God*. Grand Rapids, MI: Eerdmans, 1961.

Raschke, Carl. *The Next Reformation: Why Evangelicals Must Embrace Postmodernity*. Grand Rapids, MI: Baker, 2004.

Rawley, David G. "Revelation: General and Specific." In *Theological Perspectives: Arminian-Wesleyan Reflections on Theology*, edited by Paul R. Fetters, 83–121. USA: Church of the United Brethren in Christ, 1992.

Reymond, Robert L. *A New Systematic Theology of the Christian Faith*. Nashville: Thomas Nelson, 1998.

Ridgway, James M. "Psychology: Theology of the Human Psyche." In *A Contemporary Wesleyan Theology: Biblical, Systematic, and Practical* 2, edited by Charles W. Carter, 875–950. Grand Rapids, MI: Francis Asbury Press, 1983.

Roberts, Alexander, and James Donaldson. *The Ante-Nicene Fathers*. Translations of the Writings of the Fathers Down to A.D. 325 1. The Apostolic Fathers with Justin Martyr and Irenaeus. Grand Rapids, MI: Eerdmans, 1997. Logos Bible Software.

Robinson, Charles K. "St. Irenaeus on General Revelation as Preparation for Special Revelation." *Duke Divinity School Review* 43 (1978) 169–80.

Roccasalvo, Joan L. "Beauty, Beethoven's Fifth, and the Experience of Faith." *Irish Theological Quarterly* 73 (2008) 369–84.

Rookmaaker, Hans. *Our Calling and God's Hand in History*. Edited by Marleen Hengelar-Rookmaaker. The Complete Works of Hans Rookmaaker 6. Carlisle, UK: Piquant, 2003.

Rose, D. Glenn. "The Biblical Idea of Revelation: Its Relevance for Constructive Theology Today." *Encounter* 21 (1960) 201–17.

Ross, Hugh. "General Revelation: Nature's Testament." *Philosophia Christi* 21 (1998) 9–15.

Ryden, Hope. "Monarch Butterfly: Danaus plexippus." http://animals.nationalgeographic.com/animals/bugs/monarch-butterfly/.

Ryrie, Charles C. *Basic Theology: A Popular Systematic Guide to Understanding Biblical Truth*. 1986. Reprint. Chicago: Moody, 1999.

Sandage, Steven J., and Jeannine K. Brown. "Monarchy or Democracy in Relation Integration? A Reply to Porter." *Journal of Psychology and Christianity* 29 (2010) 20–26.

Sanday, William. *A Critical and Exegetical Commentary on the Epistle to the Romans*. The International Critical Commentary. 5th ed. Edinburgh: T. & T. Clark, 1980.

Saucy, Robert L. "Scripture: Its Power, Authority, and Relevance." In *Understanding Christian Theology*, edited by Charles Swindoll and Roy Zuck, 3–136. Nashville: Thomas Nelson, 2003.

———. "What is Divine Revelation?" In *Understanding Christian Theology*, edited by Charles R. Swindoll and Roy B. Zuck, 16–22. Nashville: Thomas Nelson, 2003.

Sawyer, M. James. *The Survivor's Guide to Theology: Investigation of Critical Issues, Survey of Key Traditions, Biographies of Major Theologians and Glossary of Terms*. Grand Rapids, MI: Zondervan, 2006.

Sayers, Dorothy L. *Letters to a Diminished Church: Passionate Arguments for the Relevance of Christian Doctrine*. Nashville: Thomas Nelson, 2004.

———. *The Mind of the Maker*. 1941. Reprint. New York: Harper & Row, 1979.

Scaer, David P. "Francis Pieper." In *Handbook of Evangelical Theologians*, edited by Walter A. Elwell, 40–53. Grand Rapids, MI: Baker Books, 1993.

Schmitt, Frederick F., ed. *Theories of Truth*. Blackwell Readings in Philosophy 13, edited by Steven M. Cahn. Malden, MA: Blackwell, 2004.

Schweitzer, Don. "Aspects of God's Relationship to the World in the Theologies of Jürgen Moltmann, Bonaventure and Jonathan Edwards." *Religious Studies and Theology* 26 (2007) 5–24.

Scott, Ernest Findlay. *The New Testament Idea of Revelation*. London: Ivor Nicholson & Watson, 1936.

Seely, Paul H. "Concordism and a Biblical Alternative: An Examination of Hugh Ross' Perspective." *Perspectives on Science and Christian Faith* 59 (2007) 37–45.

Shedd, William G. T. *Commentary on Romans*. 1879. Reprint. Grand Rapids, MI: Baker, 1980.

———. *Dogmatic Theology*. Edited by Alan W. Gomes. 3rd ed. Phillipsburg, NJ: P & R, 2003.

Sider, Ronald J. *The Scandal of Evangelical Politics: Why are Christians Missing the Chance to Really Change the World?* Grand Rapids, MI: Baker, 2008.

Smith, Christian. *The Bible Made Impossible: Why Biblicism is not a Truly Evangelical Reading of Scripture*. Grand Rapids, MI: Brazos, 2011.

Smith, David I., and James K. A. Smith. *Teaching and Christian Practices: Reshaping Faith and Learning*. Grand Rapids, MI: Eerdmans, 2011.

Smith, Donald K. *Creating Understanding: A Handbook for Christian Communication across Cultural Landscapes*. Grand Rapids, MI: Zondervan, 1992.

Smith, Gary S. *The Seeds of Secularization: Calvinism, Culture, and Pluralism in America, 1870–1915*. Grand Rapids, MI: Eerdmans, 1985.

Southgate, Christopher. *The Groaning of Creation: God, Evolution and the Problem of Evil*. Louisville, KY: Westminster John Knox, 2008.

Spencer, Stephen R. "Is Natural Theology Biblical?" *Grace Theological Journal* 9 (1988) 59–72.

Spina, Frank Anthony. *The Faith of the Outsider: Exclusion and Inclusion in the Biblical Story*. Grand Rapids, MI: Eerdmans, 2005.

Sprigg, Peter S. "Science and the Knowledge of God: From Machine to Metaphor." *Journal of Faith and Science Exchange* 1 (1997) 103–8.

Sproul, R. C. *Essential Truths of the Christian Faith: 100 Key Doctrines in Plain Language*. Wheaton: Tyndale House, 1992.

———. *Everyone's a Theologian: An Introduction to Systematic Theology*. Sanford, FL: Reformation Trust, 2014.

———. *Scripture Alone: The Evangelical Doctrine*. Phillipsburg, NJ: P & R, 2005.

Stackhouse, John G. Jr. *Evangelical Landscapes: Facing Critical Issues of the Day*. Grand Rapids, MI: Baker, 2002.

———. "Evangelical Theology Should be Evangelical." In *Evangelical Futures: A Conversation on Theological Method*, edited by John. G. Stackhouse Jr., 39–60. Grand Rapids, MI: Baker Books, 2000.

———, ed. *Evangelical Futures: A Conversation on Theological Method*. Grand Rapids, MI: Baker, 2000.

Stafford, Gilbert W. "Frontiers in Contemporary Theology." In *A Contemporary Wesleyan Theology: Biblical, Systematic, and Practical* 1, edited by Charles W. Carter, 19–54. Grand Rapids, MI: Francis Asbury Press, 1983.

Stanton, Glenn T. "Factchecker: Misquoting Francis of Assisi." http://www.thegospelcoalition.org/article/factchecker-misquoting-francis-of-assisi.

Stokes, H. Bruce, and Nathaniel P. Lewis. *Integration of Behavioral Sciences and Theology: A System-Relational Approach*. New York: Writers Club, 1999.

Stott, John. *Evangelical Truth: A Personal Plea for Unity, Integrity and Faithfulness. Christian Doctrine in Global Perspective*. Edited by David Smith. 1999. Reprint. Downers Grove, IL: InterVarsity, 2003.

———. *Romans: God's Good News for the World*. Downers Grove, IL: InterVarsity, 1994.

———. "Theology: A Multidimensional Discipline." In *Doing Theology for the People of God: Studies in Honor of J. I. Packer*, edited by Donald Lewis and Alister McGrath, 3–20. Downers Grove, IL: InterVarsity, 1996.

Street, John D. "Why Biblical Counseling and Not Psychology?" In *Think Biblically! Recovering A Christian Worldview*, edited by John MacArthur, 203–20. Wheaton: Crossway, 2003.

Strong, Augustus H. *Systematic Theology: A Compendium Designed for the Use of Theological Students*. 1907. Reprint. Valley Forge, PA: Judson, 1976.

Struthers, William M. *Wired for Intimacy: How Pornography Hijacks the Male Brain*. Downers Grove, IL: InterVarsity, 2009.

Summers, Thomas O. *Systematic Theology: A Complete Body of Wesleyan Arminian Divinity, Consisting of Lectures on the Twenty-Five Articles of Religion, Arranged and Revised, with Introduction, Copious Notes and a Theological Glossary*. 2 vols. Nashville: Publishing House of the Methodist Episcopal Church, South, 1888.

Swanton, R. Review of *General Revelation*, by G. C. Berkouwer. *Reformed Theological Review* 15 (1956) 50–51.

Swindoll, Charles R., and Roy B. Zuck, eds. *Understanding Christian Theology*. Nashville: Thomas Nelson Publishers, 2003.

Tanzella-Nitti, Giuseppe. "The Two Books Prior to the Scientific Revolution." *Perspectives on Science and Christian Faith* 57 (2005) 235–48.
Thiessen, Henry C. *Introductory Lectures in Systematic Theology.* Grand Rapids, MI: Eerdmans, 1949.
Thomas, Robert L. *Evangelical Hermeneutics: The New Versus the Old.* Grand Rapids, MI: Kregel Academic & Professional, 2002.
———. "General Revelation and Biblical Hermeneutics." *Master's Seminary Journal* 9 (1998) 5–23.
Thomas, W. H. Griffith. *The Principles of Theology: An Introduction to the Thirty-Nine Articles.* 6th ed. London: Vine, 1978.
Thompson, R. Duane. "Social Involvement: The Responsibility of God's People." In *A Contemporary Wesleyan Theology: Biblical, Systematic, and Practical* 2, edited by Charles W. Carter, 689–732. Grand Rapids, MI: Francis Asbury, 1983.
Thornbury, Gregory Alan. "Prolegomena: Introduction to the Task of Theology." In *A Theology for the Church*, edited by Daniel L. Akin, 2–70. Nashville: B & H Academic, 2007.
Thornwell, James Henley. *Theological.* The Collected Writings of James Henley Thornwell 1. Carlisle, PA: Banner of Truth Trust, 1974.
Thorsen, Don. *An Exploration of Christian Theology.* Peabody, MA: Hendrickson Publishers, 2008.
———. "Sola Scriptura and the Wesleyan Quadrilateral." *Wesleyan Theological Journal* 41 (2006) 7–27.
Todd, Stephen R. "What Evangelicals Have to Do with Athens and Jerusalem." In *For All the Saints: Evangelical Theology and Christian Spirituality*, edited by Timothy George and Alister McGrath, 73–87. Louisville, KY: Westminster John Knox, 2003.
Tomlinson, Dave. *The Post-Evangelical.* Grand Rapids, MI: Zondervan, 2003.
Towns, Elmer L. *Theology for Today.* Fort Worth, TX: Harcourt College Publishers, 2001.
Tozer, A. W. *The Knowledge of the Holy.* New York: Harper One, 1961.
———. "The Speaking Voice." http://www.the-highway.com/voice_Tozer.html.
Treier, Daniel J., et al. *The Beauty of God: Theology and the Arts.* Downers Grove, IL: InterVarsity, 2007.
Turnau, Theodore A. III. "Reflecting Theologically on Popular Culture as Meaningful: The Role of Sin, Grace, and General Revelation." *Calvin Theological Journal* 37 (2002) 270–96.
Turner, David L. "Cornelius Van Til and Romans 1:18–21: A Study in the Epistemology of Presuppositional Apologetics." *Grace Theological Journal* 2 (1981) 45–58.
Unger, Merrill F. "Revelation." In *Unger's Bible Dictionary*, edited by Merrill F. Unger, 922. 1957. Reprint. Chicago: Moody, 1967.
Vanden Berg, Mary L. "What General Revelation Does (and Does Not) Tell Us." *Perspectives on Science and Christian Faith* 62 (2010) 16–24.
Vander Goot, Henry. "Creation, Revelation, and Christian Philosophy." In *Creation and Method: Critical Essays on Christo-centric Theology*, edited by Henry Vander Goot, 137–58. Washington, DC: University Press of America, 1981.
Van Dyke, Fred, Arlan J. Birkey, and Ted D. Nickel. "Integration and the Christian College: Reflection on the Nineteenth Psalm." *Faculty Dialogue* 9 (1987) 89–96.

Van Gemeren, Willem A. *Psalms-Song of Songs*. The Expositor's Bible Commentary 5. Edited by Frank E. Gaebelein and Richard P. Polcyn. Grand Rapids, MI: Zondervan, 1991.

Vanhoozer, Kevin J. "What is Everyday Theology? How and Why Christians Should Read Culture." In *Everyday Theology: How to Read Cultural Texts and Interpret Trends*, edited by Kevin J. Vanhoozer, et al., 15–60, 254–262. Grand Rapids, MI: Baker Academic, 2007.

———, ed. *Dictionary for Theological Interpretation of the Bible*. Grand Rapids, MI: Baker Academic, 2005.

Vanhoozer, Kevin J., et al. *Everyday Theology: How to Read Cultural Texts and Interpret Trends*. Grand Rapids, MI: Baker Academic, 2007.

Van Til, Cornelius. *Christian Apologetics*. Edited by William Edgar. 2nd ed. Phillipsburg, NJ: P & R, 2003.

———. *Common Grace*. Philadelphia, PA: Presbyterian and Reformed, 1954.

———. *The Defense of the Faith*. Edited by K. Scott Oliphint. 4th ed. Phillipsburg, NJ: P & R, 1967.

———. *An Introduction to Systematic Theology*. Nutley, NJ: Presbyterian & Reformed, 1974.

———. *An Introduction to Systematic Theology: Prolegomena and the Doctrines of Revelation, Scripture, and God*. 2nd ed. Edited by William Edgar. Phillipsburg, NJ: P & R, 2007.

———. "Nature and Scripture." In *The Infallible Word*, edited by N. B. Stonehouse and P. Woolley, 255–93. Grand Rapids, MI: Eerdmans, 1953.

Van Til, Henry R. *The Calvinistic Concept of Culture*. Grand Rapids, MI: Baker, 2001.

Wainwright, William J. "Jonathan Edwards and the Language of God." *Journal of the American Academy of Religion* 48 (1980) 519–30.

Walls, Andrew F. *The Cross-Cultural Process in Christian History*. Maryknoll, New York: Orbis, 2002.

———. "Culture and Coherence in Christian History." *Evangelical Review of Theology* 9 (1985) 214–25.

———. *The Missionary Movement in Christian History: Studies in the Transmission of Faith*. Maryknoll, New York: Orbis Books, 2000.

Waltke, Bruce K., and Charles Yu. *An Old Testament Theology: An Exegetical, Canonical, and Thematic Approach*. Grand Rapids, MI: Zondervan, 2007.

Waltke, Bruce K., et al. *The Psalms as Christian Worship: A Historical Commentary*. Grand Rapids, MI: Eerdmans, 2010.

Wardlaw, Ralph. *Systematic Theology*. 3 vols. Edited by James R. Campbell. Edinburgh: A. and C. Black, 1856–57.

Warfield, Benjamin B. *Calvin and Augustine*. Edited by Samuel G. Craig. Philadelphia, PA: Presbyterian and Reformed, 1956.

———. *Evolution, Science and Scripture: Selected Writings*. Edited by Mark A. Noll and David N. Livingstone. Grand Rapids, MI: Baker, 2000.

———. *The Inspiration and Authority of the Bible*. Philadelphia: Presbyterian and Reformed, 1948.

———. *Revelation and Inspiration*. The Works of Benjamin B. Warfield 1. 1927. Reprint. Grand Rapids, MI: Baker, 1991.

———. *Studies in Theology*. The Works of Benjamin B. Warfield 9. 1932. Reprint. Grand Rapids, MI: Baker, 1991.

Warnke, George. *Gadamer: Hermeneutics, Tradition and Reason.* Standford, CA: Stanford University Press, 1987.
Watson, Richard. *Theological Institutes.* 2 vols. New York: G. Lane, 1848.
Webber, Robert E. *The Younger Evangelicals: Facing the Challenges of the New World.* 2002. Reprint. Grand Rapids, MI: Baker, 2003.
Webster, John. "Principles of Systematic Theology." *International Journal of Systematic Theology* 11 (2009) 56–71.
Weeks, David L. "The Uneasy Politics of Modern Evangelicalism." *Christian Scholar's Review* 30 (2001) 403–18.
Wells, David F. *Above All Earthly Pow'rs: Christ in a Post-Modern World.* Grand Rapids, MI: Eerdmans, 2005.
———. "An American Evangelical Theology: The Painful Transition from Theoria to Praxis." In *Evangelicalism and Modern America*, edited by George Marsden, 83–93, 193–5. Grand Rapids, MI: Eerdmans, 1984.
———. *No Place for Theology: Or Whatever Happened to Evangelical Theology?* Grand Rapids, MI: Eerdmans, 1993.
Wells, Ronald. *History Through the Eyes of Faith.* San Francisco: Harper & Row, 1989.
West, Christopher. *Theology of the Body for Beginners: A Basic Introduction to Pope John Paul II's Sexual Revolution.* West Chester: PA: Ascension, 2004.
Whidden, Woodrow W. "Sola Scriptura, Inerrantist Fundamentalism, and the Wesleyan Quadrilateral: Is 'No Creed but the Bible' a Workable Solution?" *Andrews University Seminary Studies* 35 (1997) 211–26.
Whitcomb, John C. "Biblical Inerrancy and the Double-Revelation Theory." *Grace Journal* 4 (1963) 3–20.
White, James Emery. *What is Truth? A Comparative Study of the Positions of Cornelius Van Til, Francis Schaeffer, Carl F. H. Henry, Donald Bloesch and Millard Erickson.* Nashville: Broadman and Holman, 1994.
Whybray, R. N. *Proverbs.* New Century Bible Commentary. Edited by Ronald E. Clements. Grand Rapids, MI: Eerdmans, 1994.
Wickizer, Bob. "Creation and Revelation: Two Edges of Contact Between Science and Religion." *Journal of Faith and Science Exchange* 1 (1997) 109–14.
Wiley, H. Orton. *Christian Theology.* 3 vols. Kansas City, MO: Beacon Hill, 1940–1943.
Wilhoit, Mel R. "Faith and Learning Reconsidered: The Unity of Truth." *Faculty Dialogue* 9 (1987) 77–86.
Wilkinson, Loren. "Integration and Interpretation: On Interpreting the 'Two Books' of Revelation." *Crux* 23 (1987) 11–25.
Williams, A. N. "What is Systematic Theology?" *International Journal of Systematic Theology* 11 (2009) 40–55.
Williams, J. Rodman. *Renewal Theology: Systematic Theology from a Charismatic Perspective.* 3 vols. Grand Rapids, MI: Academie Books, 1988–1892.
Williams, Stephen. "The Theological Task and Theological Method: Penitence, Parasitism, and Prophecy." In *Evangelical Futures: A Conversation on Theological Method*, edited by John G. Stackhouse, 159–80. Grand Rapids, MI: Baker, 2000.
Willimon, William H. "Answering Pilate: Truth and the Postliberal Church." *Christian Century* 104 (1987) 82–85.
———. "Jesus' Peculiar Truth: Modern Apologists for Objective Truth are Making a Tactical Error." *Christianity Today* 6 (1996) 21–22.

Wilson, Douglas. "The Sacred Script in the Theater of God: Calvin, the Bible, and the Western World." In *With Calvin in the Theater of God: The Glory of Christ and Everyday Life*, edited by John Piper and David Mathis, 83–95. Wheaton: Crossway, 2010.

Winter, Richard. "The Search for Truth in Psychology and Counseling." *Presbyterion* 31 (2005) 18–36.

Witmer, John A. "Romans." In *The Bible Knowledge Commentary: An Exposition of the Scriptures by Dallas Seminary Faculty, New Testament*, edited by John F. Walvoord and Roy B. Zuck, 435–503 Wheaton: Victor, 1983.

Wolters, Al. *Creation Regained: Biblical Basics for a Reformational Worldview*. 2nd ed. Grand Rapids, MI: Eerdmans, 2005.

———. "A Reflection by Al Wolters." In *Four Views on Moving Beyond the Bible to Theology*, edited by Gary T. Meaders, 299–319. Counterpoints. Edited by Stanley N. Gundry. Grand Rapids, MI: Zondervan, 2009.

Wolterstorff, Nicholas. "Can Scholarship and Christian Conviction Mix? A New Look at the Integration of Knowledge." *Journal of Education and Christian Belief* 3 (1999) 35–50.

———. *Educating for Shalom: Essays on Christian Higher Education*. Grand Rapids, MI: Eerdmans, 2004.

———. "True Words." In *But is it all True? The Bible and the Question of Truth*, edited by Alan G. Padgett and Patrick R. Keifert, 34–43. Grand Rapids, MI: Eerdmans, 2006.

Wood, Laurence W. "The Wesleyan View." In *Christian Spirituality: Fives Views of Sanctification*, edited by Donald L. Alexander, 95–118. Downers Grove, IL: InterVarsity, 1988.

Wooldridge, Gly. "Mathematics." In *Opening the American Mind: The Integration of Biblical Truth in the Curriculum of the University*, edited by W. David Beck, 173–88. Grand Rapids, MI: Baker, 1991.

Wright, N. T. *The Letter to the Romans*. The New Interpreter's Bible 10. Edited by Leander E. Keck. Nashville: Abingdon, 2002.

Wright, Richard T. *Biology Through the Eyes of Faith*. San Francisco: Harper & Row, 1989.

Yancey, Philip. *Rumors of Another World: What on Earth Are We Missing?* Grand Rapids, MI: Zondervan, 2003.

Young, Davis A. *John Calvin and the Natural World*. New York: University Press of America, 2007.

Young, Richard A. "The Knowledge of God in Romans 1:18–23: Exegetical and Theological Reflections." *Journal of the Evangelical Theological Society* 43 (2000) 695–707.

Ziegler, Roland. "Natural Knowledge of God and the Trinity." *Concordia Theological Quarterly* 69 (2005) 133–58.

Zuck, Roy B., ed. *A Biblical Theology of the Old Testament*. Chicago: Moody, 1991.

www.ingramcontent.com/pod-product-compliance
Lightning Source LLC
Chambersburg PA
CBHW051741230426
43670CB00012B/2110